Also available:

Mayhem at the Manor
Bedlam in a Bedsit
Ralphy to the Rescue !

SLEEPLESS IN SOHO

P.A. FENNING

Trafford PUBLISHING® www.trafford.com
North America & international
toll-free: 1 888 232 4444 (USA & Canada)
fax: 812 355 4082

CONTENTS

Dedicated to Amber and Alex
For them to compare their teenage years with those
experienced by their Grandma fifty years ago.

Introduction

A true story portraying the year from August 1964 until July 1965, as experienced by teenager Amy Brown and her best friend Pam. Continuing on from their escapades described in 'Mayhem at the Manor', the girls have now left their schooldays behind them. From their homes in suburbia, they travel up to town to begin their city jobs, where they make new friends and are drawn into the exciting nightlife on offer in London's West End. Finding themselves in an exhilarating world of clubs, music, boys and drugs, they yearn for more freedom which inevitably causes clashes with their parents and ultimately forces them into the decision to leave home.

Chapter One

August - A Job in the City

Amy sat on the hard wooden chair and twiddled her fingers nervously in her lap as she tried to avoid looking directly into the ugliest face she had ever set eyes on. What was she doing here anyway? At school she had opted for the technical course because the only alternative on offer had been the commercial course and Amy knew with a deep conviction that the one thing in life she didn't want to do was office work. Now here she sat in the manager's glass goldfish bowl of an office; a corner partitioned off from the rest of the enormous room where row upon row of heavy wooden desks stood amid Gothic architectural grandeur with stone mullioned windows and supporting columns that divided the room in two. This famous Prudential building in High Holborn housed one of the biggest offices in the whole of London.

Mr Galbraith attempted a reassuring smile to help his latest employee relax a little, but due to a paralysis of his face caused by Bell's palsy, all Amy saw was a grotesque lopsided leer. One of his baggy bulging eyes gazed at her through the thick lens of his glasses while the other perused the ceiling, Amy could empathise with his difficulty to smile as she had suffered a similar problem until recently. For more than a year she had lived with the misery of a broken front tooth which had robbed her of a smile and the ability to chat normally to boys she met at dances. Incapable of smiling properly for so long had blighted her life, but now those unhappy days were behind her.

Mr Galbraith began droning out his well-rehearsed 'Welcome to the Company' speech causing Amy's concentration to wander. Already she was missing the brief freedom she had enjoyed since leaving school a mere couple of weeks ago. Perhaps she was plunging into full-time work too soon.

*   *   *   *   *

All too clearly she could recall her final gruelling ordeal in the dentist's chair followed by the elation of walking into the Wimpy Bar where she usually met her best friend, Pam, each Saturday for lunch and giving her a big gleaming smile of even white teeth.

"That looks great, Bat," Pam had declared, as Amy flopped down opposite her, "it matches your other tooth perfectly. Did it hurt having your tooth capped?"

"It was a piece of cake, Tibs," Amy lied, remembering the hours of trying to keep her mouth wide open until her jaw felt as though it would drop off. "I'm going to celebrate this momentous occasion with a plate of egg and chips."

The girls had been best friends since their school days at the Technical High School and they still called each other by their nicknames coined at school. Amy's was short for Batty Brown, which had stuck after a teacher called her this for causing havoc while manoeuvring a chair across a crowded classroom during registration in her first year at secondary school. Pam's nickname of Tibs was simply a shortening of her surname, Tibton.

At the Technical High they had both opted for the technical course because neither wanted to end up working in an office. The commercial course seemed so horribly boring, consisting as it did of shorthand, typing and bookkeeping; but after taking their GCE 'O' levels, they had been railroaded into interviews and accepted for office jobs.

After lunch they emerged from the Wimpy Bar into the dazzling warm summer sunshine and hurried back to work. This was the last day of their Saturday jobs Pam at Macfisheries where her dad was the manager and Amy further along the High Street at Woolies. Amy couldn't wait to leave Woolies. She hated standing around all day serving customers and all for a measly 15s 9d. She envied Pam who, thanks to her dad, spent her Saturday packing shopping bags for customers and got a whopping 37s 6d though she did have to work on Friday evenings too.

"See you tonight - my house at seven - and don't be late," Pam called over her shoulder as she pushed the door of the supermarket open. "Oh, and Colin said he'd give us a lift."

Amy grimaced as she walked on. Colin was Pam's cousin who Amy had once briefly dated. With his black rimmed glasses and black curly hair he could almost pass for Buddy Holly. 'So long as he doesn't turn up in his coal lorry,' Amy thought, remembering previous embarrassing occasions when she had to clamber up into the dirty cab of his lorry outside the Scala ballroom while scores of Mods on their flashy scooters looked on in amusement.

That evening at the shabby wooden hut masquerading as a nightclub called the Inferno; the girls left Colin outside chatting to a friend and pushed their way into the crowd on the dimly lit dance floor. The external tatty appearance belied its magnetic appeal to teenagers from all over suburbia and even attracted them down from London too. A group pounded out 'Bare Footin' on the small stage and bodies gyrated to the music in the hot smoky atmosphere. Amy noticed a group of Rockers near the stage busy head banging and spotted Dennis the Menace, her next-door neighbour amongst them. She kept her distance and hoped he wouldn't see her - it would look bad for a Mod to be seen chatting to a Rocker.

The group switched to a slow number and Amy felt a tap on her shoulder. A tall, dark-haired, good-looking boy was asking her to dance. She smiled her new smile and melted into his arms. The wonderful smell of suede permeated her nostrils as her hands caressed his soft blue suede coat that reached down below his knees. He said his name was Peter and he invited her to a party later that night.

Amy bit her lip. "Sorry, but I've arranged to stay at my friend's house tonight," she lied. She would have loved to go with him but there was no way. She could never admit that her parents wouldn't allow her to go.

"Well how about you come over to my house tomorrow and cook my Sunday dinner instead? My folks are away on holiday and I can't even boil an egg," he said, giving her a little boy lost look. "You wouldn't want me to starve would you?" He smiled and Amy's heart skipped a beat.

"O.K., as long as I can bring my mate, Pam." Amy stipulated hoping there would be safety in numbers.

"It's a deal," Peter said, "I'll meet you at the bus stop in Eltham High Street at three p.m. and I'll bring my mate Dave to keep Pam company."

At the end of the dance Amy dived off through the crowd to find Pam and tell her the news.

She groaned. "Oh, but you know how much I hate blind dates."

"It'll be a laugh, Tibs," Amy coaxed, "I've never tried to cook a roast dinner before, so I'm going to need your help."

"Well I shan't be much use 'cause I've never cooked one either."

Amy was on cloud nine and even Colin's snide remarks on the way home about Peter having ulterior motives when she mentioned where she was going the next day, couldn't dampen her spirits. 'He's just jealous,' she told herself.

The girls lived in adjoining towns. Amy arrived at Pam's house after lunch next day to find her in front of the mirror in her bedroom, carefully applying her make-up.

"Hurry up, Tibs or we'll be late," Amy was so excited at the prospect of seeing the lovely Peter that she was impatient to get going.

Unfortunately she didn't pause to check the number of the bus she leapt onto, dragging Pam behind her. After half an hour or so the bus arrived in Woolwich, much to Amy's dismay. They searched and eventually found a bus that took them back to where they had started from, and they finally boarded a bus going in the right direction. Amy was getting frantic as the time neared five o'clock. She was convinced that by now Peter would have given up and gone home.

The girls jumped off the bus and Amy looked up and down the deserted High Street with a heavy heart. Then her eyes alighted on Peter emerging from a shop doorway and her spirits soared.

He just grinned when Amy explained what had happened. "Let's go home. I'm starving so I hope you two can do something with a chicken. Dave's there, waiting for us." He put his arm around Amy's shoulders and set off at a brisk pace with Pam lagging behind.

His house was only a short walk from the High Street and a path led along the side of the house to the back door where Dave met them.

"Did you get lost or something?" He asked good-humouredly. Amy looked sheepish and changed the subject. Pam brightened up at the sight of Dave who, she decided, was quite presentable. He was nearly as tall as Peter with a mop of fair hair in a Beatle cut. Amy was relieved to see the two of them chatting and Pam giggling which was always a good sign. The boys soon had the girls busy peeling potatoes while Amy told Peter to wrap the chicken in foil and put it in the hot oven.

"A couple of hours ought to be long enough," Amy said trying to sound as though she knew what she was doing. "What about veg?"

Peter thought for a moment, then opened the fridge door and rummaged in the freezer compartment. "Ah! Frozen peas!" He exclaimed triumphantly holding up a bag, "they shouldn't be too tricky."

With the dinner cooking they all retired to the lounge to listen to records. Peter opened a bottle of cider and poured it into four glasses. Then he put on some music while Pam and Dave commandeered the sofa. Amy didn't mind because Peter sat in a deep armchair and pulled her onto his lap. She got so wrapped up in kissing and canoodling with him that before she realised it, dinner was cooked. They ate off trays and the only disaster was the lumpy gravy, which Amy had tried to make while Peter had his arms around her, kissing her neck.

On the bus home Pam inspected Amy's neck and tutted disapprovingly. "Look at that love bite - better not let your parents see it or you'll be in trouble."

Amy pulled up her collar. "I shall cherish it," she said proudly, "and I don't care if my fuddy duddy old parents *do* see it."

"It might not impress your new boss when you start work in a week's time."

"Oh I'm sure it'll have faded by then," Amy said, hoping she was right. The last few hours had caused her to forget about the new job looming on the horizon. "I think Peter's nice. He asked me to go to Margate with him on Tuesday. Are you seeing Dave again?"

"He said he'd meet me at the Inferno tomorrow night. He's OK I suppose."

"You don't sound all that keen," Amy observed. She suspected that Pam was jealous because for once, Amy had the better-looking boy. While they were at school, Amy had resigned herself to always landing second best whenever boys at dances chatted them up. They seemed to prefer Pam's long dark hair, dark eyes and clear complexion to Amy's long blonde hair, blue eyes and freckles. How she hated her freckles! Perhaps now that she no longer had the additional blight to her looks of a broken front tooth, her luck was about to change.

They parted at the bus stop, a few streets from Pam's house. Amy called out: "Good luck tomorrow with the new job," as she hopped onto her bus home.

Pam's new job started in the morning at the New Zealand Insurance Company in the city. Like Amy, she didn't have much enthusiasm for it. "I'll tell you how I get on tomorrow evening," she yelled, waving good-bye.

The next evening Amy met Pam at the bus stop in her town. On the way to the Inferno several towns away, Pam told Amy all about her first day.

"It was *so* boring - even worse than school. I sat at a desk all day sorting and filing piles of paper. I tell you Bat, I don't know how long I can stick it." Pam's experience only increased Amy's misgivings about her own job at the huge head office of the Pru starting the following Monday. She pushed the worrying thoughts to the back of her mind and concentrated instead on the lovely Peter who would be waiting for her at the Inferno with Dave.

The girls dashed straight into the ladies to freshen up their make-up and tidy their hair. Only when satisfied that they had titivated themselves as best they could did they venture into the main dance hall. Being a week night it wasn't as packed as on a Friday or Saturday night. There was no sign of Peter or Dave so the girls sat on stools in the recessed cafe area and sipped cokes.

"We didn't agree a time to meet," Amy said, "but I thought they would have been here by now."

After half an hour of watching who came in, the girls joined the dancers when the Stones came blasting out of the speakers. Tonight there were no live groups to draw in the crowds.

Pam leaned over and yelled in Amy's ear: "I've just seen that sod Clive lurking by the exit with his mate John." Pam had been going out with Clive for several weeks until he stood her up one day. He apologised and had a perfectly plausible excuse but nevertheless it was unforgivable in Pam's book so she had dumped him.

Amy glanced across to the exit and found John staring back at her. She smiled and looked away. She fancied John with his dark, neatly cut hair and smart suits but he had been going out with a girl called Sue while Clive was dating Pam. Tonight there was no sign of Sue.

Suddenly John was standing in front of Amy and asking her to dance. She hesitated. What if Peter turned up? So what! No harm in one dance she told herself. At the end of the record he thanked her and walked off. Amy went to find Pam who was sitting on a bench at the side of the floor.

They sat chatting for a while and then Amy grabbed Pam's arm. "I just saw Peter go past. I'm sure he saw me. Why didn't he come over?"

"Maybe he saw you smooching with John."

"It was only a slow dance - I wouldn't call it smooching."

"Well, either way, if he saw you, he didn't like it. Was Dave with him?"

"I didn't notice Dave but I shall go and find Peter and see if he's got the hump with me." Amy jumped up and went down the hall to a set of double doors near the stage that led outside to a small, enclosed area. She thought that was where Peter had been heading. She glanced around but there was no sign of him. She went back up the hall to the exit in case he had gone that way. Outside groups of Mods hung around chatting and smoking. Amy looked for the distinctive long blue suede coat in vain.

Pam came out. "Maybe he's in the gents?" she suggested. They went back inside and sat in the hall on a side bench that gave a clear view through to the gents in the entrance lobby.

Amy was becoming agitated. "Where could he have vanished to?"

"It looks as if he's left. It's not that crowded and I think we would have spotted him or Dave by now. Are you sure it was Peter you saw?"

"No-one else has such a lovely blue suede coat," Amy said impatiently, "and anyway, of course I'd recognise him."

By the end of the evening there was still no sign of Peter so the girls left to catch their bus home.

"I've decided to go over to Peter's house tomorrow and clear things up with him," Amy declared. "Perhaps he was upset seeing me in the arms of another man."

Pam looked dubious. "Do you think that's a good idea, Bat? Dave has definitely blown it with me by not turning up tonight."

Amy sighed. "You're right, I probably shouldn't, but I need to know."

The next afternoon Amy caught the right bus to Eltham and walked to Peter's house with butterflies in her stomach. Would he think she was chasing him? A small voice kept nagging at her - go home, no good will come of this. She ignored the voice and ploughed on determinedly. She pushed open the front gate and walked up the path that led along the side of the house to the back door.

The door stood open and Amy froze at the sight confronting her: There at the kitchen sink stood a girl who Amy recognised from the Inferno. She giggled as she tried to wash dishes while Peter cuddled her and kissed her neck. How could he? Amy felt sick as she watched in horror, her stomach churning. They were so wrapped up in each other that they hadn't heard Amy approach and didn't notice her, as she stood there transfixed to the spot.

Suddenly Amy came to her senses. She *must* get away. She turned and quickly tiptoed back down the path expecting to hear a shout at any moment as one of them spotted her. She hurried back to the bus stop feeling numb and incredibly stupid. 'What an idiot you are,' she fumed to herself on the journey home. She concluded that Peter had just wanted someone to cook and clean for him while his parents were away and she had been a willing mug.

By Friday evening when she met Pam, the unpleasant episode had been pushed to the back of her mind. They caught the bus to the Inferno and Amy bombarded Pam with questions about her first week of work, hoping Pam had forgotten about her plan to visit Peter. But as the girls walked along the station approach towards the Inferno, Pam suddenly came out with: "How did you get on with Peter?"

Amy had already decided what she would say: "Er, I thought better of it and didn't go over his house after all. I've gone off him anyway. I think he was just using me to cook a meal for him." Pam seemed satisfied and changed the subject. Once they were inside the dance hall, Amy was relieved to find no sign of Peter. The place was jam-packed. They stood near the exit and peered through the gloom and smoke of the hall. A girl called Jenny with long dark hair who they knew slightly came over for a chat. She was usually there with her boyfriend Mick, but tonight she appeared to be on her own.

She leaned towards Amy and whispered, "I've got some news for you."

"Oh?" Amy said, puzzled as to what it could possibly be.

"I met Peter in town and you'll never guess what he told me."

Amy's heart sank. Had he spotted her creeping away from his house after all? "What did he tell you?" she asked dully, not wanting to know at all.

"He told me that you were the best girl he had been out with."

Amy's mouth dropped open in disbelief. That piece of news cheered her up no end, though she still hated him for what he had done. "I would hardly call cooking a meal at his house, going out with him," she said coldly.

Jenny just smiled. She was very pretty and petite which was handy as Mick wasn't very tall and a bit on the weedy side. She explained that she had had a tiff with Mick so she seemed content to tag along with Pam and Amy.

Just then John appeared in front of Amy and asked her for a dance. He looked very smart as usual in a mohair suit but the music was fast so there was no smooching. John was a good dancer and could do a lot of intricate steps so Amy felt proud to be dancing with him, aware of admiring eyes watching them. At the end of 'Heard it Through the Grapevine' by Marvin Gaye he thanked her and walked off, just as he had done the last time. Amy pushed her way back through the throng to find Pam, but then she spotted Peter hovering over by the cafe. Pam and Jenny were standing nearby so she quickly suggested they all dance. She drew them into the middle of the crowd where they could dance unseen by Peter.

Towards the end of the evening Amy was pleased when John turned up for a slow dance to Dione Warwick's 'Walk on By.' At the end of the dance he offered her a lift home.

"So long as you don't mind giving my mate Pam a lift too," she stipulated as Jenny had already left to catch her train. John agreed, so they collected Pam and went out to the car park where he led them to a smart white Beetle that looked brand new with its paintwork gleaming immaculately under a lamppost. It was obviously his pride and joy. Pam got bundled into the back and Amy was impatient for Pam to be dropped off so that she could have John all to herself.

John drew up outside Amy's house, leaned over to give her a long lingering kiss goodnight and arranged to see her the following Friday.

Amy walked indoors, her legs feeling like jelly. 'I really like John,' she thought dreamily as she got ready for bed, 'and I love the smell of his aftershave.'

Amy's big day finally arrived - the start of her working life in London. Monday morning she awoke with butterflies in her stomach. She donned the green tweed suit that she had made and checked her tights for ladders. It felt good to be well away from school uniform, free to wear her own clothes even though the office dress code dictated that no trousers could be worn.

After an hour's commute by train to High Holburn she walked towards the imposing red brick building that dominated the skyline. As she entered through the high Gothic archway and walked into the huge foyer with its glittering chandeliers, Amy felt her legs begin to twitch about the knees and her hands turn cold and clammy. Aware of this momentous occasion - her first proper job (she didn't think Woolies counted) - she was determined to hide her nervousness. She gave herself a mental pep talk: 'You are now a grown up career woman with the world at your feet.' With this thought firmly implanted in her mind, she boldly walked up to the nearest of the many uniformed commissionaires who were hovering at various vantage points. The commissionaire Amy had singled out was standing near a large glass case containing silver trophies and shields of all shapes and sizes.

"Excuse me." She looked him straight in the eye. "Would you help me please? This is my first day here and I'm not sure where to go."

He looked Amy up and down, obviously unimpressed. "That way," he said pointing to where a corridor led off from the foyer, "you'll see large red arrows directing you."

She thanked him and hurried off down the long corridor until she came to the arrows bearing a message instructing all new employees to follow them. Amy would soon discover that these arrows were a regular Monday morning feature within these hallowed precincts, which housed multitudes of employees amongst its labyrinth of corridors.

Amy followed the arrows around a corner and down a flight of stairs wondering if she would ever find her way out again. At last she arrived in what was normally the staff rest room but for now was the assembly point for new recruits prior to being dispatched to their final resting places. With her letter of acceptance and birth certificate ready for inspection as requested, she soon found herself marshalled into a small group of five girls and led off up another flight of stairs by a Miss Rogers, a sour faced spinster in tweeds and a stout pair of brogues. Amy wondered if this was how she would end up in twenty or thirty years' time when the sombre atmosphere of the place had permeated her very being. Three of the newcomers were deposited in various offices as they progressed along lengthy corridors leaving Amy and one other girl traipsing behind the formidable Miss Rogers.

Finally they were led into the enormous accounts office with its central aisle, stone columns and high windows which gave the strong impression of entering a cathedral. There were twelve sections in this department housing nearly a hundred people under its high roof.

Everyone sat in rows at the solid wooden long tables with three people to each row facing the front of the room. The other new girl was placed on the first section they arrived at on entering the room, while Amy was taken towards the far end on the opposite side of the aisle and installed in the middle of a desk on division A. She found herself one of six women as she gazed around with a sinking feeling in the pit of her stomach.

The room felt like a gigantic schoolroom with Miss Rogers sitting behind her desk at the front like a bird of prey watching with her beady eyes from behind horn-rimmed glasses, waiting for a chance to pounce on an unsuspecting victim who might have dallied too long over a chat with a neighbour.

*   *   *   *   *

Mr Galbraith was rising from his chair to escort Amy from his office, warning her to pay attention now because his obligatory speech was at an end. She quickly shook his hand and left, relieved to escape back to her desk. She gazed around the vast office reflecting on the irony of her situation. The feeling of being back at school was reinforced by a ban on smoking. If anyone fancied a quick fag they had to sneak off to the toilets.

Mr Galbraith was now ushering the other new girl into his goldfish bowl office in the far corner to give her the benefit of his welcome speech. He reminded Amy of a grotesque hunch-backed headmaster.

There was even a register where everyone must sign in each morning and sign off at night. Mr Brown, Mr Galbraith's waspish assistant, would draw a red line in the register on the dot of 8.50 a.m. Anyone arriving late had to sign in below this line. If they were unlucky enough to sign twelve times below the red line then it invoked a scolding from Miss Rogers before being despatched to the personnel department for an official warning.

Amy had an overwhelming feeling of disillusionment. All her studying and exams now enabled her to put ticks in the right places in two large ledgers, which took up most of the space on her desk. Each tick indicated that the insurance agent had collected the weekly premium from his client.

Sitting directly behind Amy was Vera, head of division A, a plump mumsy woman with a friendly smile that belied her domineering ways. Amy suspected Vera's authority had gone to her head. She could sense Vera's eyes boring into her back if she didn't have her head down working away at her ledgers. On Vera's right sat her deputy, a spindly spinster called Audrey who was a pedantic stickler for doing things properly. Amy took an instant dislike to her.

Nearest to the window beside Amy sat Joan, a smartly dressed brunette with immaculate though heavy make-up. She showed Amy the ropes as she flipped expertly through the pages of the huge ledger, her long, curved, bright red nails, like eagles talons, scouring the pages, searching for the right entry to tick. Amy watched fascinated. She had never seen nails quite so long or so curved before. She guessed that Joan was in her late twenties, and judging by the rings on her fingers, she was also married. She helped Amy by putting names to faces and explained how the office routine worked.

On the other side of Amy sat Sue, a pretty girl with long dark hair. She showed Amy where her locker was and how to find the toilets. She was in charge of supplying hand towels to everyone each Monday morning and collecting the used ones. Amy stuffed her towel into her bottom drawer and tried to remember to take it with her if she went to the ladies. She liked Sue with her easy-going friendly nature so she tended to ask her in preference to Joan if she had any queries.

The sixth person on division A was Gail, a bubbly happy-go-lucky young lady with a curly bob of unruly light brown hair and twinkling eyes who sat next to Vera at the end of the desk beside the central aisle. She and Vera were like chalk and cheese. Amy could tell that Vera disapproved strongly of Gail's slapdash way of working. She was newly married to Guy, a handsome blonde hunk who worked in the next office. Now they were married, they qualified to live in one of the many flats owned by the Pru and had just moved into one in the adjacent side street. Despite living almost on top of the job, Gail and Guy were nearly always last to arrive each morning, haring down the office to sign in, yelling at Mr Brown not to draw the red line across in the register.

Joan informed Amy that the other new girl in the department was called Jeanette and she had been posted on division H at the opposite end of the room.

The staff were divided into three lunch breaks. Amy was allocated the middle one, as was Jeanette, so they followed the crowds heading for the subsidised canteen in the basement where the food was good and very cheap.

Jeanette appeared to be a somewhat naive but pleasant girl with a ruddy complexion who came from a large family living in the East End of London. Amy couldn't help noticing that her clothes looked a little shabby.

At afternoon tea break, Joan took Amy across the aisle to division G where she introduced her to

Jennifer, a tall sturdy girl with spectacles and unruly blonde wavy hair who lived in the next town to Amy.

"I'll show you the quickest way of getting home tonight," she offered, "make sure you are ready to leave dead on ten to five."

Amy cheered herself up through the rest of the day by thinking about what she would wear to the Inferno that evening. She decided on the straight ankle-length burgundy skirt with twin vents that she had made.

Suddenly the bell was ringing signalling closing time and Jennifer was yelling at her to get a move on. As Amy signed off in the register she saw Jennifer beckoning frantically to her from the doorway. Amy dashed up the aisle and ran down the stairs trying in vain to catch her up. She ran along a corridor, through the foyer and into the street. Amy finally caught her up as she dodged through the crowds heading for the tube.

"Get your season ticket out ready to flash at the ticket collector as we run through the barrier," Jennifer panted as they galloped down the steps of the tube station.

"But my season ticket only covers me for British Rail," Amy said.

"So does mine, but if you only give it a very quick flash he won't have time to read it properly. Just do as I do."

Amy ran through the barrier behind Jennifer feeling very guilty. She fully expected the ticket collector to grab her by the collar and haul her back, but all went smoothly and they arrived on the platform as a train pulled in. Jennifer ran along the platform towards the front of the train and jumped on board as the whistle blew. Amy leapt on behind her, gasping for breath.

"You can relax a bit now until we reach Cannon Street," Jennifer said as the train sped off into the blackness of the tunnel gathering speed. They stood by the opposite doors ready to dive off at the second stop. Amy barely had time to get her breath back when the doors opened and Jennifer was off again at a gallop, up the escalator, flashing the season ticket at the barrier, running through to the mainline station and dashing across to platform one where the fast train home was about to leave. Jennifer ran along the train trying to reach the front. When the whistle blew she had to fling open the nearest door and jump in followed by a hot and dishevelled Amy. They collapsed into two empty seats as the train lurched off.

"Do you really do this run every night?" Amy panted in disbelief.

"It's worth it if we manage to catch this train as it only stops once on the journey home. It means a saving of half an hour on the journey time."

Amy wasn't sure it was worth all the effort, though it did give her time to get a bite to eat before changing and going to meet Pam at the station.

Now she had a season ticket, she intended to make good use of it. They caught a train to the Inferno and Amy told Pam all about her boring first day at work.

"Sounds as though your job is as bad as mine," she said sympathetically.

Being a Monday night the Inferno was fairly quiet. Pam and Amy perched on stools in the cafe recess watching groups of Mods dancing to the Stones 'I Wanna be your man' when a tap on Amy's arm made her jump. A good-looking blonde boy stood there smiling at her and asked her to dance. He introduced himself as Jeff. The music changed to a slow number so Amy readily accepted. She hadn't noticed him at the Inferno before though he said he came there fairly regularly. After several dances he offered her a lift home on his scooter. He had a mate called Tom who agreed to give Pam a lift home on his scooter so Amy wouldn't feel guilty about leaving

Pam to get home on her own. Jeff donned a green parka and beret and led Amy over to a lovely Chrome Lambretta with lots of mirrors that sparkled under the street lights. Amy regretted choosing the long straight skirt as she struggled to hitch it up so that she could sit on the pillion.

He dropped her off at her house and asked to see her the following evening. He wanted to pick her up from home but Amy suggested they meet at the end of the Crescent instead. She didn't fancy being ogled at by her parents and the nosy neighbours in her corner of the Crescent.

Amy's second boring day in the office only differed from the first day when Joan showed Amy how to deal with transfers and changes of address. Amy tried to concentrate on the ledgers in front of her but Jeff and his scooter kept arriving on the open pages to distract her. The day dragged by until the bell heralded the frantic dash for the station and home.

After tea Amy hurried to the end of the Crescent where her school friend, Coral, lived at number one. She found Jeff lounging on his scooter next to the phone box. Amy's heart skipped a beat. She had half expected him not to turn up, being pessimistic about her luck with boys.

He jumped up when he saw her and gave her a quick peck on the cheek. "Thought we could go over to my house - that's if you don't mind meeting my mother," he said, looking at her a little doubtfully. Amy smiled and said she didn't mind at all. In fact she was thrilled that he was actually taking her to meet his mum already. Did this mean he was serious about her?

At Jeff's house they settled down on the sofa in the lounge to watch T.V. Jeff's mum came in and Amy liked her straight away. She was plump and very smiley, wearing a neat pinafore.

"Can I tempt you to a glass of apricot brandy dear?" she asked and started rummaging in the sideboard behind the sofa.

Amy glanced at Jeff and hesitated. "Well, I've never tried it before," she admitted.

"Oh, you'll love it, I'm sure, dear." Jeff's mum handed her a full sherry glass and Amy took a sip. It tasted very sweet.

"Mmm, it's really nice," Amy said politely.

"I'll leave the bottle here then you can help yourself to more - and don't let Jeff drink any because he has got to drive you home." With that Jeff's mum tactfully withdrew, closing the door behind her. Not knowing if she might burst in at any moment, they spent the rest of the evening just watching T.V., much to Amy's disappointment, until it was time for Jeff to take her home.

"How about we go to the pictures on Thursday evening?" he asked outside her house.

"Yeah, that would be great," Amy agreed. She felt her knees wobble as he kissed her goodnight, then he drove off, leaving her to totter indoors, her head in a spin. Her heart pounded and her legs didn't belong to her. Was this her first experience of being in love? She decided it must be, as she hadn't felt quite like this before. At last she had found a nice looking boy who seemed considerate and as a bonus, even had a smart scooter.

Amy could hardly wait for Thursday evening, so when it finally arrived, she hurried to the rendezvous at the end of the Crescent. Jeff sat hunched on his scooter, his beret clasped in his hands as he fiddled nervously with it. He forced a grin and jumped off the pillion as Amy walked towards him.

"What's up?" she asked, concerned at his downcast face.

Jeff sighed. "Bad news," he said, "I got a £5 fine today for speeding so I'm flat broke. I'm sorry but that means I can't afford to take you to the pictures."

Amy had been so looking forward to cuddling in the back row, but she tried not to show her disappointment. "Why don't we have another night in at your house instead?" she suggested.

Jeff brightened up. "If you're sure you don't mind," he said putting on his beret.

"'Course I don't mind!" It was half true. As long as she was with Jeff she didn't really mind where they went. Once again they ended up at Jeff's house on the sofa. There was nothing worth watching on the TV so they listened to Radio Luxembourg. Jeff's mum popped in and poured Amy a glass of cherry brandy for her to try.

"Since you liked the apricot brandy so much the other night, I thought you might like this. What do you think?" She watched eagerly as Amy took a sip. It wasn't quite as sweet as the apricot brandy.

"Mmm, that's lovely," she said and Jeff's mum looked tickled pink.

"I'll leave you in peace now and bring some coffee in later," she said as she went out taking care to close the door behind her.

"You should tell her you don't like those brandies then she'd stop pestering you with them," Jeff said.

"But I do like them," Amy protested, "and besides I couldn't bear to disappoint her."

Jeff took Amy home at eleven and she suggested he come over to her house on Sunday.

"Why not bring your mate Tom and I'll ask Pam to come over too. With my parents away for the day in Suffolk, we could all have a really great time," Amy said eagerly.

"Sounds pretty cool," Jeff said as he kick-started his scooter. Then he paused and rummaged in his pocket and brought out a piece of paper and a pen. He scribbled on the paper and thrust it into Amy's hand. "Here's my number. Give me a ring on Saturday to let me know it is definitely OK for Sunday and I'll be able to tell you if Tom can make it."

Friday evening Amy met up with Pam on the train to the Inferno. Pam demanded to know all about Amy's dates with Jeff.

"Huh, he sounds a bit of a skinflint," Pam sneered, "just taking you back to his house."

"But he was broke - he had a fine to pay," Amy said, jumping to his defence. "Anyway it should be a laugh on Sunday, so you will come over, won't you?"

"Yeah, I suppose so," Pam said unenthusiastically.

"You liked his mate who took you home didn't you?"

"He was OK but seemed a bit shy. By the way, what's happening about John? Didn't you arrange to meet him at the Inferno tonight?"

"I still like John, but I think I prefer Jeff," Amy said, leaning back in the seat and closing her eyes. It made a nice change to have two boys to choose between. Amy realised that having her tooth crowned had made a huge difference to her life already. She could smile and talk normally now, having felt too self-conscious to do that for the past eighteen months.

At the Inferno the girls danced the night away, sometimes with boys, sometimes just with each other. Amy was disappointed that John didn't show up but she refused to let it spoil her evening. She just thought about Jeff and the fun they would have on Sunday.

Saturday morning Amy caught the train to London and Pam joined her two stations up the line.

Amy groaned as Pam flopped down on the seat next to her. "I've only gone and lost Jeff's phone number."

"Well, if you know his surname, you can look up the number in the directory," Pam reasoned.

"But that's the problem - I don't know his surname," Amy wailed, "all I can remember is his number started with KIP and an eight."

"Can you remember his address?"

"I think I might recognise it." Amy said uncertainly.

"Well when we get back I'll help you go through the directory - there can't be that many KIP numbers." Amy brightened up a little at Pam's optimism.

After a morning browsing around the shops in Oxford Street the girls fell in love with, and bought, matching soft black leather handbags. They caught the train home and Amy wasted no time in taking Pam to the phone box outside Coral's house to help her rifle through the pages of the directory. They took a page each and scanned down the list searching out the KIP numbers which fortunately, weren't too numerous. Each address was checked but rang no bells with Amy.

"Maybe he's ex-directory," Pam said after over an hour of perusing the small print.

"Oh this is hopeless," Amy moaned and pushed the book away.

"Well he knows where you live so perhaps he'll just turn up tomorrow at your house," Pam said, trying to cheer up her friend.

"But he wanted me to let him know if it will be OK. He'll probably think I've forgotten or I'm not interested."

The girls walked to the bus stop and waited for Pam's bus to come along.

"You'll still come over tomorrow won't you?"

"Yeah, I suppose so."

"We'll have the house to ourselves and if Jeff does come over he'll be bringing his mate Tom for you."

The bus drew up and Pam jumped aboard. "See ya tomorrow," she said waving as the bus pulled away.

Next day Pam duly arrived at Amy's and they relished being able to play records at full volume. Every few minutes Amy scanned the street through the bay window in the lounge but her search was in vain. The afternoon dragged on and there was still no sign of Jeff.

"It's no use," she said with a sigh, "he's obviously not coming."

"Let's go up to the phone box on the corner and hunt for some more KIP numbers," Pam suggested, "we might strike lucky." Amy reluctantly agreed and five minutes later they resumed their tedious search through the pages of the directories.

After half an hour, Amy gave a yell of triumph. "This address rings a bell. I'm sure that's the name of his road." Amy fumbled in her bag for change and quickly dialled the number. A man's voice on the other end of the line insisted no one called Jeff lived there, dashing Amy's hopes. Disheartened, they searched for another half an hour until a lady tapped impatiently on the glass.

"I'd better head for home," Pam said as they emerged into the warmth of the early evening sunshine, "I'll meet you at the station tomorrow evening and we'll go to the Inferno. Maybe you'll see Jeff there."

Amy cheered up a little at the thought. "Yeah - I'll have to explain what went wrong." She sighed. "What a waste of a whole day and an empty house."

The Inferno on Monday night was more dead than normal. There was no Jeff and no one else there who Amy and Pam knew. After dancing with a few boys they left and caught the train home. Pam alighted at her station leaving Amy looking and feeling fed up.

Next day at work as she waded through the thick wad of agent's receipts marking up the huge ledger in front of her, the phone rang. Jeff's cheerful voice was speaking to her. Her heart leapt. She quickly explained about losing his phone number, but he didn't seem to mind. He arranged to pick her up at her house the following night.

Amy was on cloud nine again and couldn't care less about the black looks she was getting from Vera and her sidekick Audrey for taking a private phone call. She rushed home with Jennifer after work and spent the evening washing and fussing over her hair. Then she experimented with her make-up, determined to make a good impression on Jeff.

At work next day, time dragged as Amy's eyes constantly flicked up to the large clock on the wall. Finally the bell rang and she could head for home with Jennifer. Tonight it was Jennifer who had a job to keep up with Amy as she flung herself down the steps of the tube two at a time.

After tea Amy changed and got ready. She waited impatiently but in vain. Jeff didn't turn up. Amy was desolate. Obviously he hadn't forgiven her for losing his phone number. This was all she could think of as the reason for him not showing up. Then another thought occurred to her: 'Maybe he's had an accident on his way over here. Maybe at this very moment he's laid out unconscious in a hospital!' Despite being worried, logic told her this was pretty unlikely. 'Why didn't I ask him for his number when he rang yesterday?' She could have kicked herself. Finally she resigned herself to the probable truth: 'You've been dumped girl!'

Feeling thoroughly fed up Amy went for a long soak in the bath and had an early night. 'The end of another brief romance,' she thought ruefully.

Friday evening Amy and Pam met up on the train en route for the Inferno. Amy decided not to mention that she had heard from Jeff and how he had then let her down. She was still puzzling over what had gone wrong and came to the conclusion that he had only rung her to find out why she hadn't been in touch with him. 'I expect his ego couldn't accept that I might have stood him up,' she reasoned.

"You're quiet this evening," Pam observed, "something on your mind?"

Amy made an effort to chat normally and allay her friend's suspicions. At the Inferno the girls danced to the loud music and halfway through the evening Jenny's Mick came over and asked Amy to dance. There was no sign of Jenny so Amy had a slow dance with him. He held her close and she discreetly checked that she wasn't taller than him. As long as she didn't wear higher heels, she was about his height. Amy had thought him to be on the weedy side but she could feel his muscles so maybe he was just very slim.

He invited her to the Wimpy Bar for a coffee, which was a five minute walk away in the High Street. As they sat sipping cappuccinos in the brightly lit Wimpy, Amy asked Mick about Jenny.

"You've been going out together for quite a while haven't you?"

Mick grunted and squirmed in his seat. He seemed reluctant to talk about Jenny. Finally he said, "we're not seeing each other any more."

"Why not?" Amy pressed.

"We don't seem to get on so well these days. We keep arguing - like the other day when she stormed off and I haven't seen her since." He glanced at Amy and grinned a boyish grin. "Let's not talk about her. I'd rather talk about you." He reached across the table and took hold of her hand. Amy met his gaze. She liked his even features and cropped Mod haircut.

"Can I see you tomorrow evening?" He asked, stroking her hand, "you will be at the Inferno again won't you?"

"Er, yeah, I expect so," Amy said, somewhat taken aback, "so long as it's really over between you and Jenny - I don't want her accusing me of stealing her boyfriend."

Mick sighed. "I told you - Jenny is in the past."

Amy smiled feeling less guilty. "We'd better get back to the Inferno - Pam will be wondering where I've got to."

They walked along the High Street and Mick put his arm around Amy's shoulders. She decided she did like him but wished he was just that bit taller.

After spending an unproductive Saturday up in town looking at suede coats, Pam and Amy arrived at the Inferno that evening. Pam was still a bit peeved with Amy for leaving her to go to the Wimpy Bar with Mick the previous evening.

"If you go to the Wimp tonight make sure you take me with you," she hissed in Amy's ear as they pushed their way through the crowd loitering in the foyer by the cloakroom. Mick was waiting just inside the main doors and grabbed hold of Amy as she entered.

"Glad you made it," he said with a smile, "come and have a dance." He took her hand and pulled her into the throng of moving bodies. She didn't have time to see Pam glaring crossly after them. Later on they were smooching to 'My Guy' by Mary Wells with arms around each other when Mick suddenly stopped and jumped away from Amy as if she had kicked him.

Jenny stood there, her eyes flashing angrily as she looked from one to the other. "I want to speak to you," she said fiercely to Mick, and grabbing his hand, headed for the main doors. Mick looked somewhat guilty and sheepish as he allowed himself to be hauled away. Amy slowly followed behind, feeling awkward. Seeing Pam chatting to Wilda, an ex-school friend of theirs, she went over to join them at the snack bar. Wilda was a spoilt only child accustomed to getting everything she wanted. While still at school she had been bought a long luxury brown suede coat and hush puppy shoes that Amy and Pam could only dream of owning until they were out at work and earning a wage. She had an air of self-confidence, her shiny black hair cut in a crisp Cleopatra style with heavy black eye liner to reinforce the look. Amy told them what had just happened.

Wilda frowned. "You're lucky Jenny didn't hit you for taking her boyfriend away from her," she said.

"But Mick told me he wasn't seeing her any more," Amy protested.

"Huh, - and you believed him?" Wilda said scornfully.

It was Amy's turn to be cross. "How was I supposed to know he was lying," she said defensively.

"Yes, be fair Wilda," Pam chipped in coming to her friend's defence, "Amy wouldn't deliberately steal Jenny's boyfriend."

"No I would not!" Amy said defiantly.

Just then Jenny joined them. She was crying. "I hate him!" she sobbed, wiping her eyes with a tissue.

"What did he say?" Wilda asked, putting an arm around her.

"He - he's packed me up," she mumbled into the tissue as she wiped her nose, "the sod!" Then she turned to Amy. "It's all your fault, you know," she said accusingly.

Amy's mouth dropped open. "W-what? What have I done?"

"He says he wants to go out with you and not me." She sobbed again.

"Well he told me that you and him were through - that you walked out on him - and that's the truth," Amy said.

Jenny looked at her for a moment. "Yes, I expect he would say that," she said, "lies drip readily off his tongue. Well you're welcome to him. I'm glad to be rid of him." She turned and walked off towards the exit.

"I'd better go after her," Wilda said and hurried away.

"Let's go and get a coffee at the Wimp," Pam suggested, seeing her friend looking worried. As they left the Inferno Amy glanced around but could see no sign of Mick.

In the Wimpy Bar, sitting over a cup of coffee, they discussed the recent trouble.

"'Course you won't have anything to do with that Mick now you know he lied to you," Pam said vehemently.

"I don't know what to do," Amy said with a sigh. "He seems nice enough and I do quite like him. Perhaps he really did think Jenny had finished with him."

"Hummph!" said Pam, disbelief written all over her face.

"Why can't I have a nice uncomplicated boyfriend?" Amy said wistfully, "why do boys have to lie and cheat?"

"It's what they do best," Pam said perceptively. She finished her coffee, then added, "I don't feel like going back to the Inferno - let's catch a bus home."

As they stood at the bus stop in the High Street who should come along but Mick with some of his friends. He came over to Amy and drew her to one side.

"I'm glad I found you - I have to explain you see. Jenny wouldn't accept that we were through so tonight I told her in no uncertain terms. Now she has got the message loud and clear."

"So I gathered," Amy said coldly.

"It's you I want for my girlfriend," he pleaded giving her a puppy dog look. She couldn't stay angry with him for long so he persuaded her to meet him the next afternoon. Just then the bus arrived. "I promise I'll make it up to you," he said. As she started to walk away, he pulled her back and gave her a quick kiss before she ran to the bus and jumped on board.

'Maybe he's OK after all,' she thought as she joined a disapproving looking Pam on the long three-seater.

Amy walked into town Sunday afternoon and met Mick, as arranged, outside the Scala dance hall. They walked round to the Wimpy Bar for a coffee and Mick suggested going back to his house for tea.

"It's OK, mum will be out so we'll have the place to ourselves," he urged when Amy hesitated. They walked to the car park and Mick, on his best behaviour after the previous evening, helped her into the passenger seat of his Hillman.

He told Amy a little about his family as he drove. He was an only child and his dad had recently been killed in an accident at work. Amy was shocked to hear this and felt immediate compassion and warmth towards him as he told her how he and his mum were coping. "It was in all the local papers - you might have read about it. Mum goes out a lot now - doesn't like to sit in the house alone."

"I don't usually read the papers," Amy admitted, "and besides, I've only now found out your surname."

At Mick's house they searched through the kitchen cupboards and decided to make some cheese on toast as an easy snack. Mick played an R&B record of Georgie Fame live at the Flamingo. They sat on the sofa in the lounge with plates on their laps.

"Have you been to any West End clubs?" Mick asked.

Amy shook her head. "Not yet, though Pam is thinking of asking her aunt who lives in Plaistow in the East End, if we can spend a weekend with her so that we can try out one or two."

Mick shook his head and tutted. "Some of these clubs aren't safe places for girls to be on their own. I'd be worried if I thought you were in a West End nightclub. Promise me you'll just stick to the Inferno - it's got a good atmosphere and you'll be OK there."

Amy felt quite touched by his concern for her welfare but didn't feel inclined to make any rash promises.

After an evening of kissing and cuddling on the sofa Amy decided it was time to go home so Mick gave her a lift and arranged to meet her Monday evening at the Inferno.

Monday, being the last day of the month, was also payday. For two weeks work she received the princely sum of sixteen pounds, three shillings and eight pence. She was thrilled to receive her first pay packet but had to endure a stern lecture from Miss Rogers about not spending it all at once, as it had to last her a whole month. Amy was annoyed at being treated like an irresponsible schoolgirl so she decided to spend it anyway, just to spite Miss Rogers.

That night Pam and Amy arrived at the Inferno and found Mick loitering just inside the doors with the same group of mates he was with on Saturday night. He introduced them to the girls and Pam took a liking to a tall good-looking mate called Dick wearing a long tan leather coat. He seemed keen on her too because he asked her to dance several times during the evening. Where Mick was short and puny, he was tall and broad shouldered with light brown hair that kept flopping in his eyes. Amy hadn't noticed him at the Inferno before but Mick said he was one of his best friends. Wilda and Jenny arrived but kept their distance and didn't speak.

Mick took Amy round to the Wimpy Bar in the High Street for their usual cup of coffee. Amy was fast gaining the impression that Mick was a creature of habit and obviously liked frequenting Wimpy Bars. Afterwards, instead of returning to the Inferno, Mick borrowed the keys to his friend, Eric's, old convertible car. He had brought his mates to the Inferno in it, as it was so large. They cuddled up on the long front bench seat, and enjoyed a snogging session.

At the end of a pleasant evening, Mick went and spoilt it at the bus stop by just saying good-bye with a casual: "See you in the Inferno on Friday."

On the bus Amy fumed as she and Pam rummaged around in their bags for the bus fare. "What a sod! He hasn't even got the decency to arrange to meet me outside the Inferno so he can pay for me to go in."

Pam was only half listening, being absorbed by thoughts of Dick.

"Dick said he'll be there on Friday too," she said dreamily, "I think he's really nice."

"Mmm, yes he does seem quite well mannered, though if he knocks around with Mick, it doesn't bode well," Amy said crossly. "I think I shall teach Mick a lesson. I'm going to get him to really like me and then I shall sod him around - maybe two-time him 'cos he deserves it."

After Amy got off the bus, she still had a good half-mile to walk home. She cursed out loud when her heel caught on a kerb and broke, leaving her to hobble the rest of the way.

Chapter Two

September - The Wedding

Amy rushed home Friday evening after an uneventful week at work, gulped down her tea, washed and changed, before hurrying back to the station. In her haste she jumped on the wrong train, which didn't stop at Pam's station. She eventually arrived at Pam's house to discover that Pam had already left so she had to head for the Inferno alone.

In the gloom of the smoky dance hall she finally met up with Pam who was chatting with Mick, Dick, Eric and several others. Pam spent the entire evening in Dick's company so Mick whisked Amy off to the Wimpy Bar for their usual coffee followed by another snogging session but this time in Mick's car. At the end of the evening he offered the girls a lift home, so Pam and Dick got to kissing in the back seat while Mick and Amy tried to ignore them by making small talk.

After spending many hours in London on Saturday, searching for the elusive perfect suede coat, without any success, the girls gave up and caught the train back to Pam's in order to get ready for another evening at the Inferno in the company of Mick and Dick. As they left Pam's house heading for the station, Pam's cousin, Colin, pulled up beside them. He offered them a lift to the Inferno which they happily accepted since he was driving his car and not his dirty coal lorry.

He dropped them off outside the Inferno and Amy was relieved to see him drive off instead of wanting to come in with them.

The evening fell into the usual routine of dancing followed by Mick taking Amy to the Wimpy Bar and then back to Mick's car for a snogging session.

The girls got a lift home to Pam's because Amy had arranged to stay there overnight. Mick and Dick kissed them goodnight and said they would see them in the Inferno Monday evening.

Indoors, it was Pam doing the moaning. "I think they are a right pair of cheapskates," she said crossly as they got ready for bed, "you'd think they would arrange to pick us up and take us to the Inferno instead of meeting us in there."

"Then they won't have to pay for us to get in," Amy reasoned, "it's about time they took us somewhere else for a change."

The girls squeezed into Pam's single bed and Monty, the black and white mongrel, joined them, as was his custom - much to Amy's dismay. She found it difficult to get comfortable with hot doggy breath blowing in her face or down her neck - or worse if he was suffering from one of his bouts of flatulence.

Sunday morning the girls were up bright and early. Mrs Tibton dished up hard-boiled eggs. She didn't do soft-boiled apparently so Amy resigned herself to the discomfort of indigestion for the rest of the morning.

"Did you two sleep well?" she inquired with a wink at Amy as she passed her a thick slice of bread. Amy now knew her winks were only facial tics so these days she just ignored them. When she first met Pam's mum she had found the winking somewhat unsettling.

After breakfast the girls caught the train to London en route for Petticoat Lane with its many suede and leather shops and stalls.

After a morning spent trying on various suedes, Pam finally chose a bottle-green single-breasted three-quarter length coat. It was love at first sight for her, whereas Amy was becoming disheartened at ever finding the right suede. As they walked back down the market, Pam suddenly stopped and pointed to a coat hanging from a shop doorway on a corner.

"Wow, look at that lovely suede, Bat, I can just see you in that."

Amy gazed up at the coat. It was deep maroon, single breasted with a rear vent, covered buttons and tie belt. "Mmm, it's nice but I bet it's not my size," she said trying not to get too excited.

"Let's go in and see," Pam said and dragged her into the cramped shop. It was packed with rails of suedes and leathers. The smell was almost intoxicating.

A small man emerged from a back room and Pam asked him about the maroon suede.

"Ah yes," he said shaking his head. "That was a special order, tailor-made for a customer who has let me down. I guarantee there isn't another coat like it in the whole of London." He unhooked it from above the door and held it out for the girls to admire. "Just feel the soft nap - this is one of the finest suedes I have ever worked on," he said proudly, giving it a loving stroke. Amy tingled with excitement as he helped her try it on. It fitted her perfectly. "It could have been made for you, my dear," he said guiding her over to a full-length mirror so she could admire herself.

"Ooh Bat, it really looks great on you," Pam drooled, "and that vent up the back is terrific." Amy turned to get a glimpse of the rear and tied the belt around her waist. She felt good and the suede felt wonderful.

Without further ado she bought it. Mum had lent her the extra money she needed so now she would be broke for a whole month or more until she had repaid her mother.

That evening the girls headed for the Black Prince feeling ecstatic in their new suede coats. Because they arrived late the man on the door let them go in for free. A group they didn't know was playing some pretty good R&B so they danced in their coats for the remainder of the evening. A boy called John came over accompanied by his mate and chatted to them. John asked Amy for a dance and she soon discovered he was Wilda's boyfriend and he had recognised them from the Inferno. His mate danced with Pam and at the end of the evening they offered the girls a lift home. Being broke, they gladly accepted.

As Amy stepped out of the car at her house, she paused then leaned in the window. "Er - it might be for the best if you don't mention to Wilda that you met me and Pam and gave us a lift home - she just might get hold of the wrong end of the stick."

John grinned. "My lips are sealed," he said and drove off.

Monday evening the girls headed over to the Inferno to show off their suedes to Mick and Dick. Dick came over but there was no sign of Mick.

"Mick asked me to apologise to you," Dick said to Amy, "his car broke down so he's busy towing it down the motorway." Amy felt annoyed, so when a good-looking boy called Tony asked her to dance, she readily agreed. As she smooched to a slow number with him she saw Dick watching her and hoped he would tell Mick about Tony.

Jenny and Wilda were there and came over for a chat later in the evening. Amy was relieved to see that Jenny didn't appear to be holding any lasting grudge against her for stealing her boyfriend and Wilda didn't mention John, though she realised Wilda might not have seen him yet.

When Pam arrived at Amy's house on Wednesday evening she had a message for her from Mick. The girls were in the kitchen taking turns at washing their fringes in the sink. Amy sat on the kitchen table with its protective oilskin cloth, rubbing her fringe with a towel while Pam was busy shampooing hers. Luxemburg faded in and out on the Bakelite wireless that squatted on the windowsill, its warm glowing dial like a smiling face beaming out.

"I bumped into him at the station and he asked me to apologise to you about Monday. He says he'll see you at the Inferno on Friday," she mumbled dousing her fringe in the bowl.

"Oh does he!" Amy said derisively, "I think he deserves to be two-timed, and then I'll pack him up."

"Who are you going to two-time him with Bat?" Pam asked grabbing the towel from Amy and dabbing at her hair.

"Well, maybe that Tony I danced with on Monday - he was quite dishy, or even John. I'm fed up being messed around by Mick."

"How about we go up to the Marquee next week, Bat. I've heard it's got a terrific atmosphere and fantastic groups."

Amy brightened up. "Sounds like a good idea - that's in Soho isn't it?"

"Yeah - I'll give my Aunt Anne a ring and see if we can stay at her house overnight as she lives in the East End."

Friday evening found Amy and Pam at the Inferno dancing to The Stones' 'Satisfaction'. Amy glanced towards the stage and spotted Tony weaving his way through the crowd of dancing bodies, heading in their direction. Pam suddenly dug Amy in the ribs. "Don't look now, but Mick's just arrived and he's coming over," she yelled, leaning towards Amy's ear so she could be heard.

Mick and Tony both reached Amy at the same moment from opposite directions. She decided to pretend she hadn't seen Mick and turned to smile at Tony. But before Tony could ask for a dance, Mick had grabbed hold of Amy's arm and pulled her round and into his arms.

"Hi, babe," he said and gave her a squeeze, "am I forgiven yet for Monday night? I really couldn't help it, you know, and I did ask Dick and Pam to apologise for me."

Amy saw Tony taking Pam in his arms for a dance and felt a pang of jealousy. She was irritated at the way Mick had grabbed her as though he had a right to her. She would have much preferred to be where Pam was right now, smooching with Tony to 'My Guy' by Mary Wells.

She gave Mick a cold look. "I'm not sure you deserve to be forgiven that easily," she said snootily but allowed Mick to dance with her all the same.

At the end of the dance Dick arrived. He stood near the entrance, head and shoulders above the throng, scanning the faces. Pam quickly left Tony and pushed her way through to him. After a few more dances the four of them felt in need of fresh air and refreshment so they walked down to the Wimpy Bar. Amy was still giving Mick a hard time, barely speaking to him, which left him struggling to make conversation.

"How about we all go to the flicks tomorrow night?" he suggested passing Amy a cup of coffee.

"Depends if there's anything worth watching," Amy said moodily.

"I think I saw a Hitchcock film advertised at the Granada as we were coming here," Pam said.

"Sounds good to me," Dick declared. He raised his cup to his lips and paused, trying to gauge Amy's reaction.

She shrugged. "Yeah, Hitchcock should be OK," she agreed, "better than some 'B' rated horror movie."

Later the boys waited to see the girls onto their train home and arranged to meet them on the same platform the next evening.

As the train rumbled and swayed on its journey, Amy leaned back in the seat and sighed. "You know, Tibs, I really don't know why we bother with those two. I'm sure if they could get away with meeting us inside the cinema after we'd paid to get in, they would, after all they never pay for us to get into the Inferno."

Pam nodded. "Yeah, I think you're right, Bat. Much as I like Dick, he doesn't exactly push the boat out when it comes to showing a girl a good time."

"Saturday night at the flicks is hardly an exciting night on the town," Amy said bitterly, "I'd still like to two-time him and then ditch him."

The train ground to a bumpy halt at Pam's station. "See ya here in the morning, Bat," she called out and slammed the train door shut behind her. Amy waved goodbye to her friend, cheered by the thought of a morning spent shopping in London.

Late next morning the girls staggered into the gloom of the Macabre Coffee House in Wardour Street, their eyes taking a few seconds to adjust after the bright daylight. They were laden with carrier bags from a successful shopping trip to Oxford Street and were now in need of refreshment. They ordered cappuccino coffees and sat down at a black coffin shaped table. In fact everywhere was black - the walls, ceiling and even the windows. The only light came from candles - some flickered ghoulishly inside skulls on each of the tables causing the eye sockets and mouth to glow ominously.

"I'm glad we managed to find this place," Pam said gazing around appreciatively, "someone at work told me about it."

The waiter brought over the coffees and introduced himself as Demis. He was quite good looking in a swarthy continental way with his black hair and tanned skin. Amy tried to place his accent but her curiosity finally got the better of her. "Where are you from?"

"I come from a small island off the Greek mainland," he said flashing a wide smile of even white teeth.

"You mean to say you gave up all that warm Greek sunshine to come and work in this dark morbid place?" Amy said with a hint of incredulity in her voice.

"I love London and I love working here. There is so much life here. This is where it all happens. Nothing ever happens back in Greece. The biggest bit of excitement is a goat breaking wind!" He returned to the bar leaving the girls giggling into their coffees. They flicked the ash from their cigarettes into the skeleton hand ashtray and discussed their morning's purchases. Pam had bought a navy twin set and a pair of Hush Puppy shoes.

"I think I'll wear these with my ski pants tonight and annoy Dick - He told me he doesn't like girls to wear trousers - prefers them in skirts."

"What a Chauvinist!" Amy exclaimed scornfully with a frown. "I might as well wear my new dress then." She had tried on the dark green woollen dress and loved the way it hugged her figure; the wool felt so soft to the touch. She was sure Mick would appreciate it.

Amy had to be back home by 2 p.m. as Katy had arranged to come round for a final fitting of her bridesmaid dress so after finishing their coffees they headed for the station.

Amy and Katy had been best friends since childhood. The dress, although beautifully made, wasn't exactly what a Mod would be seen wearing with its fitted waist and full skirt in shiny peach satin material but nevertheless Amy was excited at the prospect of being a bridesmaid.

"You look lovely in it," Katy said smiling approvingly, as she carefully examined the fit around the waist, "it really shows off your figure. I think mum has done a terrific job making all the dresses. Have you managed to get some white court shoes yet to go with it?"

"I'll try and get a pair tomorrow up Petticoat Lane," Amy said half-heartedly. She hated white shoes and knew they would never be worn again after the wedding. Keith, Katy's intended, sat in a chair watching the television and puffing on a cigarette. He obviously didn't want to get involved in the finer details of dresses and shoes, judging by his occasional bored glances in their direction.

As Katy and Keith were leaving, Katy turned to Amy. "Don't forget to come over early on my wedding day as we've got to get to the hairdressers. I've decided we'll all have our hair set in French pleats." She was plainly pleased with her decision and didn't see the shocked look on Amy's face as she walked down to the front gate.

'A frumpy fifties hairstyle! I'll be pulling it down for the evening knees up,' Amy vowed grimly. She had never been a bridesmaid before so when Katy had asked her a year ago, she had been thrilled and accepted without any second thoughts. There would be herself and an ex-school friend of Katy's as the older bridesmaids with two little bridesmaids and a page.

Amy pushed the forthcoming wedding to the back of her mind and went upstairs to get ready for, what she was sure would be, a boring evening at the pictures. At least her new green dress felt good. She gazed in the mirror, admiring the smooth outline and hoped it wouldn't seat and make her bum look big. She put her hair up in a half bun as she thought it gave her a more sophisticated look.

The Hitchcock film turned out to be 'Marnie' and everyone enjoyed it. Amy was very impressed with

Mick, who had made the effort to dress in a smart dark grey suit. He admired her new dress but poked fun at her hair and tried persuading her to take it down. She refused, annoyed by his jibes. At the end of the evening, as the girls caught the train home to Pam's house, Amy decided that she liked Mick a bit more now.

The girls squashed into Pam's single bed and Amy had her usual struggle with the dog who wanted to sleep on top of her with his wet nose pressed into her neck.

"I reckon it was the suit that made you fancy Mick a bit more tonight," Pam said with a chuckle. "I was right about Dick - he didn't appreciate my ski pants one jot." She turned over to go to sleep leaving Amy with the dog puffing doggy breath in her face.

The girls were up early Sunday morning and after a rushed breakfast of hard-boiled eggs and toast, followed by the inevitable indigestion for Amy, they hurried off to the station to catch the train to London Bridge and then a bus to Petticoat Lane.

Pam helped Amy search for a suitable pair of white shoes to wear with her bridesmaid's dress and eventually they found a passable pair on a stall at the far end. Amy tried them on and as they didn't pinch she bought them without further ado.

Pam bought another pair of ski pants and then the girls caught a bus to Piccadilly for a quick coffee in the Macabre before catching the train home.

That evening Amy met up with Pam at the bus stop in the next town. She hopped off the bus to find Pam leaning against a wall, chewing gum and twirling her hair absently while she waited. The girls were heading for the Black Prince and could catch a bus from the same bus stop.

"We've got about quarter of an hour before our bus is due," Pam told Amy.

"We could always try thumbing a lift instead," Amy suggested. She hated waiting around on draughty street corners.

"I thought you'd gone off thumbing lifts after your experience in the sports car to Swanley with Yvonne last year," Pam remarked. Yvonne had been the scatty one in their gang at school.

"That was Yvonne being her usual impetuous self. She....." Amy was cut short by a black car squealing to a halt in front of them.

"It's Colin!" Pam exclaimed and dived across the pavement. She tugged the passenger door open.

"Do you girls want a lift?" Colin demanded with a grin.

"You bet! We're going to the Black Prince," Pam said.

"Thought you might be," he said, "hop in - that's where I'm going too."

Amy and Pam both squashed onto the front bench seat and Colin jammed the gear stick protruding from under the steering wheel into first. The car lurched off round the corner and quickly gathered speed. Not for the first time, Amy wished Colin would take a bit more care with his driving. Another bend taken too fast sent the girls sliding along the bench. Amy was glad it was Pam and not her who crunched into Colin's side. Amy hauled herself back to the side window and held onto the door handle to stop herself from sliding across again.

They pulled into the car park at the Black Prince and were surprised to see a crowd standing around talking animatedly. As they got out of the car a friend of Colin's came over.

"Guess what!" he said, looking shocked, "the Inferno lived up to its name and burnt down last night."

Amy and Pam were horrified.

"How did it happen? Amy asked.

The boy shrugged. "Dunno. Some say it was a cigarette butt that got kicked under the stage."

"Well the place was no more than a glorified wooden hut so I'm not surprised," Colin said casually.

"Since you hardly ever went there, I don't suppose it would bother you if it did burn down," Pam said coldly. "Come on Bat." She linked arms with Amy and they walked off towards the entrance to the dance room.

An R&B group that they didn't recognise was hammering out 'Walking the Dog'. The girls were in no mood for dancing so they made their way through the crowd to the rear of the room. Pam went off to the bar to get some drinks while Amy found an empty table and quickly bagged it. Pam reappeared with two vodka and limes and plonked them down.

"I can't believe we won't be going to the Inferno any more," Amy said, gazing into her drink and shaking her head.

"Maybe they'll rebuild it," Pam said without conviction.

"Huh, I wouldn't get your hopes up - it probably wasn't even insured," Amy said despondently.

"I wonder where everyone will go instead," Pam said with a sigh.

"We'll have to find out," Amy said, glancing around in the hope of seeing a familiar face. Just then two boys approached and sat down uninvited on the two other vacant chairs at the table. The taller one wearing a black leather Beatle jacket grinned at Pam.

"Can we buy you lovely girls a drink?" he asked, "you look as though you could do with cheering up," he added, glancing at Amy's long face.

"Yeah, why not," Pam said and managed to give him a forced smile. "Vodka and lime and the same for my mate Amy." The boys introduced themselves as Pete and Dave. Dave, the shorter boy with mousy hair that hung below his ears was dispatched to the bar for the drinks while Pete extolled the virtues of the group on stage. The girls made an effort to be polite as they had been bought drinks but as soon as they could they made their excuses and headed for the ladies.

"Let's go and find Colin and ask him to give us a lift home," Pam said as she combed her hair in front of the mirror, "I'm not in the mood for dancing this evening."

"Hope we don't bump into those two again," Amy said, waiting by the door for Pam to finish tidying her hair. "Pete was OK but I definitely didn't fancy my one."

"Come on then." Pam nudged Amy out through the door and they cut across to the side exit, avoiding the dance room. They spotted Colin lounging in the bar chatting to a group of friends. Pam hurried in with Amy in her wake and grabbed Colin's arm, smiling sweetly. She knew Colin would be putty in her hands. He drained his glass of beer and reluctantly followed Pam and Amy out of the bar.

On the way home he told the girls that as far as he could find out, most people from the Inferno were talking about going to the Harrow at Eltham the following Friday.

"Never been there - is it any good?" Amy asked.

"It can't be as good as the Inferno else we'd have heard about it," Pam surmised.

"I've just had a thought," Amy said, grabbing Pam's arm. "We're supposed to be meeting Mick and Dick at the Inferno tomorrow night."

"Well we can still do that," said Pam, "what's the betting they won't even know it's been burnt down?"

So the next evening the girls caught the train over to the Inferno - or what was left of it. The roofless shell minus its doors looked dismal in the evening gloom. Pam's prediction was right. Mick and Dick arrived in Mick's car just after them and they couldn't believe their eyes.

"Now what do we do?" Mick asked looking as though his whole world had collapsed around him.

"Well me and Pam might try the Harrow on Friday night as everyone else from here should be there," Amy said.

Mick gave a derisive snort. "I've heard it's a bit of a posh dump," he said, "what d'you reckon Dick?"

Dick just shrugged. "Never been so can't say, but if it was any good I think the word would have spread."

"That's what I say," Pam agreed, "but it still might be worth a try if everyone else is going."

"Well, the night is young," said Mick, "how about we all go over to my house and listen to some records?"

"So long as your mum won't mind," Amy stipulated, "don't want to upset her."

Mick assured her it would be OK as they piled into his car. It wasn't exactly the exciting evening Amy had been hoping for, lounging on Mick's bed with the others listening to records, but Mick's mum was in a good mood. She popped in with coffees at eleven thirty and hinted that it was getting late and everyone had work in the morning.

Thursday evening Pam arrived at Amy's house around seven thirty and they sat in the kitchen listening to Luxemburg.

"I'm fed up," Amy said moodily, "Mick and Dick still don't take us out anywhere exciting. I mean, what a cheapskate taking us back to his house on Monday night."

Yeah, they are a bit tight-fisted," Pam agreed. "I phoned Dick yesterday from work and he said they want to meet us at Woolwich on Saturday and take us to the pictures."

"What a nerve!" Amy exclaimed. "Pictures!" she added contemptuously, "can't they think of anywhere else?"

"Oh, I nearly forgot. Dick gave me a message for you from Mick - he wants you to ring him this evening as early as possible."

Amy glanced at the clock on the windowsill. It was nearly eight o'clock.

"I don't feel like running when he clicks his fingers," she said grumpily.

"Oh, let's have a walk to the phone box. The fresh air might put you in a better mood," Pam said with a grin.

"You can bet Mick won't cheer me up," Amy declared sliding off the kitchen table.

Round at the phone box Amy got through to Mick's mum only to be told that Mick had gone out. Amy thanked her and asked her to tell Mick that she had rung.

"What a sod!" she stormed as they pushed open the door of the booth, "why do we bother with those two losers?"

Pam shrugged. "Probably because we've got no-one better at the moment."

Amy grunted in agreement. "Pity we're not going to the Marquee tomorrow night."

"I'm still waiting to hear from Aunt Anne. Hopefully we might get to stay at her house for a whole weekend."

"D'you think she'll be OK about us going out to West End clubs?"

"Oh I'm sure she won't mind and what's more mum won't worry because she'll trust her sister to look after us."

The girls returned to Amy's for coffee and discussed what they would do on their weekend away in London - what clothes to take and where to go.

The following evening they met up at Eltham station. Quite a crowd got off the train with Amy and many she recognised from the Inferno. Pam spotted her and waved from behind the ticket barrier.

"Hiya Tibs," Amy said, flashing her season ticket at the gruff looking inspector as she hurried through the gate, "if we just follow this lot, we should find the Harrow easily - I bet that's where they're all going."

Pam agreed and they fell into step behind a group of four giggling girls. It only took five minutes to reach a large building that looked like a fairly posh hotel set in its own grounds. A queue had formed that wound round the side to a back entrance where the dance hall was situated. Loud music was thumping inside and the girls received a bit of a shock on reaching the door where a large bouncer demanded an entrance fee nearly double the Inferno's fee.

"This place had better be good to justify that sort of money," Pam said peevishly as she was jostled into the ladies. After tidying their hair and handing in their coats they manoeuvred around the groups of gossiping girls until they reached the dance hall. Amy gazed at the flashing coloured lights making patterns on the walls and ceiling in the dimly lit room.

"Reminds me of the Scala," she commented standing on tiptoe in a vain attempt to see the stage at the far end of the room where the music was coming from.

"Not even a live group," Pam grumbled, sounding somewhat disappointed. A petite girl with long dark hair walked by holding a boy's hand.

"Hiya," she called out without pausing. Amy looked round and recognised the girl as Jenny, Mick's ex-girlfriend.

She nudged Pam. "Jenny's here and she sounds in a good mood. P'raps that's her new boyfriend."

Pam craned her neck around Amy to catch a glimpse of the pair as they vanished into the crowd.

"He's an improvement on Mick," she remarked, "taller at any rate."

"I don't feel so guilty if she's happy again," Amy said. Just then Mick's friend Eric appeared in front of them.

"Hi girls. How d'you like this place?"

"It's not the Inferno is it," Pam said gloomily.

"Doesn't have the atmosphere of the Inferno even though most of the crowd come from there," Amy said. She looked around to see which of Eric's mates were with him but he seemed to be alone. "Where's Mick and Dick tonight?" she asked casually.

Eric shrugged. "Your guess is as good as mine," he said and leaned towards them. "If you ask me, I think two nice girls like you deserve better than them." He gave a wink and a smile before melting into the crowd again.

"Eric's right," Amy said, "he's......" She tailed off as a familiar blue suede coat distracted her. Pam had spotted it too.

"Isn't that the dishy Peter?" she asked watching the coat swish through the exit. Amy's stomach gave a lurch. Suddenly she didn't want to be there any more.

"I really don't think much of this place," she said, "let's not waste any more time here, Tibs." She gave Pam's arm a tug and shoved her way out to the ladies to reclaim her coat. Pam followed and tactfully didn't mention Peter again, guessing it had touched a raw nerve with Amy.

The next day, being Saturday, Amy had a lie-in before walking into town after lunch to meet Pam. They went into Woolies to see some of Amy's ex-workmates. Bing, the supervisor was very chatty, and Maggie on baby-wear came over to say hello. The girls left to catch the train over to Pam's house where they had tea and got ready before leaving to meet Mick and Dick at Woolwich. Mick apologised for being out when Amy had phoned. Feeling in a better mood, she forgave him and received a hug in return. The horror film was 'Castle of Terror', which they quite enjoyed.

Mick couldn't take Amy home because his car was off the road and since Dick didn't even possess a car, the boys saw the girls onto their train home.

Mick asked Amy to ring him on Wednesday. "By the way, are you really going through with being a bridesmaid next Saturday?" he asked with a cheeky grin.

"Of course I am," Amy snapped irritably, "and if you and Dick can't behave properly, I shan't bother to try and get you invitations to the reception."

"We'll be the epitome of good manners," Mick assured her, adding: "I'm sure we'll have a really great time."

"I've known wedding receptions to get a bit out of hand once the relatives have had a few drinks," Pam said dubiously.

"Well I'm sure this one won't," Amy retorted. Then the train gave a sudden lurch causing Mick and Dick to fall off the step by the carriage door. The boys were busy brushing themselves down as the train gathered speed so they missed the girls waving goodbye.

"Another exciting Saturday night," Amy said sarcastically and pulled out two sticks of chewing gum from her handbag. She gave one to Pam and unwrapped the other.

"At least next Saturday should be better because of the wedding," Pam said optimistically. Amy just grunted and gazed out at the dark night whizzing past the window. Pam changed the subject. "Coming over to the Black Prince tomorrow evening?"

"Dunno - who's on?"

"Dunno," Pam said, mimicking Amy's lacklustre tone. Amy stirred and looked round at her friend, then realised Pam was taking the Mickey.

She made an effort to sound a bit more enthusiastic. "Yeah, all right - we might as well go since we're not doing anything else. No chance of Mick and Dick wining and dining us, that's for sure!" The girls laughed.

Sunday evening the Black Prince proved to be a bit dead, lacking a decent group. They saw a few familiar faces including Pam's other cousin, John Prescott, and Eric. Amy also spotted their zany Scottish friend Yvonne giggling with some chap in the corner. They hadn't spoken since leaving school or at least Yvonne hadn't contacted them and they had no idea what they had done to upset her - probably nothing as Yvonne had sent them to Coventry before for no apparent reason. Pam and Amy decided to ignore her until she made the effort to speak first but Yvonne was too wrapped up with her boyfriend to notice anyone else.

Next day at lunchtime Amy headed for the row of phone booths in the basement of the Pru to make a call to Katy. She wanted to check with her that it would be OK to bring Mick and Dick to the reception on Saturday. Katy had already agreed that Pam could go though Amy sensed Katy wasn't too keen on Pam. "I think she uses you," Katy once pronounced after a visit to Amy's when Pam arrived and proceeded to rush Amy off to a dance.

Today Katy was in a good mood. "Of course they can come but it's up to you to keep them under control."

Amy thought she made them sound like badly behaved dogs but refrained from saying as much.

Wednesday evening Amy enjoyed the cool autumnal air on her face as she walked to the phone box on the corner of the Crescent to phone Mick. She told him the good news about Saturday and he sounded pleased. Amy guessed it was probably because it meant a free evening for him. He was still having trouble with his car. "Shan't get it back from the garage until Saturday," he said despondently, "please give me a ring tomorrow evening and cheer me up." Amy promised she would and then dawdled home to a mundane evening of hair washing.

Next morning she received a letter from Katy. She had changed her mind so Mick and Dick were no longer invited to the reception. She sounded very apologetic explaining that Keith wasn't keen on the idea of strangers at the reception. Amy cursed Keith on the train to work; he was inclined to be very possessive where Katy was concerned.

She rang Mick that evening and told him of the change of plans. He didn't seem too disappointed and suggested they meet at Woolwich Friday evening for a night at the flicks. Amy tried to sound enthusiastic at the prospect but Mick's dates had a definite ring of repetitiveness about them. She walked home feeling fed up.

The following evening the girls met Mick and Dick at Woolwich. They had all arrived by train as Mick's car was still out of action. They watched 'Love with the Proper Stranger' and 'Wheel of Fire' which made a change from the usual horror flick.

Afterwards, as they huddled together on the platform to keep warm while waiting for their trains, Mick announced unexpectedly: "We've decided to come to the reception tomorrow regardless."

"But you can't," Amy said with a gasp of surprise, "you'll be barred or kicked out."

"We'll take our chances - maybe they'll be too busy to notice us creeping in. If we keep a low profile, then once everyone's had a few drinks, we won't need to worry."

"Keith has got several brothers," Amy warned.

"Maybe they're not as big as me," Dick boasted, puffing out his chest.

"I shall act surprised when you turn up," Amy said, "I don't want to fall out with Katy, though I think it's Keith who's behind the ban."

"That's settled then," Dick said, giving Pam a hug.

"I bought their wedding present today - a set of tumblers. I hope they like them because they weren't cheap," Amy said flicking back her hair.

"D'you think we ought to buy wedding presents too?" Pam asked looking conscious-stricken.

"No, of course not, after all you're only coming as my guests - you don't really know Katy and Keith."

"Amy's right," Mick quickly agreed.

The boys' train drew up at the platform so it was the girls' turn to see them off first for a change. The guard didn't waste any time in waving his green flag and blowing his whistle. They barely had time for a quick peck before Mick and Dick were whisked away.

Amy sat in the hairdressers next morning watching apprehensively as the stylist twirled and tweaked her hair into a French pleat. She managed to force a smile for Katy's benefit as she sat next to her having a headdress fitted into her hair, which would hold the veil in place. On the other side of Katy sat her old school friend, Christine, also having her hair scrunched up into a pleat. Katy was excited; her big day had arrived and she intended to enjoy every moment.

With their matching hairdos all neatly lacquered into place, the girls hurried back to Katy's first floor flat to start getting ready. The wedding was booked for 2p.m. at the church, so everyone was flapping around in a mild panic. There was make-up to be carefully applied and dresses to don. Mrs Bullen clucked like an old mother hen fussing over everyone and worrying in case any drinks got spilt and spoilt an outfit. Charlie, Katy's younger brother, strutted around in his hired morning suit trying to be helpful but generally getting in the way. Jean, Katy's older sister, was making last minute adjustments to the bouquet and buttonholes. Katy was the only one who looked relaxed and enjoying herself. She sat in her bedroom wearing frilly white underwear and sipping tea while applying more mascara.

Mrs Bullen hurried in with a plate of cheese sandwiches. "You ought to try and eat something - I don't want you passing out from hunger during the service," she said thrusting the plate under Katy's nose. She sighed and took one to keep the peace. She wasn't hungry but it was wisest not to argue with her mother.

Amy came in wearing her bridesmaid's dress. She and Christine had been busy changing in Jean's bedroom. Mrs Bullen quickly forced a cheese sandwich onto her too and then took a step back to admire her handiwork.

"Turn round Amy, let me see how the dress hangs at the back." Amy obliged with a twirl feeling vaguely surreal in the peach satin dress. Christine came in and Mrs Bullen gave a satisfied grunt.

"Don't my bridesmaids look a picture?" Katy said swivelling round on her stool to grin at the pair with their matching hair, dresses and white shoes. Amy felt like a fish out of water in her bridesmaid's outfit but put on a brave face for her friend.

In the lounge Mr Brown had arrived. He felt very honoured to be asked to give Katy away. The Bullens had lived across the Crescent from the Browns ever since they all moved into the houses as new in the late 1940's. When Mr Bullen died of Leukaemia while the children were still young, Mr Brown became the father figure they automatically turned to in times of need. Now he stood patiently munching on a cheese sandwich while Charlie attached a carnation to the lapel of his jacket.

"These teeth are playing havoc with my gums - I knew they would, but mother insisted I must wear them. She said I can't give Katy away with no teeth."

Charlie grinned. "No-one will notice if you want to take them out Mr B," he said, then cursed as he pricked his finger.

"No, no, it's more than my life is worth to disobey the wife. I shall have to suffer in silence, but I might slip them out so that I can enjoy the wedding breakfast."

Then it was time to get Katy into her dress and attach the veil to her headdress.

"The cars have arrived," Charlie called out from his vantage point at the lounge window. Mrs Bullen became even more flustered as she organised everyone into groups for each car, leaving Katy and Mr Brown to wait for the last car.

At the church Amy and Christine waited in the entrance foyer with the two younger bridesmaids and the pageboy, shivering in the chill of early autumn. Through the doors Amy spotted Keith with Barry, his brother and best man, hovering at the front of the pews in their matching morning suits. Keith kept tugging nervously at his collar as though it was strangling him.

Katy's car drew up and she carefully alighted with a helping hand from Mr Brown. He looked very proud as Katy took his arm. Amy, Christine and the other bridesmaids and page moved into position behind them and the organ began to play the bridal march. The wedding went off without a hitch; Amy felt like she was in a dream as the vicar droned through his address.

The ceremony over, everyone trooped up the aisle and huddled outside for the photo session, which seemed to go on forever. Amy smiled a frozen smile through chattering teeth and then made a dash for the nearest car as soon as the photographer had finished. It was only a short ride to the reception at a local hall which reminded Amy of the scruffy green huts where both she and Katy had first attended infant school together. This too was a single storey wooden structure with a stage at the far end and a room at the opposite end where all the food and drink was stored.

The tables were arranged in a U shape with Kay, Keith and their immediate families across the top table. Amy sat with her mum, dad and brother, Ray. There were the usual toasts and speeches after the meal. Then the cake was cut and handed round and eventually the tables were moved to the side to make room for dancing and the party began. Up on the stage a Dansette record player was plugged in, as this constituted the main entertainment. There was no live group, but the music was quite good and pretty loud. Barry came over and dragged Amy onto the floor for a dance.

"I think me and you should go out together sometime," he whispered in her ear as he gripped her tightly around the waist. Amy suspected he had already been imbibing rather freely. "I think you're lovely," he mumbled nuzzling her neck.

Amy pulled away. "I don't think my boyfriend would approve," she said coldly adding, "in fact he'll be arriving here any time now - I think I'll go and look for him." She hurried away leaving Barry swaying slightly in the middle of the dance floor looking bemused. She had arranged to meet Pam and the boys outside the hall at 7p.m. and it was nearly time so she hung around at the entrance hoping Barry wouldn't come looking for her.

At 7.15p.m. they rolled up in Mick's car. Amy had to endure the jokes and comments about her hair and clothes. She envied Pam in her Mod gear with her hair hanging loose on her shoulders.

She took them over to an empty table on the far side of the room, well away from her parents, because she didn't relish the prospect of them wanting to be introduced to Mick. "You boys get the drinks in," Amy said and then dragged Pam off into the ladies to help remove all the pins from her hair. She brushed it out and back to its usual long loose state. "Oh that feels a lot better," she said shaking her head and then gazed down at the dress. "Pity I haven't got other clothes to change into though," she said with a sigh.

They re-joined Mick and Dick and enjoyed the next couple of hours drinking and watching the antics of some of the inebriated guests as they tried to dance.

Katy came over looking hot and happy in her white dress. There was no sign of Keith. Amy introduced the boys and she smiled sweetly and said how pleased she was that they had made it to the reception. She sounded sincere but Amy couldn't help feeling a little uncomfortable because she had ignored her friend's wishes.

"If Katy says anything to me later, I shall say I never received her letter," Amy said to the others after Katy had gone. She decided this was the best strategy.

Half an hour later Amy felt a tap on her shoulder. It was Katy again. She beckoned to Amy and took her to the rear of the hall. "How d'you fancy doing something a bit daft?" she asked with a giggle.

Amy looked puzzled. "Like what?"

"Let's catch a bus back to the flat so that we can change - I've asked Christine and she's up for it."

Amy glanced down at her dress then at Katy in her full-length wedding dress and veil. She grinned. "Yeah, why not - it'll be a laugh." Then a thought occurred to her. "But what about Keith? Have you told him where you're going?"

"'Course I haven't," Katy said scornfully, "if he knew, he'd try and stop me - that's why we need to sneak away quickly. My Keith is lovely but he's a bit old-fashioned."

Katy went to fetch Christine while Amy returned to the others to tell them she would be gone for a while to change.

Outside the girls all held hands and ran down the middle of the road until they reached the High Street. A bus was just pulling away from a bus stop.

"That's the bus we want," gasped Katy breathlessly and without thinking dragged her two friends in front of it and flagged it down. The bus braked sharply and Katy blew a kiss to the startled driver. The conductor stood speechless on his platform as the girls hopped on board. All heads turned in their direction as they flopped down on the three-seater inside.

"Oh blimey," Katy blurted out, "I haven't brought any money for the fare!" The girls could only giggle at their predicament. The bemused conductor just grinned and let them off from paying.

The bus stopped a few yards from the flat and the girls were soon changed. Katy found some money for the bus fare back to the reception and they arrived just in time for the last few dances before the evening drew to a close.

Keith came steaming across the dance floor to Katy looking none too pleased, and when she explained what she had done, he looked even more put out. "You should have taken a car," he said peevishly, "there was no need to go and catch a bus in your wedding dress."

"Yes, I know, dear," Katy said patiently. "But I wanted to be different and fancied catching a bus. Besides it was much more fun," she added with a hint of defiance.

Amy left Katy pacifying Keith and went to drag Mick onto the dance floor for a smooch to a slow dance since Pam was doing the same with Dick.

She leaned across and grinned at Pam. "I reckon Keith is going to have his hands full with Katy."

Chapter Three

October – A New Friend

Amy and Pam plodded up the hill to Amy's house feeling pleased with their purchases.

"When this skirt is made, it will go well with the green twin set I bought up Oxford Street on Thursday," Amy declared, puffing slightly from the exertion. It was Saturday afternoon and the girls had met up in town to buy some grey material to make a long straight skirt each. In Sherry's they had found some material they both liked and bought two lengths. "I'm glad I bought that yellow roll-on while I was in Marks," Amy added, "I think I'll need it to give me a smoother look if this skirt fits tightly."

Pam switched her shopping to the other hand. "You must show me your twin set, Bat, 'cause I think I'll get one too only I'd better get a blue one just to look a bit different, after all we've got a lot of matching clothes already and now we'll have the same grey skirts."

The girls arrived just as Mrs Brown was laying the dining room table for tea. "You'll be staying for some tea won't you Pam?" Mrs Brown invited, "it's only Welsh rarebit on toast - one of Mr Brown's favourites."

"Sounds lovely," Pam said politely, then she and Amy retreated to the lounge to study the dress pattern they were going to use.

"Since it's the same pattern we used for the maroon skirts, it should be straight forward," Amy said, "only last time I had a double vent and this time I think I'll just put in a single rear vent."

"Mmm," Pam said thoughtfully, stroking the grey material. "I think instead of a pleated vent, I'll just make a slit," she said, "then at least our skirts will be slightly different."

After tea the table was cleared and Pam helped Amy to pull out the extension so they could lay out the material properly. After carefully pinning on the pattern pieces, they used Mrs Brown's pinking shears to cut each piece out.

"How did you get on with Mick last night?" Pam mumbled through a mouthful of pins.

"Oh the usual," Amy said and sighed, "we met up at Woolwich and went to the flicks - it was a boring old cowboy film, and then he brought me home in his car."

"Why didn't he take you there in his car?" Pam asked sharply, her mouth now empty of pins.

"You know Mick - he's not exactly the gentlemanly type - probably wanted to save petrol."

"Do you realise, Bat, that tomorrow we'll have been going out with Mick and Dick for five weeks and five days."

"You've been keeping check?" Amy asked in surprise, "well it may not be for much longer," she added gloomily, "that sod made some weak excuse about not being able to see me tonight so he says he'll come over here tomorrow evening with Dick and pick us up."

"It's not good enough Bat," Pam grumbled, "boyfriends are supposed to take their girlfriends out on a Saturday night, not go on the razzle with their mates."

Amy grunted in agreement as she concentrated on cutting out the waistband of her skirt. She finished and held it up for careful inspection. "That looks good," she said, satisfied with her effort. "You know, Tibs, we ought to tell Mick and Dick when we see them, that we went to a really wild party tonight."

Pam giggled. "That'd make them jealous, and serve them right too."

Sunday afternoon Pam arrived at Amy's and the girls continued working on their skirts. They had pinned and stitched the side seams the night before and now they were busy fitting the zips and waistbands.

Mrs Brown popped her head round the door from the kitchen. "It's tongue for tea today, I take it Pam will be here."

Amy glanced at Pam and saw her give a slight grimace. "Er, we'd prefer beans on toast. Don't worry - I'll make it," Amy offered helpfully. Pam looked relieved as Mrs Brown just nodded and vanished back to the kitchen. Just then there was a knock at the front door. Mrs Brown went to see who was there and called out in her Sunday posh voice: "Amy, dear, it's for you."

"Surely it's far too early to be Mick and Dick," Pam said looking alarmed, "I haven't even changed yet."

Amy jumped up and hurried to the door where she found a sheepish looking Eric on the doorstep. "Er, Mick asked me to stop by and tell you he's sorry but he can't make it tonight - nor Dick either."

Amy scowled. "He's done this once too often," she said crossly, "I've had enough of his unreliability."

"He wants you to ring him this evening," Eric said apologetically, looking uncomfortable, then he muttered goodbye and hurried back to his car.

A fuming Amy returned to Pam in the dining room and repeated Eric's message.

"How dare they!" Pam snapped indignantly, "they're really pissing me off – oh – er, sorry Mrs Brown," she added hastily as Amy's mum appeared in the doorway with a disapproving look on her face.

"I need the table now for tea," she announced so the girls quickly packed away the sewing machine and their dressmaking bits and pieces.

After tea they walked round the Crescent to the phone box on the corner to ring Mick. As Amy expected, he was full of apologies and claimed to be stony broke.

"Give me a ring Wednesday evening," he said, "and we can make arrangements to meet at the Falcon Hotel - it's supposed to be pretty good there."

"Maybe I will and maybe I won't," Amy said irritably and banged down the receiver.

"Let's get ready and go over to the Black Prince," Pam suggested as they walked back around the Crescent, "we need to forget about them and enjoy ourselves." Amy nodded in agreement.

They caught a bus to the Black Prince and were pleased to find the Pretty Things were on stage playing some great R&B. The place was packed out but the girls managed to find a small space to dance their latest Mod dance to the music. A boy who Amy had seen there several times came over and asked her to dance. Pam gave her a subtle shove towards him and then turned to find her cousin John grinning at her. He whisked her off for a dance as Amy melted into the arms of the dishy boy wearing a smart blue mohair suit. He introduced himself as Tim and she soon discovered that he was a bit of a nutter when he insisted he had an invisible parrot perched on his shoulder.

"Go on, give him a stroke, he won't peck you," he coaxed. Amy, feeling a bit silly, gave the air above his shoulder a quick stroke.

"Oh, he likes you," Tim said, "but better not stroke him there any more or he'll get too excited. It doesn't do to get him too excited."

Amy felt herself flushing. "Why not?"

"Well, for one thing he starts talking loudly and then he shrieks and swears."

"Oh," Amy giggled, "I'd better leave him alone then." As they chatted Amy learnt that Tim lived only a few streets away from her.

"I'll accompany you home if you like," he offered and Amy happily accepted. At the end of the evening, Tim and Amy walked to the bus stop outside the Black Prince with Pam and she caught her bus home.

"I'll ring you at work tomorrow," she yelled to Amy as she jumped on board.

Tim and Amy waited for their bus, which arrived five minutes later. When they alighted from the bus, Tim walked Amy to her door where he left her with a vague: "Maybe I'll see you at the Black Prince next week." There wasn't even a goodbye kiss.

"Yeah, maybe," she said, trying to sound carefree as she walked up the garden path and gave him a wave, but her heart was sinking. He hadn't exactly been falling over himself to ask her out, so she didn't hold out much hope for next Sunday at the Black Prince.

At work Monday morning, Miss Rogers ushered in a well-dressed new girl with a swarthy complexion and straight black hair that reached to her chin. She introduced her as Mary Romano and placed her on D division, two rows in front of Amy. The dark rings under her eyes gave her a haggard look. She turned round and flashed Amy a quick smile of even white teeth. Amy smiled back, feeling sorry for her, stuck as she was, on such a dead division, full of old crones. It appeared to be even worse than A division.

At lunchtime Amy invited Mary to join her and Jeanette in the canteen. As soon as they were out of the office and in the lift to the basement Mary lit up a Benson & Hedges using an expensive-looking silver lighter. "I've been gasping for this all morning," she said and took a long drag on the cigarette. She spoke in a cockney accent with a twang of Italian.

In the canteen over lunch Mary chatted easily about her family. They had emigrated from Italy many years ago and lived in a large house at Finsbury Park. She was the baby of the family with two older brothers who spoiled her by inundating her with presents.

"They gave me this," she said proudly stroking the green twin set she was wearing, "it's real cashmere." Amy and Jeanette looked suitably impressed. "My brothers can get me anything I want," she boasted, pushing the packet of cigarettes towards Amy. Amy took one and Mary pushed the packet towards Jeanette who shook her head and tucked into a yoghurt. Mary continued, "P'raps I shouldn't be telling you this, but Thursday night is their thieving night."

"You're not serious!" Amy said unable to hide the shock on her face.

Mary grinned. "Yeah, 'course I am. You should see the stuff stashed down in our cellar."

"Do your parents know what they do?"

"Leave it out! They'd go barmy and chuck 'em out of the house. No, they never go down to the cellar - just as well! How d'you think I got this twin set? It'd take at least a couple of weeks wages to buy it."

"Don't they ever get caught?" Jeanette piped up in her soft lisping voice having finished her yoghurt.

"They've had a few near misses but that just makes it all the more exciting," Mary said with a laugh. Amy couldn't decide whether Mary was telling the truth or just exaggerating to impress her new workmates. She liked Jeanette with her plain, uncomplicated ways but Mary she wasn't so sure about.

"So where do you hang out of an evening for kicks?" Mary asked Amy as they sipped their coffees.

"It used to be the Inferno at Welling - it had a great atmosphere until it burnt down."

Mary laughed. "That's good - the Inferno getting burnt. I think I've heard of the place."

"Everyone regrouped at the Harrow Inn but it's not the same," Amy said with a sigh.

"My favourite haunt is the Scene Club up West. You should come down there one night - I know you'd love it even though it's a bit of a dive, but the music's great with fantastic R&B sounds and they sometimes have live groups on stage. The Animals have appeared there and even the Who when they used to call themselves the High Numbers. I know a lot of the regulars who go there."

Amy nodded. "Yeah, me and Pam must give it a try one night."

The talk moved on to boyfriends and Jeanette felt a bit left out of the conversation, as she had never had a boyfriend.

"I've got this sod of a boyfriend called Trevor," Mary said grumpily and dragged hard on her cigarette. "He pisses me off most of the time - always messing about like a big kid. Don't think I'll see him for much longer."

Amy grunted. "Mm, know what you mean. Me and my mate Pam are supposed to be going out with a pair called Mick and Dick - a right couple of cheapskates. They're always complaining about how broke they are. They can never afford to take us anywhere decent."

Mary's eyes lit up. "Mick and Dick? I know a Mick and Dick who go down the Scene quite a lot."

"Well it can't be the same two," Amy said flatly.

"These two hang around with several mates; I often have a laugh and a joke with them."

"You don't happen to know the names of any of their mates?" Amy asked feeling a twinge of suspicion.

"Well, one of them is called Eric. He's got this big old convertible car that they all drive up in from South London."

Amy's mouth dropped open in a gasp of disbelief. "It's them! Is Dick tall and wears a long tan leather coat?"

Mary chuckled. "Yeah, that's him - practically lives in that coat."

"The lying, conniving bastards!!" Amy blurted out going red with anger. "How dare they. All the times they've told us they're broke and can't see us, they were really skiving off to the Scene. No wonder Mick tried to put me off from going to the clubs up West. He was probably afraid I'd bump into him. That does it. Wait 'til I tell Pam - she'll be furious too!"

"Well at least I can keep an eye on them and tell you what they get up to down there."

Back in the office that afternoon Pam rang Amy as she had promised and Amy quickly told her what Mary had said. Amy heard Pam gasp. "The sods!" she spat down the phone.

"I've been thinking, Tibs, let's not tell them that we've found out about their nights out in London."

"Well I've no intention of speaking to Dick again, so it's not a problem," Pam said bitterly.

"Yeah - we'll just snub them if we happen to bump into them - and serve them right!"

They arranged to meet up Wednesday evening at the Falcon Hotel.

"Meanwhile Bat, let's get our skirts finished so we can wear them there."

"Of course you do realise that those two will be there," Amy pointed out.

"Yes, and we will simply ignore them," Pam said emphatically.

Wednesday evening they met up outside the Falcon Hotel, wearing their new grey maxi skirts.

"Mick will probably guess I'm not speaking to him because I didn't ring him," Amy said as they queued to get in.

In the large dance hall the group on the stage at the far end sounded pretty feeble. Pam nudged Amy and pointed across the room to where the familiar figures of Mick and Dick were hovering with a few of their mates. They spotted the girls but looked uncertain whether to come over so Pam and Amy made it clear they didn't want their company by glaring and turning their backs on them. Then Amy's heart gave a flutter as she saw someone she recognised.

She nudged Pam. "Look Tibs, isn't that the lovely Tony from the Inferno over there?"

"Yeah, and he looks pretty wrapped up with that girl he's dancing with," Pam observed.

Amy sighed. "Just my luck."

They stayed for a few dances, and then decided to head for home. They were feeling fed up because every time they pushed through the crowd they kept meeting up with Mick and Dick, and had to make a quick detour.

The weekend arrived and, needing to economise, Amy stayed home Friday and Saturday night watching T.V. But by Sunday she could stand it no longer. She had to get out of the house or she would go stir crazy so she borrowed £2 from her dad and persuaded Ray to give her a lift over to Pam's on the back of his tandem. No easy feat in her long straight skirt, which she had to roll up around her waist.

The girls got ready and caught a bus to the Black Prince. Amy wasn't feeling optimistic about seeing Tim after the casual way he had said goodbye to her.

The group playing on stage weren't much good and the room wasn't as packed as usual. Halfway through the evening Amy spotted Tim dancing with Jo Reynolds, an attractive girl from her class at school. Amy watched her stroking the imaginary parrot on Tim's shoulder. She giggled and nestled coyly against him as they smooched to a slow number.

Amy turned to Pam. "I'm getting fed up Tibs - I think we ought to leave."

"A couple more dances, Bat - we might as well get our money's worth."

Amy agreed half-heartedly. She didn't want to spoil Pam's evening, as she seemed to be enjoying herself. Amy forced a smile and made sure they danced well away from Tim and Jo.

Monday, after work, Amy discovered the tube trains were on strike so she didn't get home until nearly seven. She just had time to dash in, change and dash out again as she was meeting Pam at the Railway Tavern.

All the usual faces from the Inferno were there including Mick and Dick who Pam and Amy again ignored.

A fairly dishy boy came over and asked Amy to dance. As they smooched together she was pleased to catch sight of Mick looking across at them with a peeved expression on his face. The boy turned out to be Polish and Amy had difficulty understanding his broken English so she made an excuse to get out of a second dance with him and went in search of Pam. She found her propping up the bar, chatting to her cousin Colin over an orange squash. He quickly bought Amy a drink and they stayed for a while chatting to Colin and a couple of his mates who came in and joined them. Colin offered the girls a lift home.

"We accept providing you've not got your dirty coal lorry parked outside," Amy stipulated doubtfully.

"You know I only keep it for high days and holidays," Colin replied with a grin.

Amy and Pam met up on the train to Woolwich on Saturday. They bought some red nail varnish to share between them and Amy fell in love with a gorgeous brown velvet paisley dress displayed in a shop window so she dashed in and tried it on. It fitted perfectly, though the sleeves were too long. As it was a one off, the assistant offered to have the sleeves shortened for her. A thrilled Amy paid the deposit and arranged to collect it the following Saturday.

"I'm getting really fed up with the lousy local clubs," Amy grumbled once the girls were on the train home.

"Yeah, they're not much cop," Pam agreed. "Someone at work was telling me about a club at Lewisham that's supposed to be pretty good - the El Partido - and what's more it's an all-nighter – not that we'd be allowed out all night!"

"Well why don't we give it a try tonight, Tibs?" Amy suggested, "it's got to be better than the Harrow!"

The girls returned to Pam's and after tea got themselves ready for the evening ahead.

They found the club in the High Street at Lewisham. A narrow doorway between two shops with steep stairs leading up to a very dark first floor where a large room with blacked out windows had a stage at one end. Tables lined the walls, which were also painted black. The music was deafening but good with the promise of a decent group coming on stage later.

Lights flickered off a glass ball rotating on the ceiling. A small bar in the corner served drinks so the girls got themselves an orange each and found an empty table to sit at.

"This is more like it," Amy said gazing round approvingly at the groups of people chatting or dancing.

"It's not all that crowded though," Pam observed, "and it makes a change not to see anyone we recognise."

"I expect a lot of people come later as it stays open all night." Amy said.

The girls got up to dance and were quickly joined by a couple of smartly dressed boys in mohair suits. They introduced themselves as Robert and Brian. A slow number came on and Amy found herself in Robert's arms. They were both tall, good looking boys and the girls were happy to spend the rest of the evening in their company.

"I come here quite a lot but I haven't seen you here before," Robert said in Amy's ear.

"It's our first time," Amy explained, "thought we'd try it out."

"How d'you like it?"

"So far so good. Does it fill up later on?"

"Once the band is on stage, it'll be that packed you won't be able to move."

Robert was right and the band was even more deafening making talking impossible.

The girls had to leave in order to catch the last train home so the boys accompanied them to the station and arranged to see them at the El Partido the following Saturday.

Back at Pam's house it was nearly 2 am before the girls squeezed into Pam's little bed with Monty, as usual, insisting on joining them.

"That was a pretty good evening," Amy pronounced with a yawn, "I quite like Robert. How did you get on with Brian?"

"He was OK," Pam said laconically. "Did you notice they arranged to meet us inside the club next week, so they won't have to pay for us to get in."

"I've had enough of cheapskates. If that's what they are then they can get lost," Amy said with a grimace, pushing Monty's bottom out of her face.

Next morning the girls had a lie in and got up late morning. Amy stayed at Pam's all day, as she didn't fancy going home to an empty house. Her parents and brother were away all day visiting Aunt Nora, her mum's eldest sister. That evening Amy borrowed a skirt and jumper from Pam. Although Pam was slightly taller, her clothes fitted Amy fairly well.

They caught a bus to the Black Prince in the next town, anticipating a good night ahead as the Graham Bond Organisation was billed to appear. They weren't disappointed. The small dance room was jam-packed and hot. The music was loud and sounded great. Graham Bond thumped away on the Hammond organ and did most of the vocals with a chamber pot at a raunchy angle on his head. There was a lot of appreciative cheering, whistling and clapping. John Prescott, Pam's dishy cousin, was there and asked Amy for a dance. They shuffled around with difficulty in the crowd. He was in a jubilant mood and left Amy gobsmacked when out of the blue he suddenly proposed to her. She noticed a twinkle in his eye, so she grinned and told him she'd think about it. He gave a theatrical bow and kissed her hand as he left.

"I think John's been drinking," Amy told Pam when she repeated what he had said.

Just then two boys pushed their way through the crowd and asked Pam and Amy for a dance. Pam danced with a tall, gorgeous looking blonde boy while Amy danced with his mate, Ken, who had a dark Beatle hair-cut and black leather jacket. They hovered next to the girls when the number finished and offered them a lift home. Pam seemed quite taken with the blonde one whose name was Ritchie, so they accepted their offer, but no firm dates were made to see them again, which disappointed the girls.

Amy wore her hair up in a half bun for a change when she went to meet Pam at the Railway Tavern Monday evening. It was well lacquered to prevent it from moving, even in a gale.

The dance room was crowded and the girls enjoyed themselves dancing to the music until Pam noticed Dick standing near the doorway staring dolefully across at her. Mick stood next to him, hands thrust down into his pockets. The girls decided it was time to leave. They pushed through the crowd and left the room without a glance in the direction of Mick or Dick, but they heard the distinct sound of clapping.

"Those sods had the cheek to clap as we walked out!" Amy exclaimed crossly.

"Oh just ignore it, Bat, we've hit them where it hurts - in their egos!" They left the Railway giggling and caught their respective buses home.

Amy was none too pleased when she arrived home next evening to be informed that Great Auntie Gertie was about to descend on the Brown household for her annual visit. Amy's parents were collecting Auntie Gertie in the morning, which would mean Amy vacating her bedroom to move in with her mother so that her aunt could have her bedroom. Dad was being dispatched to share Ray's double bed.

"Why is it always me and not Ray who has to move out?" Amy grumbled to herself as she rummaged through her wardrobe pulling out clothes she would need. "She'd just better not nail her combinations to my bedroom door."

During Auntie Gertie's visits, her combinations were regularly washed and hung out to dry on the line - much to Amy's embarrassment. She had never seen such voluminous underwear. There appeared to be a trap door in the seat and dad firmly believed (tongue in cheek), that the only way into them was to nail them to the door and back in through the trap door!

Auntie Gertie was a very sweet old lady, but also very deaf, making communicating difficult. Next day she offered to help mum with the washing up after the evening meal. She insisted on washing the dishes, which she did at break neck speed, leaving food still sticking to them. Mum waited until Auntie Gertie had retired to bed and then discreetly re-washed them.

Amy met Pam at the Falcon Hotel Wednesday evening. As they queued to get in, she spotted Tony from the Inferno standing about four feet in front of her. He had his arms around a blonde girl's shoulders. Amy wished she had chosen him instead of Mick when she had the chance. 'At least he has the decency to meet a girl outside a dance hall,' she thought despondently.

Once inside the loud music soon had them dancing, when who should turn up and ask them to dance but the gorgeous Ritchie and his mate Ken. This cheered up the girls no end until Ritchie announced that he had to leave early as he had arranged to do something for a friend. He apologised and left Ken to give them a lift home in his car.

Ken drew up outside Pam's house to drop her off and invited them to a party on Saturday night.

Pam looked dubious. "My parents don't like me going to parties, but if I don't tell them and I'm not too late in getting home then it should be OK."

"And if I stay over at your house Saturday night, then my parents won't know where I've been," Amy added.

Saturday morning the girls met up on the train to London. They stopped off at Woolwich so that Amy could collect her brown paisley dress and then they headed for the West End to search the shoe shops until Pam eventually found a pair of black suede shoes that she liked enough to buy. Their shopping done, they made for the Macabre coffee house for a much needed rest and a cappuccino.

"Have you heard back yet from your aunt?" Amy asked spooning the froth off the top of her coffee and licking it, "I can't wait to try the West End clubs."

"Oh, I'm a twit!" Pam exclaimed, "I forgot to tell you. I got a message from Aunt Anne to say we can go and stay with her anytime we like. She's looking forward to seeing us."

"That's great Tibs. How could you forget to mention something as important as that? How about we go next weekend?"

Pam nodded. "Why not - it'll be a laugh. I'll tell her to expect us Friday evening." Amy's spirits soared considerably, especially when added to the good news that Great Auntie Gertie was going back home.

"Do you realise Tibs, that our poor cat cops it every time Auntie Gertie farts, which is pretty often. Dad tries to save her blushes by blaming the cat!" Pam giggled into her coffee.

They caught the train home and arranged to meet up that evening at Pam's house. Ken and Ritchie were going to pick them up at Blackfen station to drive them to the party.

Back at home Amy found her parents were out, taking Auntie Gertie home. Pleased to get her bedroom back again, she flung open the window to get rid of the vague odour of old person that hung around, and couldn't resist inspecting the back of the door for signs of nail holes.

Amy arrived to collect Pam from her house that evening, so they could catch the train to Blackfen where they had arranged to meet Ken and Ritchie. Pam told her parents they were off to the El Partido once more, which they didn't mind too much because it was a club. Mrs Tibton objected to parties because, as she so often pointed out with a wink, there were bedrooms at parties and that spelt danger. "You girls are boy mad these days and boys definitely don't need any encouraging," she said disapprovingly as Pam and Amy were leaving.

The party was a bit of a disappointment. Everyone stood around in groups talking and nibbling on bits of cheese and pineapple. The music wasn't very loud and the boys were more interested in watching a football match on a TV in the back room.

"C'mon Bat, I've had enough of this party," Pam said after a half-hearted dance where they were the only ones dancing, "let's sneak off and walk into Welling." Amy agreed and they left without bothering to say goodbye to Ken and Ritchie.

In Welling they made a beeline for the Wimpy Bar and a rest with a refreshing cup of coffee.

"I enjoyed that walk. How about we walk as far as Bexleyheath and catch a bus from there back to my house?" Pam suggested.

"It's not like you to get all energetic," Amy observed with a grin, "these shoes aren't very good for walking, but I'll give it a go."

They finished their coffee and set off on the three-mile hike but it took them longer than they anticipated in their high heels. At Bexleyheath, having missed the last bus, they found themselves walking the rest of the way back to Pam's house. They limped indoors at 12.30am tired out and collapsed into bed.

"You and your bright ideas," Amy grumbled, but the only reply she got from Pam was a grunt. An exhausted Amy couldn't even be bothered to push the dog's wet nose away from her neck.

Chapter Four

November - West End Clubs

The next week at work seemed to drag for Amy. She could hardly wait for Friday and the exciting prospect of a weekend spent seeing what the West End clubs had to offer.

Thursday evening, as she carefully packed a suitcase, she was surprised when her normally tight-fisted mother appeared in the doorway and gave her ten shillings spending money. "Mind you behave yourself and don't forget to thank Pam's aunt for having you for the weekend," she said primly eyeing the new stockings Amy was pushing into the suitcase.

She lugged the suitcase to work on Friday morning and managed to stow it in her locker. After work she met Pam at the tube station where they caught an underground train to Plaistow in the East End.

Pam, also with a suitcase in tow, was as excited as Amy. "How about we try the Marquee in Wardour Street tonight?" she suggested, "I've heard they get top names there playing Blues and R&B."

"Sounds great," Amy said, "I wonder who's playing there tonight."

"We'll soon find out," Pam said as they alighted at Plaistow station and she led the way to an estate several streets away where her aunt and uncle lived in a small neat mid-terraced house.

Pam's aunt was very easy going and welcomed them both with a hug. She showed them up to the spare bedroom dominated by a large comfortable-looking double bed.

"Dinner will be ready in half an hour," she announced and then left them to unpack and change.

The girls got themselves ready for the evening ahead and could hardly face the large meal that Aunt Anne placed in front of them, such was their excitement, but they made the effort so as not to appear rude.

Pam's Uncle Fred didn't say a lot. After a brief "hello" and "how are you," he ate his meal in silence. Aunt Anne made up for his reticence by chatting non-stop, asking Pam how her sister - Pam's mum - was keeping and how little Ronnie was doing at school. Pam informed her that her brother was far from little these days, towering over her by almost a foot. By the time Pam had sated her aunt's curiosity, dinner was over and it was time to leave. Her aunt said she didn't mind what time they got back but to try and be quiet if she and Uncle Fred had gone to bed.

As they walked to the tube station, Amy turned to Pam looking amazed. "I could just see my mum going to bed if I was still out," she said, adding, "I like your aunt."

"She's OK," Pam agreed, "a lot more relaxed about us being out late than my parents."

The girls arrived outside the Marquee and joined a short queue waiting to get in. The hoardings on the walls announced that Sonny Boy Williamson would top the bill along with the resident group, the Yardbirds.

"Should be a good night," Pam observed, "my cousin Rob would be dead envious of us as the Yardbirds are his favourite group."

"Who's Rob?" Amy asked curiously, "you've never mentioned him before."

"Haven't I? He's my Aunt Bessie's son. They live not all that far from Aunt Anne. Perhaps we could go and pay him a visit tomorrow and see if he can recommend a good club for us to go to tomorrow night."

"You seem to have an unending stream of male cousins," Amy said a little enviously. She only had two boy cousins her age and they lived in the north of England.

The Marquee was packed with little room for dancing so they stood as near to the stage as they could get and drank in the atmosphere of the smoky dimly lit room. The music was loud. The Yardbirds played 'I Wish You Would' with its pounding guitar solo thumping through the speakers. Sonny Boy Williamson sang mostly slower Blues numbers and received noisy applause with much whistling and foot stamping. The evening drew to a close and as the girls queued at the cloakroom for their coats, Pam suddenly gave a yell.

"Look, Bat, over there - leaning against the wall - it's Rob!"

Amy saw a handsome young man wearing a dogtooth checked coat. He was gazing earnestly at everyone walking past him.

"I wonder what he's doing here," Amy mused vaguely.

"We'll soon find out," Pam said passing Amy her coat and pushing her way through the crowd towards Rob. He gave Pam a broad grin of recognition as she arrived beside him.

"Aunt Anne said you were here so I thought I'd come and escort you both home," he said leaning around Pam to get a glimpse of Amy who was suddenly feeling a bit shy and hovered behind Pam.

Pam introduced Rob to Amy and he shook her hand. Amy gazed at his even features, admiring his aquiline nose. She adored aquiline noses. Rob suggested they go for a coffee before heading home, so they walked down Wardour Street to the Macabre. Rob bought the coffees, and then he and Pam caught up on family news while Amy quietly sipped her coffee and tried not to stare across the table at Rob. Pam asked him about a club for Saturday night.

"I've got a great idea," said Rob glancing at Amy, "how about I ask my mate Jim to come with us tomorrow night and we'll take you down the Flamingo. We're both members so you can get in as our guests." The girls looked at each other and grinned.

"Sounds great," said Pam.

"Well I suggest you try and get some sleep tomorrow because you'll be up all night."

Rob took the girls back to Aunt Anne's house. They arrived at nearly 2 a.m. and he arranged to collect them at 4 p.m. and take them back to his house for tea.

The girls were so excited they lay awake discussing what to wear.

"I just hope this Jim is O.K. I don't fancy getting lumbered with a nerd," Pam said sounding a bit doubtful, "by the way, what did you think of Rob?"

Amy's heart gave a flutter. "Oh, he seems quite nice," she said with deliberate offhandedness. She didn't want Pam to guess that she was becoming besotted with her cousin so soon. She had already been out with two of Pam's cousins and it hadn't worked out. She hardly dared to hope that this time it might be third time lucky.

Next morning the girls went to the local street market and browsed amongst the stalls of clothes, records and bric-a-brac. They returned to Aunt

Anne's for lunch and had barely finished when Rob arrived early. Amy's heart skipped with excitement.

"Is it O.K. to take these two lovely ladies to an all-night party tonight?" he asked his aunt putting an arm around her shoulders and giving her a playful squeeze.

"Of course it is, dear. I know I can trust you to look after them and bring them home safely."

Pam and Amy exchanged quick smiles then Rob was ushering them out of the house.

"Don't forget when we get back tomorrow that we've been to a party," he reminded them, "Aunt Anne isn't keen on Soho nightclubs."

"You lied so easily, Rob," Pam teased pretending to scold him, "you must do it a lot." He just grinned and ushered them onto a bus that had drawn up at the bus stop. They sat on the three-seater and Rob insisted on paying the fares. The short bus ride took them to Jim's house.

"I thought it would be a good idea for you to meet Jim before tonight - that's why I came round early," Rob explained. Amy fervently hoped Pam would like Jim because if she didn't then all their plans for going out in a foursome could quickly collapse.

Jim's dad was caretaker of a school so they lived in the house next door to the school, which went with the job. Amy's fears soon disappeared at the sight of Jim - a tall good-looking boy with a mop of dark hair in a Beatle cut. He reminded Amy of Dan - Pam's first love when she was fifteen. Pam went all coy and giggly with him - always a sure sign that she was smitten. Amy had seen it before with boys that Pam fancied so it all boded well for the night ahead.

They spent the afternoon in a small back room playing records and chatting. Jim's mum brought in a tray with mugs of coffee and a plate of biscuits. She was short, plump and very pleasant and she didn't seem to mind the loud music one bit.

"There you are," she said setting the tray down on the coffee table and beaming at Pam and Amy. Jim told her of their plans to go out that evening to a nightclub.

"Well you boys must be sure to take care of these lovely girls. I've heard that some of those clubs can get a bit rough."

"They'll be fine with us," Jim assured her, "we shan't be going to any rough old dives."

Jim's mum shook her head and smiled. As she left the room she paused to remark: "You young people - I wish I had half your energy!"

At five o'clock Rob and the girls left Jim after arranging to meet up with him later that evening back at his house. They caught a bus to Rob's house as his mum was expecting them for tea.

Rob lived in a maisonette on a small estate with his mum and dad. His older sister was married and lived a few streets away. Amy felt a bit nervous at meeting more of Pam's relatives but she needn't have worried because Pam's Aunt Bessie made her feel very welcome. The table at the far end of the lounge was laid out for tea. After everyone had sat down, Rob's dad came ambling in wearing rolled up shirtsleeves and braces holding up his baggy trousers.

"Oh Alf, you might have made more of an effort," Bessie said crossly giving his clothes a disapproving look.

"Don't fuss, girl. I'm sure Pam and her friend don't mind," he said amiably, sitting down on the empty chair at the head of the table.

Rob told his parents the same story he had told his Aunt Anne and they didn't seem to mind the fact that Rob and the girls would be out all night.

As soon as tea was finished Rob took the girls to the nearby bus stop to catch a bus back to Aunt Anne's.

"At least if my mum and Aunt Anne meet up our cover stories will match," Rob said as the bus drew up. The girls waved goodbye and as the bus moved off Rob called out: "Don't forget to be ready by 8.30."

The girls could hardly contain their excitement, as they got ready for the night ahead. They giggled and chattered up in the bedroom and had to remember to talk about the party when within earshot of Aunt Anne and not mention nightclubs.

"What do you think of Jim?" Amy asked as she sat in front of the dressing table mirror applying mascara. She glanced in the mirror and saw a dreamy look spread over her friend's face.

"Oh he seems O.K.," Pam said with deliberate casualness.

"Come off it," Amy scoffed, "he's just your type."

"All right, I admit he is rather dishy," Pam conceded. "I'm *so* looking forward to a whole night in his company."

"I just know it's gonna be a great night," Amy said imagining herself in Rob's arms all night, "I wonder who'll be topping the bill at the Flamingo."

"Dunno, but it's a well-known and popular club so they ought to have someone pretty special on a Saturday night."

8.30 finally arrived and the girls paced up and down the lounge peering impatiently out of the window for a sign of Rob. Amy wore her new paisley dress and suede coat. Pam wore a new knitted dress under her green suede coat. Their flick-ups were well flicked and make-up applied with great care ready for the night ahead. The doorbell rang and both girls grabbed their handbags and dashed to the door calling out goodbye as they went.

Rob stood on the step grinning and Amy thought he looked more handsome than ever. He was wearing his dogtooth checked coat with the collar turned up against the chill November air.

They caught a bus over to Jim's house and were soon relaxing in the back room again with cups of coffee. Jim put an L.P. of R&B music on the record player. "This is the sort of music they play down the Flamingo," he told the girls as Graham Bond started singing 'Hi Heel Sneakers' in his unmistakable throaty voice.

"That's great - I love the Graham Bond Organisation. We see them from time to time at the Black Prince near where we live," Amy said, stretching her legs out as she sat on the sofa. Rob had removed his coat to reveal a maroon Fred Perry top. He sat next to Amy and she felt a tingle run through her as his arm brushed hers.

"I'm sure we can find something to do for the next couple of hours," Rob said slipping his arm around Amy's shoulders. Jim switched on a table lamp in the corner and then switched off the main light giving the room a subtler glow. He sat in the armchair and pulled Pam onto his lap. Amy didn't see what they did next because Rob's lips met hers in a tender kiss. She closed her eyes and sank back into the sofa; her heart skipped a beat and her head whirled in ecstasy. They came up for air eventually and Amy saw Pam snuggled up on Jim's lap in a tight embrace.

The arm was up on the record player and Graham Bond was starting his second rendition of 'Hi Heel Sneakers'. Amy was in heaven as Rob pulled her back down onto the sofa for another long snogging session.

All too soon Jim roused them by switching off the music.

"It's 11.15 - time we made a move," he said replacing the record in its sleeve. Rob and Amy sat up and Amy quickly rummaged in her bag for a comb to tidy her hair. Pam was busy brushing her hair and looking very happy.

They donned their coats and headed for the tube station. Rob had his arm around Amy's shoulder and Jim did the same with Pam. Amy barely noticed the chill night air. Her mind was bubbling at the prospect of the whole night ahead in Rob's company.

They emerged from Piccadilly Circus underground and found themselves amongst a lively throng of colourful people, mostly teenagers, all out to enjoy themselves in the West End. Rob's grip tightened protectively on Amy's shoulder as they turned into Wardour Street. Crowds loitered outside the Discotheque where loud music throbbed from the doorway. Across the street more crowds hovered around the entrance to the Marquee.

"Saturday night there's not usually much on at the Marquee," Rob told Amy as they sidestepped around a group of West Indians who were offering blockers to all and sundry passing by. Amy felt a little nervous and was glad of Rob's presence beside her. They arrived at the small entrance to the Flamingo. On the first floor large letters across the windows announced the Whisky A Go-Go Club. Rob took hold of Amy's hand and drew her through the black throng at the doorway. Amy felt her handbag being tugged. She grabbed it firmly and hurried after Rob. Glancing back she saw Pam being pulled through the crowd by Jim. She too looked nervous but managed to give Amy a quick smile. Steep narrow stairs led down to a small table where passes and membership cards were checked and entrance money was taken. As non-members and guests of Rob and Jim, the girls paid fifteen shillings each and then found themselves inside the dimly lit basement with its low ceiling and black walls. The music thundered off the walls and ceiling - it had nowhere else to go. The group on stage were playing a John Mayall number. The floor was packed. Amy saw black faces everywhere and only the occasional white face. She held on tight to Rob as he weaved through the tightly packed crowd. There was very little space for dancing. Amy felt hands tugging at her arm. Rob arrived down the front near the stage where there were several rows of plush red velvet cinema chairs with seats that sprang up, but they were all occupied.

"As soon as we spot some empty chairs we'll grab them," he yelled in Amy's ear, "it's a long night to be standing for hours on end."

Amy's hair was already sticking to her forehead in the close, sweaty and smoky atmosphere. Her clothes felt damp. She looked at Pam. Her face was flushed and shiny and her hair hung limply around her shoulders.

"D'you think we should hand our coats in at the cloakroom?" Amy yelled at her.

Pam shook her head. "No way. I'm not parting with my new suede. Besides everyone else seems to be keeping their suedes and leathers on - even the ones trying to dance."

Amy looked around. It was true. Those that could find a small space to dance were sweating profusely in their coats. Over against a side wall Amy noticed a raised platform with a metal barrier to prevent anyone falling off onto the dance floor. Steps led up at one end and a few tables and chairs were arranged along by the barrier. Amy suddenly recognised a few familiar faces sitting at one of the tables. She nudged Pam and pointed. There was Mick, Eric and a few of their mates, but no sign of Dick.

"They look very at home up there," Pam said sourly, "I bet this is where they get to every Saturday night."

They spent half an hour standing listening to the group. Rob informed Amy that they were the Original Topics.

"They're just the warm-up group before the main act comes on," he explained.

"They're not bad but who's topping the bill tonight?" Amy asked.

"I spotted a poster on the wall as we came down the stairs - tonight it's Zoot Money and his Big Roll Band. Should be great!"

"Wow! I can hardly wait," Amy said excitedly.

The group finished their turn and records were played while they cleared their equipment off the stage.

Jim leaned over to Amy. "Zoot Money was on the R&B record I played this evening. He sang 'Walking the Dog'.

Amy nodded. "We should be in for a terrific night."

A group in the seats in front of Rob stood up to leave. Rob tugged Amy's arm. "Come on - we've got to be quick, these seats are like gold dust." He jumped over the back of the seats and quickly bagged four chairs before the group had even moved away. Jim followed Rob but Amy and Pam inched their way round to the front of the seats. They didn't fancy trying to clamber unladylike over the backs in their dresses.

As they settled into their seats the compere arrived on stage to announce the main act and suddenly there was Zoot Money seated at a large Hammond organ with his assorted band members tuning and checking their instruments.

Amy loved the earthy throb of the R&B music and the mellow yet stabbing notes from the organ.

Rob leaned in and whispered in Amy's ear. "This is one of the best acts they get down here though there is one that's even better - Georgie Fame and the Blue Flames - they're fantastic. He really gets the audience going and the atmosphere is electric when he plays. I'll try and find out when he's appearing here next."

Amy didn't think anything could top the sheer joy she was experiencing right now as she sat next to Rob listening to great music.

After a couple of hours Zoot Money took a break and the compere returned to announce that the

Animals were in the house and had been invited on stage to do a few impromptu numbers. This was an unexpected bonus. Amy had been having trouble keeping her eyes open. Tiredness swept over her in waves, but she fought against it. Now the loud cheers and applause that greeted Eric Burdon and the rest of the group revitalised her sagging energy as Alan Price took his place at the Hammond organ vacated by Zoot Money. They were soon thumping out their hits to shouts and whistles of approval from the audience.

Eventually Zoot Money and his band returned for the final session of the night. As they started into Hoochie Coochie Man, Pam prodded Amy. She needed to go to the loo but didn't want to go alone so Amy went along to keep her company. The boys said they'd meet up with them over at the bar on the far side of the dance floor for a drink.

The ladies toilet was small and crowded. Amy and Pam emerged after a fruitless attempt to liven up their damp hair.

"Oh Bat, it's so hot in here," Pam exclaimed wiping her forehead with a tissue, "maybe we should have taken off our coats after all."

"But just think of all the weight we've sweated away," Amy said with a grin, "isn't this a fantastic night!"

"It definitely knocks the Railway Tavern into a cocked hat," Pam said and pushed her way through the crowd towards the bar with Amy clutching the back of her coat so as not to lose her.

Rob and Jim were leaning on the bar with four bottles of coke in front of them. Amy was glad of the ice cold drink to slake her thirst but was horrified when a glance at the price list behind the bar showed a bottle of coke cost two shillings. There was no alcohol for sale, which was probably just as well, and the choice of soft drinks was very limited.

"Look at those extortionate prices," she whispered to Pam.

"They know there's not many places open at this time of night to buy drinks," Pam whispered back.

Their drinks finished, the night was drawing to an end. A few people were leaving making a bit more room on the dance floor. A slow number started up so Rob and Jim took the girls for a smoochy dance until the club closed at 6a.m.

They emerged from the nightclub into the grey dawn of early morning. Amy shivered in the cold damp air. She felt washed out and was sure she looked as bad as she felt in the unforgiving morning light. She glanced at Pam and could tell that she was feeling the same. The boys seemed unfazed by the sleepless sweaty night and didn't look any different.

"We'll have to walk to Aldgate in order to catch an early bus since there aren't any other buses around at this hour," Rob explained as Amy held on to his arm.

"So long as you know how to get there," Amy said keeping her gaze averted to the wet paving slabs in order to avoid him seeing her shiny face. She was thankful for her long hair, now minus its flick-ups, which helped to veil her face.

"Sounds like a long way," Pam said from behind. She was holding Jim's arm tightly and, like Amy, staring hard at the pavement to hide her mascara smudged sweaty face.

As they walked towards Holborn Amy noticed loads of policemen strolling around in pairs. "They're the R&B coppers," Rob informed her, "they're always around making sure there's no trouble when the clubs turn out on Sunday mornings."

At 6.45a.m. they passed the imposing red brick Gothic frontage of the Prudential. Amy shuddered. 'It doesn't seem real that in just over 24 hours' time I'll be back here for another week of drudgery,' she thought.

They reached Aldgate and had a ten minute wait until a bus arrived that took them back to Plaistow and Aunt Anne's cosy terraced house. Jim didn't stop; he headed back to his own house after arranging for everyone to meet up at his place that evening.

Rob flopped out on the sofa while Pam and Amy each curled up in an armchair. After dozing for about an hour they were roused by Aunt Anne who had come downstairs and was busy in the kitchen making everyone a cup of tea. She didn't seem to mind them being out all night. No-one could face eating breakfast, so after the tea Aunt Anne found a blanket for Rob. He went back to sleep on the sofa while the girls, reluctant to go upstairs to bed, dozed on and off in the armchairs and Aunt Anne and Uncle Fred ate their breakfast in the kitchen.

At 10a.m. Pam got up and stretched then looked at Rob and smiled. He was sound asleep. She shook Amy and beckoned for her to follow her into the dining room.

"There should be a tape recorder in here if I remember correctly," Pam said opening a cupboard. She moved a few things then gave a satisfied grunt and pulled out a portable tape player.

"What d'you want that for?" Amy asked looking puzzled.

Pam grinned. "I want to play a little trick on Rob," she said giggling. She flipped open the lid and checked there was a cassette in it. "Now, when I press record, I want you to make some really loud snoring noises into the microphone," she said.

Comprehension dawned on Amy. "Why me? You can do pretty noisy snores yourself - don't forget I've had to share your bed with you and Monty."

Pam scowled and sighed. "Oh all right if I must." She pressed the red button and started making loud snorting and snuffling noises into the recorder but soon had to turn it off when both girls got a fit of the giggles. "I think that should do it," Pam said after calming down and replaying the tape, "just wait 'til Rob wakes up."

Rob finally roused at 11a.m. and was immediately confronted with the tape recording. He looked sheepish and mumbled an embarrassed apology, accepting without question that he had made the noises. Amy took pity on him and told him the truth; consequently Pam immediately received a battering with a cushion.

Rob took his leave and arranged to meet up with them at Jim's that evening. The girls went to bed all afternoon catching up on some of their lost sleep and got up in time for tea. Then, having washed and changed, they packed their bags, thanked Pam's aunt and uncle for having them and said their goodbyes.

They arrived at Jim's and Amy's heart skipped when Rob answered the door. They spent a glorious few hours listening to records while kissing and cuddling - Amy and Rob monopolising the sofa once more while Pam and Jim snuggled in the deep armchair. There was no interference from Jim's parents who were keeping out of the way in the lounge watching T.V.

All too soon it was time to leave. Rob and Jim escorted the girls to the station. Rob gave Amy his works phone number and asked her to ring him on Thursday to make arrangements for the following weekend.

On the journey home, as the girls excitedly exchanged opinions on the weekend and on the boys, it became obvious that Pam was as besotted with Jim as Amy was with Rob.

"This next week at work is going to drag on forever," Amy moaned.

"Never mind Bat," Pam said trying to console her friend, "it's been a fantastic weekend and the next one should be just as great."

Monday morning at work Amy still felt washed out from lack of sleep. Mary came over and wanted to know how her weekend had gone. Amy loved talking about Rob - how sweet he was, not to mention gentlemanly, considerate, good looking and good company - she could have gone on for ages but noticed Audrey out of the corner of her eye frowning and tapping her desk impatiently so with a muttered, "tell you more at lunchtime," she knuckled down to the huge pile of accounts overflowing from her in-tray.

The week dragged by just as Amy knew it would. Thick fog Tuesday evening meant a very slow journey home finally arriving at 8p.m.

Wednesday Amy was greeted at work by an excited Mary. "I've got some news for you - tell you at lunch," she said grinning mischievously at Amy's puzzled expression.

In the canteen Amy and Mary finished their lunch off with coffee while Jeanette had a yoghurt.

"Come on then Mary, what's this news you're dying to tell me?" Amy asked impatiently. Mary had refused to say a word all through the cottage pie. She pulled out her Benson & Hedges and offered one to Amy before lighting up and taking a long drag.

"I've been stirring things up with Eric and his mates," she announced with a twinkle in her eye.

"What d'you mean by that?" Amy asked suspiciously.

"I got chatting to them last night down the Scene. Told them how I work with you and that you and your mate Pam had got new boyfriends and had spent the whole weekend with them. You should've seen the look on their faces." Mary giggled.

"What did they say?" Amy asked, unsure whether to be pleased or cross with Mary's meddling.

"Eric said he'd tell Mick and Dick when he sees them next."

"I couldn't care less what Mick thinks - he's not a patch on my lovely Rob." Amy sighed and sucked dreamily on her cigarette. Then she came back down to earth with a bump. "I've just remembered - I've got to give Pam a ring to make arrangements for tonight."

She grabbed her bag and hurried off to the phone booths with the other two tagging along behind. The phones looked old fashioned in their wooden booths tucked away in a corner of the basement. Amy had been shown how to tap phone numbers on this old type of phone by her friend Yvonne, sometime ago. All three squeezed into the booth and Amy carefully counted out the taps and dialled the zeroes while Mary chatted loudly to hide the noise of the tapping just in case anyone should hear and get suspicious. Jeanette looked uncomfortable to be a part of something slightly dishonest. Her eyes darted around nervously and her cheeks were flushed a deeper red than usual.

Amy got through to Pam and told her what Mary had done. Pam, like Amy, didn't really care though she was a bit peeved that her morals might be brought into question if Dick heard she had been with another boy for a whole weekend. They made arrangements to meet up later at the Falcon and then it was time to get back to the boring drudge of the office.

Pam and Amy arrived on consecutive trains that evening. The Falcon proved to be pretty dead with an unknown group playing not very good music to a half empty dance floor. Amy spotted Mick with one of his mates over by the exit and wondered whether Eric had told him about her weekend.

"I'm fed up already," Pam moaned, "let's make a move." Before Amy could stop her Pam headed for the exit and bumped into Mick. He grinned and looked pleased to see them.

"Surely you're not going already?" he asked. Pam just nodded and pushed past him, followed by Amy who avoided looking at him.

Suddenly he grabbed Amy by the arm. "Would you two like a lift home? I've got my car outside." Amy hesitated and looked at Pam.

"That would be great Mick," Pam said quickly in case he changed his mind. The three of them headed outside. Mick paused to explain to his mate who said he'd get a lift home with someone else.

On the way to Pam's Amy told Mick about seeing him down the Flamingo on Saturday night but didn't mention who she was with. Mick sounded surprised so Amy guessed that he hadn't heard from Eric yet.

After dropping Pam off at her house the journey to Amy's house passed quickly as they sang the praises of Zoot Money.

"Does this mean I might see you sometime down the Flamingo?" he asked.

Amy wasn't sure if he was pleased or worried at the prospect. "Maybe," she said vaguely as his car drew up outside her house.

"Oh by the way," Mick said as Amy was getting out, "I'm going out with Jenny again."

"Well I'm glad to hear it," Amy said, genuinely pleased. She smiled and couldn't resist adding: "And I've got a gorgeous new boyfriend - a real gentleman, which makes a nice change!" She walked away feeling smug with her parting shot.

Thursday morning Amy's restless eyes kept glancing at the clock on the office wall. Rob had asked her to ring at midday when he took his lunch hour. At eleven forty five she could wait no longer and hurried out of the office and down to the telephone kiosks in the basement. After checking that no-one was around she carefully tapped out the Maryland number. A man's gruff voice answered. Amy nervously asked to speak to Rob. There was a pause and a muffled shout then Amy heard Rob's voice talking in her ear and her heart began racing. She arranged to meet him at his home on Saturday with Pam.

"If you and Pam don't mind a bit of a boring evening, you can come and watch our band playing. We've been booked to play at a dance hall."

"Sounds great - can't wait to hear you playing the drums." Rob was drummer and Jim played the bass guitar in a group calling themselves 'The Tribe'. Amy had never been out with anyone who actually played in a group before. The pedestal that Amy had Rob teetering on top of, got taller by the minute as she became further infatuated with Pam's cousin. She reluctantly said goodbye but consoled herself with the thought that it was only two days until she would see him in the flesh.

During her lunch hour she phoned Pam to tell her of the arrangements for Saturday.

Pam was in a bad mood. "Some bugger pinched my purse on the train to work this morning," she growled.

"Did you lose much money?"

"About four pounds I think. What a sod! I shall have to borrow some money off dad for the weekend."

"You're still coming then?"

"You bet. Wouldn't miss it for anything."

Amy spent Friday evening on cloud nine, as she got ready for the weekend. She altered her grey skirt so it fitted better, washed her hair and packed a case.

After lunch on Saturday she met up with Pam at the station and they caught the train to London.

"By the way Bat, I've arranged for us to stay at my Aunt Bessie's this weekend."

"You mean we're going to stay at Rob's?" Amy asked in surprise.

"Yeah - Aunt Bessie said she'd manage to squeeze us in somehow."

"I don't mind being squeezed in with Rob," Amy said with a giggle.

They finally arrived at Rob's house mid-afternoon. Rob looked as pleased to see Amy, as she was to see him. Pam's Aunt Bessie welcomed them both with a hug and bustled off to the kitchen to make a pot of tea.

"Don't forget we must have an early tea this evening," Rob said to his mum as she set a tray of cups and saucers down on the coffee table, "we need to be at the gig by seven and before that the van has got to be loaded up. When we get to the hall, we've got to set up all the gear and then test it. Hope you girls don't mind being cramped up in the back of the van amongst all the gear."

"We'll help you load up and unload at the other end, won't we Pam?" Amy offered with a smile. She was looking forward to roughing it in the group's van.

"Yeah, 'course we'll help," Pam said before adding, "when is Jim coming round?" As if in answer to her question the doorbell rang.

"That should be him now," Rob said jumping up to open the door. Jim came in and gave Pam a hug. They looked equally pleased to see each other again.

After tea the van arrived with the remaining two members of the group. Dave played rhythm guitar and John played lead plus the vocals. All the equipment was stored in the cellar at Jim's house so everyone piled into the van and John did the driving.

With everyone helping it didn't take long to load up the back of the van. There wasn't much room left to sit amongst all the gear so Amy and Pam sat on Rob and Jim's laps. After an uncomfortable but fairly short journey, they drew up outside a large hall. Amy and Pam helped with the unloading and carried instruments and amplifiers into the hall.

The equipment was set up on the stage at the front of the hall and the boys were soon busy checking everything and tuning their guitars. The girls perched on the edge of the stage and Amy felt so proud to be Rob's girlfriend as she watched him sitting amongst his drum kit tapping and adjusting drums and cymbals.

The hall slowly filled up and the chairs grouped around tables along each side of the dance floor became occupied mainly by young people but also a fair number of older people too. A small bar opened at the rear of the hall and the tables were soon clinking with bottles and glasses.

The dance organiser came onto the stage and introduced The Tribe. After some polite applause and a few whistles there came a loud crash from Rob's drums as the group launched into their first number - 'Poison Ivy'. Pam and Amy jumped up and began dancing their Mod jive. Amy felt a bit self-conscious as they were the only ones dancing and she could sense Rob's eyes watching her. Before long others joined them on the dance floor and the evening got under way with a swing. The singer, John, had a pretty good voice. Amy thought he sounded like Paul Jones of Manfred Man. He even bashed on a tambourine as he sang when he wasn't playing his guitar. They had a good repertoire of songs, mainly R&B, but included some pop and played a few requests too.

Pam and Amy were glad when the interval gave the boys a short rest while records were being played. Jim and Rob took the girls to the bar and bought them drinks. They perched on bar stools and Rob slipped his arm around Amy's waist.

"Your group sounded really great," she enthused, "just like real professionals."

"I'm surprised we were even in tune," Rob admitted, "'cause we don't bother to do much practising. I've got a drum solo coming up in the next session,"

"Can't wait to hear it," Amy said, and received an appreciative peck on the cheek from Rob by way of a reply.

They had time for one dance before the boys had to return to the stage to play for the rest of the evening.

"I think Jim looks a bit like Paul McCartney, especially the way he holds his bass guitar," Pam said dreamily as the girls watched from the side of the stage.

"Yeah, I see what you mean," Amy agreed. Jim did look good in his dark green suede jacket. Then came Rob's drum solo and the rest of the group left their instruments on the stage and came off leaving Rob and his drums at centre stage. Amy couldn't help puffing up with pride as the drums throbbed and the cymbals clashed for what seemed like ages. The audience began to cheer and whistle while Rob looked cool and composed as the drumsticks flicked around from drum to drum. He seemed to be enjoying the attention, and then the others returned and joined in to end the number, after which Rob stood up and bowed to deafening applause and more whistles. Amy and Pam joined in the applause then went onto the dance floor to jive to a few more numbers.

The evening drew to a close and the girls went on stage to help dismantle the equipment. The group were buoyed up and seemed well pleased with their evening's performance.

Amy showered praise on Rob for his drum solo as they loaded up the van. Somehow they found room to squeeze in the back. Again the boys sat on the floor with the girls on their laps, which suited Amy just fine.

The van pulled up outside Rob's maisonette and Rob, Amy, Pam and Jim spilled out the back doors. Jim kissed Pam goodnight while Rob and Amy walked up the path to the front door. They paused in the porch for a kiss while waiting for Pam.

It was twelve thirty when the three of them finally arrived indoors leaving Jim and the others to unload the van back at Jim's.

Aunt Bessie was waiting up for them. She quickly made a pot of tea and some sandwiches for their supper.

"Now then, I've made up a bed on the sofa for you, Rob, so that the girls can have your bed tonight. I hope you girls don't mind sharing a single bed," Aunt Bessie said handing round the cheese and pickle sandwiches.

"Me and Amy are always cramming into my bed so we're quite used to sharing," Pam assured her aunt taking an offered sandwich.

"Even the dog manages to squeeze in with us," Amy added with a grin.

"Well that's all right then," said Aunt Bessie, "and you'll be fine on the sofa for one night," she added turning to Rob.

"I'm so tired I could sleep on a clothes line," Rob said with a yawn.

"I think that drum solo must have exhausted you," Amy said sympathetically.

"He's always tired," his mum said offhandedly, "needs at least eight hours sleep a night."

The girls finally squashed into Rob's bed and Amy felt a tingle of excitement to know she was lying where Rob usually laid. She kissed the pillow before falling asleep.

Sunday was spent lazing around reading the papers and listening to the radio while the delicious aroma of roast beef wafted out from the kitchen. Amy was content to share the sofa and newspaper with Rob while Pam fidgeted restlessly as she gazed out the window, obviously missing Jim.

After the traditional Sunday lunch the girls helped Pam's aunt to wash up while Rob and his dad popped out to the pub, which irked Amy, but she hid her irritation. Afterwards she and Pam packed their bags.

By the time Rob and his dad returned the girls were ready to take their leave and said goodbye to

Pam's aunt and uncle, being careful to thank them for their hospitality.

Rob did the gentlemanly thing by carrying their bags to the bus stop where they all caught the bus to Aunt Anne's.

"I thought I ought to pop in and see her and Uncle Fred while I was in town this weekend," Pam said.

"Yes, I suppose she might have got a bit peeved if she knew you stayed at our house and didn't bother popping round to see her," Rob agreed.

Aunt Anne gave each of them a hug and insisted they stay to tea. Pam was itching to get to Jim's - they had arranged to meet at his house that afternoon but she hadn't got the heart to refuse her aunt's kind offer so they stayed for ham salad and home-made fruit cake and eventually arrived at Jim's in the early evening.

"I was wondering where you had got to," Jim said looking relieved to see Pam at last. They hugged and kissed before making for the back room to listen to records. This time Jim and Pam grabbed the sofa so Amy was happy to snuggle up on Rob's lap in the armchair. After about an hour Jim's mum popped her head round the door and called them into the lounge.

"Come and watch T.V. The Beatles are on and I know you ones will want to see them."

For once Amy would have preferred not to watch the Beatles. She was already in her own seventh heaven snogging with Rob.

"We'd better go in and keep them happy," Jim said reluctantly getting up and pulling Pam to her feet.

They squashed together on a three-seater sofa and Jim's mum handed round mugs of tea. The Beatles were topping the bill at the London Palladium but Amy didn't feel like swooning over Paul tonight, not with the gorgeous Rob pressed up against her, his arm around her shoulders.

They escaped back to their little room as soon as possible trying not to appear too eager to go. After another glorious hour of snogging and cuddling to a background of music, it was time for the girls to head home.

At the station, as the boys said their goodbyes, they arranged to meet the girls the following evening at Tottenham Court Road.

The train sped off into the night and Amy leaned back in the seat with a contented smile on her lips. "Wow, Tibs, another great weekend."

"Yeah, but I wish I could have seen more of Jim," Pam said wistfully.

"Well at least we've only got to wait less than twenty four hours until we see them again," Amy said trying to console her friend.

"They mentioned taking us to the 100 Club - I think I've heard of it," Pam said cheering up a little, "should be good."

Monday evening after work Amy met Pam at Chancery Lane tube station and they went down to the ladies toilets in the basement of the Prudential to get ready for the evening ahead. They carefully applied make-up and combed their hair while chattering excitedly. When they were all spruced they headed for the nearby Wimpy Bar and ordered toast and coffee to pass the time until they caught the tube to meet the boys.

The girls arrived outside the Dominion in Tottenham Court Road at exactly eight o'clock - the time they had agreed with Rob and Jim. They waited impatiently watching the passengers alighting from every bus that stopped there. By eight thirty there was still no sign of them and Pam was beginning to get cross. Then, five minutes later, the boys hopped off a bus and hurried over, full of apologies for being late.

All irritation melted away as they walked up Oxford Street holding the arms of their respective boyfriends. Rob was wearing his usual dogtooth checked coat and Jim his green jacket which toned well with Pam's green suede coat.

The entrance to the 100 Club was a narrow doorway, much like the entrance to the Flamingo. The name was lit up above the door and steps led down into the gloomy depths under Oxford Street. Like the other clubs, the decor was black walls festooned with posters advertising coming events. There was a short queue up the stairs but it didn't take long to reach the cubicle where the entrance fees were paid. Rob and Jim were members so Amy and Pam were signed in as their guests. The man in the booth shoved an application form at each of the girls.

"Fill those in and hand them back to me and you should get your membership cards in a couple of weeks," he said gruffly.

They kept their coats on, as the room wasn't all that full and cool air circulated spasmodically from a fan in the ceiling. Rob led them across the room to the far side where they leaned against the wall and watched the group tuning their instruments.

"It's the Birds tonight," Rob said to Amy. "They're fantastic and even louder than the Who."

"I thought the Birds were an American group," Amy said.

"You're thinking of the American Byrds spelt with a Y," Rob said, "these are the British Birds - a really terrific R&B group."

Suddenly the group burst into their first number and any further talking became impossible as the sound waves coming out of the huge amplifiers hit Amy square in the chest. She was glad to have the wall at her back or she was sure she'd have toppled backwards.

The long-haired singer draped himself over the microphone - his diminutive stature meant he only just reached the mouthpiece. He reminded Amy of his simian ancestors as he bellowed into the mike, his hair covering his face. He occasionally peered out from beneath his unruly locks to leer at the girls in the audience. Amy suddenly found her eyes locked on to his and felt decidedly uncomfortable so she quickly looked away.

The lead guitarist was a different proposition - Amy willed him to glance in her direction because he was absolutely gorgeous - in fact the most handsome bloke she had ever set eyes on. He was tall and slim with long straight black hair and piercing dark eyes. He played his guitar brilliantly with breath-taking solos that had the audience gasping.

"That's Ronnie Wood," Rob yelled in Amy's ear. He had noticed her watching him doing his solo piece. "Good, isn't he?"

Amy just nodded trying to look casual. She didn't want Rob to see her ogling some other dishy bloke. Over by the side of the stage two willowy girls with long straight blonde hair stood giggling together. Amy thought they must be models with their immaculate make-up and stunning looks. She soon realised that one was Ronnie Wood's girlfriend and the other was the drummer's girlfriend when the interval arrived, and they all went off together. Even though she was with her beloved Rob, Amy couldn't help a pang of jealousy searing her heart as Ronnie Wood put his arm around his beautiful girlfriend and vanished up the stairs with her.

During the interval another group called the Loose Ends came on stage and played a few numbers. They were good but not a patch on the Birds. Pam and Amy had a couple of dances then Rob and Jim made the effort to join them for a slow smooch before the Birds were back on stage for the final part of the evening. The room noticeably filled as everyone crowded round the stage. They were obviously very popular.

The singer leaned on the mike and Amy was sure he winked at her as he mumbled about a single due to be released, which they would now perform. Like the rest of their music it was very loud with a raunchy R&B sound. It ended to enthusiastic applause and whistles.

"I shall have to get that when it comes out," Amy yelled in Rob's ear.

He nodded. "Yeah, me too. Glad you like them."

Amy felt like she was walking on air as they emerged from the club at the end of the evening. Oxford Street was still brightly lit and bustling with people who had been to the West End theatres and cinemas and were now heading for their favourite restaurant or the tube station and home.

The four friends jumped on a bus that took them to Charing Cross Station. Pam and Amy's train was delayed by half an hour as it didn't have a driver so the boys waited with them and discussed their evening at the 100 Club. Rob promised he would ring Amy next day at work and they finally kissed goodbye as the train driver arrived and climbed into his cab.

Next afternoon Amy phoned Pam in a bad mood. She was taking advantage of the fact that today was Vera's birthday and she was in a very good mood so didn't mind Amy making a private phone call.

"He hasn't rung me - the sod!" she snarled quietly into the mouthpiece so the others on her section wouldn't overhear her. To rub salt into her wound, Pam cheerfully informed her that she had just had a long chat with Jim.

"Their group has got a gig on Saturday evening and they want us to go with them."

"Huh, Rob had better ring me first and apologise for not ringing today."

Talking to a cheerful Pam made Amy feel even more fed up. Then a beaming Vera plonked a large piece of cream sponge wrapped in a sheet of A4 paper in front of her. Amy thanked her; unsure whether the

new Vera was real or just an act she put on for her
birthday once a year.

She leaned across to Sue and whispered: "Why
has Vera given everyone a piece of cake?"

"It's what everyone does on their birthday," Sue
whispered back.

"But surely we should be the ones to buy her a
present and give her cake on her birthday," Amy said
looking puzzled.

Sue grinned. "Vera said she didn't want us
spending money on a present for her so we have
taken her at her word. Just think, when it's your
birthday, you'll have the pleasure of buying cakes for
everyone on the section."

"I can hardly wait," Amy muttered with a
grimace. She eyed the piece of cake suspiciously. She
would prefer not to have this gift from Vera. Now she
was expected to eat it, enjoy it, and then thank Vera
for the dubious pleasure.

Amy's stomach was in a knot thanks to Rob, but
she forced the dry sponge down her throat anyway
and turned to smile a thank you at Vera who sat in
her chair radiating smugness. She had even given
slices of sponge to Miss Rogers and Mr Galbraith.

'What a creep!' Amy thought trying not to choke
on the last crumbly piece.

Next day Amy's spirits sank lower with each
passing hour until finally at 2.30 the phone rang.
Amy pounced on it and - yes - it was Rob! She forgot
to be cross with him for not ringing the day before
and he soon had her giggling into the phone.

Joan heaved a sigh of relief. "Thank goodness
you're back to normal and even smiling again," she
said as Amy hung up. "Glad I'm no longer a teenager."

Amy was back on cloud nine. The weekend was
arranged and she could hardly wait.

On Friday she rang Pam in her lunch hour and
arranged to meet her next day at her house.

As she alighted from the train that evening, Amy heard her name being called. She turned to see her old school friend, Coral, hurrying towards her, her lank dark hair still looked as greasy as it did at school. Her friend looked as prim and proper as ever only nowadays Amy was grateful that she no longer wore metal bands to straighten her front teeth, which used to cause projectiles of spittle whenever she spoke. They walked home together as they both lived in the Crescent: Coral at No. 1 by the phone box and Amy at the second bend by the large green. Amy stopped at the newsagents to collect her Melody Maker and bought twenty Piccadilly. Coral tutted her disapproval, being a bit of a prude. She had always tried to play the part of Amy's conscience. Amy ignored her and instead talked non-stop on her favourite topic - Rob. She told Coral all about the nightclubs and weekends spent in London knowing that Coral would be suitably shocked. As they parted outside Coral's house, she eyed Amy suspiciously. "You don't take drugs do you, to stay awake all night?"

"Haven't needed to yet," Amy said as she walked on with a farewell wave, hoping she implied that she could if she wanted to, even if it wasn't true. She and Pam had never been offered drugs and she knew Pam would be dead against taking them anyway.

Next day, lugging her suitcase, Amy met up with Pam at her house and they caught the train to London, both filled with anticipation at the weekend that lay ahead.

"We're sleeping at Jim's tonight," Pam told Amy as they left Charing Cross Station and headed for the District Line. "His mum is going to make us up a bed on the divan in their back room."

"I don't mind. I'll sleep anywhere if it means seeing Rob for the weekend," Amy said as she jumped into a waiting train. She was impatient to see her beloved Rob once more.

At Jim's Pam got a hug and a kiss from her beloved which left Amy feeling decidedly lonely.

"Rob will be over a little later with the van as we've got to get the gear loaded up," Jim told Amy.

Jim's mum bustled in with a tray of tea things and Amy, desperate to make the time pass more quickly, helped to lay the table.

Rob and the other two group members arrived in the van after tea. Amy was on cloud nine once again as Rob greeted her with a hug and a quick kiss looking a little self-conscious to be demonstrating affection in front of his mates.

All the group's gear had to be hauled up the stone steps from the cellar and loaded into the van. Pam and Amy mucked in and the van was soon packed and ready to leave.

Rob and Jim made makeshift seats on the amplifiers, and the girls managed to squash onto their laps.

The gig was a 21st. birthday party being held in a hall slightly smaller than the previous Saturday. After only a ten minute journey, the van had to be unloaded and the equipment set up on the small stage. The group went through their repertoire of songs, adding several new ones. During the interval, after a drink at the bar, Rob asked Amy if she'd like to go outside for some fresh air. It wasn't particularly stuffy or smoky in the hall but Amy quickly said she would. Holding Rob's hand, she followed him through the crowd and out into the darkness of the badly lit side street.

"I've missed you," Rob whispered pulling Amy towards him and holding her close in his arms. He kissed her tenderly and Amy felt all the strength leave her legs. She put her arms around Rob, partly to support herself, and wanted that moment to last forever. She was oblivious to the chilly November wind. Nothing else mattered except that Rob was giving her his undivided attention.

Then a shout brought her back down to earth. "Come on, Rob, we're due back on stage." Jim had poked his head out of the door and was calling impatiently to his friend.

Rob's arm lingered around Amy's shoulder as they walked back inside then Jim whisked him away to the stage.

Pam gave Amy a knowing smile. "And what have you and Rob been up to?"

Amy grinned and gave a sigh. "Oh Pam, I am *so* in love and it's fantastic! You'd better be ready to catch me if I swoon."

Rob was soon into his drum solo. Pam and Amy pushed through the crowd to stand and watch his frantic drumming. He spun his drumsticks and tossed them in the air, caught them deftly and began battering the cymbals. The crowd cheered and clapped as the speed of his solo built up to a crescendo of noise, his hands flitting around the drums, the sticks becoming a blur and then he slowed up ready for the rest of the group to join in again. Amy felt the pride well up inside her again as it had the last time.

"He doesn't even break out in a sweat," she observed as she and Pam joined in with the applause.

At the end of the evening, the 21 year old girl was caught and received the customary bumps. She protested but in vain as six strapping men began to toss her towards the ceiling. Each toss was emphasised with a crash on the cymbals from Rob. Afterwards the birthday cake was cut and pieces handed round to everyone, including Amy, Pam and the group.

The party-goers all seemed very pleased with The Tribe and the evening drew to a close around midnight. The gear was safely stowed in the van and the girls once more perched on the boy's laps, as they headed for Jim's house.

Suddenly there was a scream of brakes and the van lurched sideways just missing a car that swerved across the road out of control. Through the van's back windows Amy saw the car plough into a lamppost and flip onto its side. She and Pam gave involuntary shrieks. The van stopped and the boys piled out.

"You two girls stay here," Rob said tersely, "We'll go and see if they're O.K."

Amy was shaking and she could feel Pam doing the same next to her. They watched in silence as the four boys ran down the empty street to the upturned car with its wheels still spinning. They tugged open a door and two young men hauled themselves out looking shaken and dazed.

"Thank goodness," Amy gasped in relief, "I can't see any blood. They look as if they're not too badly hurt."

After standing, talking to the two young men for a while, the boys returned to the van. "They're O.K., just a bit shaken up," Jim said as they retook their seats on the amplifiers, "apparently their car went out of control and just shot across the road - or so they say."

"If they'd hit our van we'd have copped it," John said over his shoulder as he drove off.

"Yeah, we were pretty lucky there," Rob agreed and gave Amy a squeeze. "You O.K.?" he asked looking concerned, "you look a bit pale."

Amy managed a smile. "It was a bit frightening but I'm O.K. now. What are those two chaps going to do about their car?"

"A friend of theirs has got a garage a few streets away so they're going to give him a ring and ask him to bring a tow truck."

At Jim's everyone helped unload the gear and take it down to the cellar. All too soon Rob had kissed Amy goodbye and left with the other two in the van.

Jim's mum had already made up the divan in the back room for the girls so Amy went off to the bathroom to wash, leaving Pam plenty of time for a lingering goodnight kiss with Jim.

The girls lay in bed chatting about the evening's events, too excited to be sleepy.

"Oh Pam, I think Rob is really lovely." Amy gave a sigh. "Can't wait to see him tomorrow."

"Mmm, I know the feeling," Pam said softly, "Jim makes my legs go weak when he kisses me."

The girls woke late on Sunday morning. As they dressed, an appetising aroma of bacon wafted out of the kitchen. Jim's mum insisted they have a cooked breakfast, which they didn't really want but thought it might look rude or ungrateful to refuse. They had almost finished their breakfast when Jim finally put in an appearance looking tousled and tired.

His mum eyed him critically. "Too many late nights my boy," she said putting a plate of egg and bacon in front of him.

After breakfast they all caught a bus over to Rob's where they sat listening to records and chatting. Pam's aunt cooked a Sunday roast while Pam and Amy helped by laying the table. Amy was relieved the dinner wouldn't be ready until 2p.m. as she was still full from breakfast.

After dinner they all walked to the bus stop and Rob kissed Amy goodbye promising to see her later at Jim's. First he had to pop round to see a mate. Amy felt downbeat at having to leave him but tried not to show it.

Back at Jim's house Pam and Jim kept their kissing and canoodling to a minimum so that Amy wouldn't feel too left out. She whiled away the rest of the afternoon by browsing through Jim's record collection and playing his music. How the time dragged as she yearned to hear Rob's knock at the door. Finally at 6p.m. he arrived and all was right in Amy's world again. Rob said he was feeling a bit out of sorts.

"Funny you should say that," said Jim, "I've been feeling a bit queasy this afternoon. How do you two feel?" he asked turning to Pam and Amy.

Amy hadn't felt too good but had put it down to being apart from Rob.

"Now you mention it, I do feel a bit off," Pam said rubbing her tummy.

"Must be my mum's lousy cooking," Rob said with a grin.

"That was a lovely dinner your mum made us," Amy said coming to her defence.

"Well something seems to have upset us all," Rob said. They decided to have a quiet evening so watched T.V. in the lounge with Jim's mum and dad. All four of them squashed together on the sofa and Amy was in heaven feeling Rob so close to her.

The boys walked the girls to the bus stop at the end of the evening. They had decided to catch a bus home for a change, which entailed changing at Woolwich. They arranged to meet the boys Monday evening at Leicester Square then all too soon the bus arrived and whisked them away.

"I don't know how I'll survive 'til tomorrow evening," Amy said craning her neck for a final glimpse of Rob in his dogtooth checked coat with the collar turned up, "another great weekend, Pam!"

"Oh Bat, I think I'm in love - swoon, swoon," Pam said dramatically clutching at her heart in a bout of overacting.

"Yeah, swoon and thrice swoon," Amy agreed joining in and pretending to faint.

"Fares please," snapped the conductor. A stern, disapproving face glared down at them and brought them crashing back to earth.

Pam finished work earlier than Amy so she caught a bus to Holborn the next evening and arrived at the Pru just as Amy was signing off. They headed for the ladies wash-rooms in the basement where they had the sinks all to themselves. As they washed and put on fresh make-up their excitement grew at the prospect of spending another dreamy evening with their gorgeous boyfriends.

"You know Pam, I have to keep pinching myself in case it's all a fabulous dream and I might wake up," Amy said as the two of them trotted along the corridor, through the foyer and out onto the pavement of High Holborn. They crossed the busy road clutching each other's arms and hurried into the Lyons cafe for a snack of buttered toast and tea.

"I'm feeling peckish Bat," Pam said studying the menu, "I think I'll have a poached egg on my toast today."

"I've totally lost my appetite," Amy said. "I'm too excited at the thought of another whole evening in my darling Rob's company."

Nevertheless she still managed to swallow a large heap of buttered toast and then the girls were ready for a long walk to the West End as they had over an hour to kill. Tonight they were meeting the boys at Leicester Square because they were going to see the Moody Blues at the Marquee in Wardour Street. It reminded Amy of that wonderful evening when she saw Rob for the very first time.

The girls waited impatiently by the bus stop in Leicester Square and the two boys eventually hopped off a bus from Plaistow half an hour late. All irritability faded away to be replaced by sheer elation as Rob put his arm around Amy and gave her a quick kiss. Each blamed the other for being late but Amy didn't care any more.

The Marquee was packed. They handed in their coats and pushed through the tightly packed bodies until they had a good view of the stage. The Moodies were great and sang a number of songs including 'Go Now' before taking a break while another group went on stage.

Rob whispered in Amy's ear: "Let's shoot off to the Macabre for a coffee." He took her hand and pushed through the crowd with Pam and Jim following. The Macabre was only along the street so they braved the cold night air without their coats. After the close, humid heat in the club, the air outside struck them like a bucket of ice-cold water.

They huddled round a black coffin-shaped table in the dim candle-lit blacked out cafe and sipped cappuccinos. Then Rob stunned Amy with a suggestion out of the blue: "How about me and Jim come down to Kent and spend the weekend with you? You can show us some of the hot places you frequent down there."

Amy gulped. She could hardly believe her ears. She glanced at Pam.

"That's a great idea," Pam said quickly smiling at Jim and gave his hand a squeeze next to the skeletal hand ashtray, "only," she hesitated, "we don't have a spare bedroom to put you up."

Amy wasn't prepared to allow a fantastic weekend to slip away from her. "You can both sleep at my house - it shouldn't be a problem," she said rashly trying not to visualise her parents' predictable horrified reaction when she informed them of her arrangements.

"But where can you put them up?" Pam asked looking puzzled.

"We've got the divan in the lounge which converts into a double bed."

"Are you sure your parents won't mind us dossing down in your lounge?" Jim asked looking a little dubious.

"'Course not," Amy said, hoping she sounded more confident than she felt.

"Then it's settled," said Rob squeezing Amy's hand, "I shall be able to meet your family and you can show me the delights of your home town."

"Hmm, I think you'll find it pretty dull after London," Amy said. They finished their coffee and then dashed back to the Marquee to catch the next session with the Moody Blues.

There was no room to dance but Amy was happy feeling Rob's arms around her waist as he stood behind her enjoying the group. At the end of the evening, the boys walked the girls to Charing Cross Station and arranged to come down to Kent on Friday evening.

On the train home Pam and Amy made excited plans for where they would take the boys at the weekend.

"Just imagine Pam, us walking into the Railway with Rob and Jim to find Mick and Dick are there. Wouldn't they be sick seeing us with two such gorgeous fellas!"

"That would be great Bat, I think we should take them there on Friday night - there's a good chance those two sods might be hanging out in there." Pam grinned and added: "It would serve them right!"

It wasn't until Amy was nearly home that she began to have serious misgivings about whether her stuffy parents would even allow her to have, not one, but two blokes staying in the house all weekend. She also needed Pam there for moral support because she didn't fancy looking after both of them on her own. Pam would have to cram into her single bed with her.

After getting up late next morning, Amy gulped down some cornflakes for breakfast. Between mouthfuls she explained to her mother the arrangements she had made for the weekend, trying to make it sound a *fait accompli* and irrevocable.

Her mother immediately launched into a tirade of negative reactions. "How am I supposed to put up two total strangers <u>and</u> feed them for a whole weekend?" she wailed waving her hands in the air in exasperation.

"They're not strangers," Amy retorted crossly, "Rob is Pam's cousin and we've been going out with them for a while now."

"Well they are strangers to your dad and me!"

"Once you've met them they won't be will they?"
Amy reasoned and dashed out the back door before
her mother could put her foot down and refuse to
have them stay. Amy hoped that by the evening her
mother would have had time to chew it over and
become reconciled to the arrangement.

That evening Pam arrived at the Pru as usual
only tonight they weren't going clubbing. The
Pru was putting on a production of South Pacific
in the theatre on the top floor. Gail, on Amy's
section, was playing the leading female role and
had been bubbling over with excitement for weeks
giving everyone a blow-by-blow account of how
the rehearsals were going. Because she and her
gorgeous blond hunk of a husband, who worked in
the adjoining office, were renting one of the Pru's
courtesy flats just across the road, it was easy for her
to get to rehearsals. She had given Amy a couple of
free tickets for that evening's show.

After their tea and toast in the Lyon's cafe, the
girls returned to the Pru and made their way up
in the lift to the theatre on the top floor. Amy had
never been up there before. She and Pam were very
impressed by the plush furnishings and pale oak
carved woodwork everywhere. The luxurious seats
had thick cushions covered in red velvet and banked
so that everyone had a clear view of the stage. The
production was extremely professional. Amy and Pam
had their doubts about whether South Pacific was
their sort of show but soon found themselves totally
wrapped up in it.

"I didn't know Gail could sing like that - she's
really good," Amy whispered as Gail launched into
"I'm gonna wash that man right out of my hair."

During the interval the bar opened just outside
the theatre's doors and the girls got themselves a
drink.

"I wish my firm had all this on its top floor," Pam said wistfully.

"I had no idea it was as good as this up here," Amy said gazing around. "The theatre is sold out; there are no empty seats left. Everyone seems to know these productions are worth coming to see."

The second half was as good as the first with a grand finale to end. Amy's hands became hot and sore from all the applauding and encores that carried on for ages.

On the train home Amy told Pam her parents were coming round to the idea of having a houseful at the weekend. It wasn't strictly true but Amy felt sure her parents just needed time to adjust to the idea.

They had retired to bed when she arrived home but next morning Amy found her mother scowling at her across the breakfast table.

"Your dad's not very happy at you wanting to bring boys here," she said.

"Dad won't mind - he'll like Rob and Jim." Amy assured her. She could tell she had got her way, albeit very grudgingly.

Sitting on the train to work, she heaved a sigh of relief as it entered the tunnel at Woolwich and she gazed at her reflection in the window. She carefully tucked in a stray strand of hair that had escaped from the half bun she had hurriedly styled that morning. She had felt like making a bit of an effort because payday had finally arrived.

She received forty four pounds twelve shillings and eight pence for one month's work. During the lunch hour she hurried to Leather Lane Market, next door to the Pru, to indulge in a bit of Christmas shopping. She bought two pairs of black leather gloves; one for herself and one as a present for Pam. She also bought her mother a box of chocolates. 'That'll help to bring her on side for the weekend,' she thought as she arrived back at the Pru and dashed down to the basement to phone Rob.

After several attempts at phone tapping she finally got through and thrilled at the sound of his voice on the other end. He told her he couldn't make Friday evening so he and Jim would come down on Saturday instead. Amy said it was fine, trying to hide her disappointment, and Rob promised to ring her on Friday.

Next day, being Friday, Amy waited on tenterhooks for the phone to ring. But she waited in vain. Rob didn't ring.

"What a sod!" she fumed as she walked home from the station, her stomach twisted in knots with worry. She hoped and prayed that the weekend was still on.

Saturday morning she met Pam in town and her fears were put to rest.

"I rang Jim last night and he wants us to meet them off the train this afternoon," she said.

Amy's spirits soared once again. "Come and help me buy a housecoat. I need one for when I'm staying at Rob's." She also treated herself to a new bra and roll-on as well as the Stones latest record of 'Little Red Rooster.'

"I love its great bluesy sound," Amy enthused as they walked up the hill back to her house.

Pam nodded, "I think it's one of their best so far."

After a quick tidy of their hair and touch-up of the make-up they headed back down town to the station, excited at the prospect of the boys company for the rest of the weekend.

Amy saw the familiar dogtooth checked coat emerging from one of the carriages. It was her beloved Rob followed by Jim in his green suede jacket. They carried overnight bags and grinned when they saw the girls waving to them from the other side of the ticket barrier.

"Aren't we lucky Tibs," Amy whispered as they waited impatiently for a hug and a kiss.

They walked up the hill arm in arm laughing and joking. Rob didn't mention why he hadn't phoned the previous day so Amy decided to forget it. It didn't matter now he was here with her once again.

They all sat down to tea around the dining room table and Amy was so pleased, not to mention relieved, that the boys, and especially Rob, made such a good impression on her parents. He had her mother giggling like a schoolgirl and even Ray seemed to enjoy their company.

Rob worked at a printers and dad was keen to know what his work entailed so Rob happily explained all the details of his work to him.

After tea the four of them walked back down to the station and went into the Railway Tavern. Despite it being Saturday, Amy hoped Mick and Dick would be there and as they walked in she scanned the crowd but couldn't see any familiar faces. She was devastated to discover that tonight of all nights the dance room had been booked for a cricket dance. They were still in the middle of the speeches, so they lingered for a while over a few drinks in the bar and then slowly walked back home.

Mum had made up the divan in the lounge into a large double bed for Rob and Jim.

"Don't you girls be too long getting to bed," she said as she and dad prepared to go upstairs.

"We're just going to have a nightcap," Amy said and went out to the kitchen to put the kettle on.

After a quick drink they all sprawled on the bed and Rob switched the light off. Amy was in seventh heaven kissing and cuddling with her beloved - and in her own house with her parents upstairs. She could hardly believe it.

Suddenly there came a loud thump on the ceiling. Amy sighed. All good things must come to an end. "That's dad, telling us to get upstairs," she said to

Pam. After a final kiss goodnight accompanied by more knocks on the ceiling, the girls reluctantly left the boys.

"D'you realise it's two in the morning," Pam whispered as she took off her watch and laid it on top of her clothes. They squeezed into Amy's bed and rolled together in the dent. Amy loved her bed with its dent which felt as though the bed was hugging her but it had its drawbacks when she shared with a friend.

"I could have stayed downstairs with Rob all night if dad hadn't spoiled things. I think Rob is lovely."

Pam gave a sigh. "Mmm, and Jim is really gorgeous - and a great kisser."

"Yeah, I love the way Rob kisses me," Amy mumbled with a yawn.

Next morning the girls were up and waiting impatiently in the dining room for the boys to put in an appearance. Mum was busy frying bacon in the kitchen and the appetising aroma wafted through and succeeded in luring the boys out of bed.

After breakfast they listened to records in the lounge. Rob said how much he liked 'Little Red Rooster' so Amy impulsively insisted he have it. She got a thank you kiss and she was happy.

To keep in her mother's good books, Amy went to help with the Sunday roast. She made the Yorkshire pudding - she had always made it since she was very small and considered herself something of an expert now. Besides she wanted Rob to sample her cooking.

Rob dutifully went into paroxysms of delight over her Yorkshire until Amy gave him a gentle kick under the table to shut him up.

Pam suggested they go over to her house in the afternoon so Rob could pay his respects to his aunt, uncle and Cousin Ronnie, Pam's younger brother.

On the bus to the next town where Pam lived, Jim confessed to the girls that they sometimes took hearts.

"Only when we're staying out all night and want to keep awake," Rob added hastily, trying to justify taking them.

"Does that mean you took some when we were at the Flamingo with you all night?" Pam demanded suspiciously.

"Oh no, we didn't take anything then," Jim insisted, "if we had, we would have wanted to dance all night instead of just sitting around."

"Perhaps we all should have taken some then we could have danced the night away together," Amy said with a laugh.

Rob looked at Amy in surprise. "I didn't think you girls took hearts," he said.

"We don't - at least we haven't as yet."

"Well maybe next time we're out all night," Rob said with a grin. Pam gave a disapproving frown so Rob quickly changed the subject.

They stayed for a teatime meal of beans on toast at Pam's house. Mrs Tibton winked at Amy almost every time she asked her a question. Amy knew it was only a tic but she still found it rather disconcerting.

After tea they all sat in the lounge chatting over mugs of tea until Pam announced they had to leave to catch a bus to the Black Prince.

The Graham Bond Organisation was on stage so at last they had a decent place to take the boys with a great band performing. Amy anticipated a terrific night ahead and wasn't disappointed. The Black Prince impressed Rob and Jim. It had a good atmosphere and was crowded with fans. Amy scanned the crowd in the hope of seeing some familiar faces so she could show off her gorgeous boyfriend but couldn't spot anyone she knew. They managed to find enough room on the dance floor for a few dances and when the heat got to them they moved into the saloon bar for a cold drink. As they leaned on the bar sipping their drinks, Rob nuzzled into Amy's neck and whispered the magic words in her ear: "I love you." She felt a shiver of excitement go up and down her spine. 'Oooooh!' she thought, 'the feeling is definitely mutual.' But instead of passionately declaring her undying love for him as she desperately wanted to, she just smiled what she hoped was an enigmatic Mona Lisa smile. She thought Rob looked a little disappointed but the moment was lost when Pam and Jim dragged them back to the dance hall for a final dance before the boys had to leave to catch their train home. It made a change for the girls to accompany them to the station and see them onto their train.

They arranged to meet up the following evening in Oxford Street as usual for the 100 Club. As the girls walked to the bus stop, Amy told Pam what Rob had said.

"He obviously expected you to say the same to him," she said, "now he probably thinks you don't really care about him."

This devastated Amy. "But nothing could be further from the truth," she said feeling alarmed, "I'm sure Rob must know how I feel about him."

"I think boys are pretty insecure and need to be told - it's good for their egos," Pam said trying to sound as though she knew more about boys than she actually did.

"Have you told Jim that you love him yet?"

"Well, no - not in so many words but I will as soon as he declares his love for me," Pam said with a decisive flick of her hair.

On the bus home all Amy could think of was her missed opportunity. She was mortified that Rob might think she didn't love him. Maybe she would be able to put things right tomorrow evening.

Monday evening the girls met up at the Pru as usual for a tidy up followed by tea and toast in the cafe before the long walk to the West End. They were too early for Rob and Jim so they went to the

Macabre for coffee and chatted to Demis the Greek waiter. They helped him finish his crossword in the evening paper and then it was time to meet the boys over in Oxford Street. Amy's heart sank when Jim jumped off the bus alone.

"Rob wasn't ready so I came on without him," he explained, "he said he'd catch the next bus."

The three of them waited for two more buses to arrive but there was no sign of Rob. Amy put on a brave face and after twenty minutes they gave up and headed for the 100 Club.

Inside they stood by the wall watching the Birds setting up their instruments. Even the sight of dishy Ronnie Woods tuning his guitar with his long black hair hanging over the frets couldn't lift Amy's spirits. She felt totally empty. Pam was in Jim's arms next to her. Why wasn't Rob here with her now? Did her lack of response to his declaration of love the previous night have something to do with it?

Just as the Birds launched into their record of 'Next in Line' with a deafening intro, Amy spotted the familiar dogtooth checked coat coming through the crowd towards her. Rob looked sheepish. Amy was so relieved and happy to see him she couldn't be cross with him.

"Where did you get to?" Jim yelled at his friend. He also looked relieved that Rob had finally arrived. Amy guessed Jim didn't much fancy having to look after two girls all night.

Rob put his arm round Amy and gave her a kiss. Suddenly everything was fine again.

"Sorry I'm so late," Rob whispered in her ear, "I had to do some overtime at work."

Amy gave him a smile and a kiss. "You're here now and that's all that matters," she said and remained firmly on cloud nine for the rest of the evening.

Chapter Five

December - Love is in the Air

Amy woke Monday morning and decided to take a day off work.

"You know I don't approve of you skiving off work when you're not ill. I won't go to the phone box and ring the Pru to tell lies for you," her mother snapped when Amy mentioned her plans at breakfast.

Amy shrugged. "I'll do it myself," she said offhandedly, and grabbing her bag and coat, went out the back door still munching on a piece of toast. She walked down the hill into town intending to buy a weekend case but couldn't find one. On her way home she stopped at a phone box and rang Pam at work to ask her to call the Pru.

"Just tell them I'm feeling sick but should be in tomorrow." Pam agreed to do this favour for her friend though she sounded a little peeved that Amy was having a day off without her.

Amy continued home and decided to go via her Aunt Ruth's and pop in for a cup of tea and a chat. Her aunt and Uncle Henry lived in a semi-detached Edwardian house with steps leading up to the front door. She had always been able to talk to her aunt about things she wouldn't dream of mentioning to her mother. She found Uncle Henry, her aunt's second husband, somewhat daunting. He was fat, bald and extremely ugly with a drooping bottom lip, but at least today he would be out at work. She had bought some fags in town and her aunt didn't mind her smoking so she offered her one and they puffed away together over cups of tea in the small back room where a fire crackled in the grate giving the room a cosy feel.

Aunt Ruth appeared interested when Amy mentioned the clubs in London so she told her all about the Flamingo, Marquee and 100 Club. The subject of drugs came up and her aunt wanted to know if Amy had taken any.

She shook her head. "With my hand on my heart I can honestly say I haven't." She thought it wiser not to add that if the opportunity arose she might be tempted.

Back at work on Tuesday, Amy phoned Rob in her lunch hour but he was out. To console herself she went next door to Gamages and bought a weekend case ready for her next visit to Rob's.

The moment her lunch hour started on Wednesday, Amy again dashed downstairs to the basement to ring Rob. Her heart skipped a beat when he answered the phone. He was in an exceptionally good mood because his group had secured a booking for a wedding reception. He larked around putting on different voices which kept Amy in fits of giggles and before hanging up she arranged to meet him at his house on Saturday. She spent the rest of the lunch hour in the canteen with Jeanette, as Mary was absent from work. She couldn't stop herself from boring Jeanette with how lovely and gorgeous her beloved Rob was and what a wonderful weekend she was going to have as he had promised to take her to a party on Saturday night.

Amy met Pam at the station on Saturday and they headed for Oxford Street to do some shopping, as Amy wanted something new to wear to the party. She bought a beige hipster skirt, maroon Fred Perry and a pair of patent leather shoes. Pam bought a pinafore dress and black suede shoes, then the girls caught a bus to the East End.

Pam was staying at Jim's house. "Jim didn't mention anything about a party when I rang him yesterday," she said rummaging in her handbag for the bus fare.

"I'm sure Rob said it's Jim's cousin's engagement party so he must know about it."

"Jim can be a bit vague and forgetful at times," Pam said, "so I expect we'll see you both at the party tonight."

Amy got off the bus a few stops before Pam and walked the short distance to Rob's house with the hit song by Vic Damone running through her head:

'I have often walked down the street before .... on the street where you live.'

Rob opened the door and greeted her with a hug before taking her weekend case and carrier bags. Amy was back on cloud nine. The only fly in the ointment was Rob's mum telling Amy she would be sharing her bed, as Rob's dad would be sleeping on a put-you-up in Rob's bedroom.

After tea Amy changed into her new clothes and got appreciative comments from Rob on how lovely she looked which made her flush with pleasure.

The party was a family and friends get together at a semi-detached house about twenty minutes away by bus. Amy was pleased to find Pam and Jim already there when they arrived. The lounge diner was packed and the music blared loudly but there was no room to dance. Rob fetched some drinks and Jim found a spare dining chair and put it next to his. Amy spent most of the evening perched on Rob's knee and Pam did the same with Jim.

Rob kept sneezing into a large handkerchief. "I think I've picked up a rotten cold," he told Amy, "perhaps you'd better keep your distance if you don't want to catch it." Amy could think of nothing nicer than sharing Rob's cold and to prove it she gave him a kiss and a cuddle. Rob took courage from this and asked Amy if she loved him.

She desperately wanted to scream "YES!" at the top of her voice and tell the whole world how she felt, but she hesitated, and then Jim was asking Rob something and the moment had gone yet again.

At 2a.m. they caught a taxi home and Amy kissed Rob goodnight before summoning up the courage to crawl into bed with his mum. She crept into the bedroom in the dark, undressed, and slipped under the sheets, keeping to the edge of the bed so as not to disturb Rob's mum who was gently snoring, her hair a mass of rollers silhouetted in the moonlight shafting in between the curtains.

Amy got up at 11.30 Sunday morning with a sore throat. 'Looks like I'm getting Rob's cold,' she thought as she dressed.

There was a buzz of excitement in the lounge. Rob's married sister, Carol, was expecting her first baby and it was due today. Rob's mum had her coat on. "I'm going over to Carol's to check she's O.K.," she said, "Rob, you'll have to look after Amy, and dad can cook the dinner." With that she hurried out the front door.

"She's like an old mother hen," Rob's dad said shaking his head, "can't believe I'm gonna be a granddad."

"So you're going to be an uncle," Amy said to Rob giving him a gentle nudge in the ribs as they sat on the settee.

"Yeah, hope it's a boy then I can play footy with him."

After a lunch of grilled chops, Rob took Amy to the pictures where two horror films were showing.

They snuggled together in the back row sharing a large box of popcorn. Amy loved having Rob all to herself for once. All too soon the films had ended and she was saying goodbye to him at the bus stop before heading back home. She had arranged to see him on Thursday at the 100 Club but that felt like light years away as she watched his check coat disappear from view round a corner.

At work next morning Mary rushed over to Amy's desk looking very excited.

"The Scene got raided on Saturday night," she said, "I wasn't there but a mate of mine was. The fuzz swooped and made the blokes and girls form two lines. The girls were taken into the ladies toilets and searched for drugs and the same was done to the blokes in the gents toilets. Quite a few people got arrested."

"Don't suppose Dick and Mick were there," Amy said hopefully.

"Dunno, but I might be able to find out," Mary said. Just then a loud cough from behind Amy warned her that Vera was getting annoyed so Mary retreated back to her seat.

Amy rang Pam at lunchtime and arranged to go over her house that evening.

She arrived at Pam's only to find herself being propelled backwards out of the front door. "Let's go and visit my gran," Pam said fiercely grabbing Amy's arm.

Pam's gran lived a few streets away in a small ground floor flat. She was a sweet old lady who Amy had met a couple of times before.

"What's up?" Amy asked seeing her friend's flushed face.

"It's my flippin' mother. I've just had a blazing row with her. She doesn't like me staying at Jim's all weekend and is trying to stop me from seeing him."

"She can't do that!" Amy gasped in horror.

"She can try but she won't succeed," Pam said through gritted teeth. "She spoilt things for me with my lovely Dan when she made me pack him up just because I was still at school. She's not going to split up me and Jim - I'd leave home first."

The girls compared notes on their weekend, as they hadn't seen each other after the party.

"Rob is so lovely – I've decided to marry him," Amy said emphatically.

"Does Rob know of this arrangement?" Pam asked with a wry smile.

"Er, no - not exactly, but I'm sure he knows how I feel about him."

Pam's gran greeted the girls warmly, pleased to have their company as she lived alone in her small ground-floor flat. She gave the girls a snowball each to try. Amy had always regarded these as old ladies drinks but she was pleasantly surprised how nice it tasted.

Pam could talk to her gran the same way that Amy could confide in her Aunt Ruth. She poured out her woes and had a good moan about her mother.

"Never you mind, pet," her gran said patting her on the shoulder, "your mum is still my daughter and not too big to put across my knee if she gets out of hand." The girls burst into giggles at the thought of it.

The following evening Amy stayed in and shortened her hipster skirt. Her mother gave her £4 for Christmas which cheered her up somewhat as she was feeling fed up waiting for Thursday.

Thursday finally arrived and she hadn't heard from Rob but Pam rang her at work and arranged for them to meet up that evening. Amy accompanied Mary to Oxford Street in their lunch hour as Mary wanted to buy some new shoes. Amy had a discreet swoon as they walked past the 100 Club, imagining being there with her delectable Rob in a few hours' time.

Pam arrived at the Pru after work and they enjoyed their usual tea meal in the Lyons cafe before the long trek to Oxford Street to meet Rob and Jim. Once again Rob was late but this time only one bus behind Jim.

Tonight the Pretty Things were playing at the 100 Club. Amy thought they were good but not quite as raunchy or loud as the Birds.

On the train home Amy's mind was in a whirl. She was so head over heels in love and Pam appeared to be equally smitten by Jim. "He reminds me of Gorgeous George," she said with a sigh.

"Mmm," Amy agreed absently, "but he looks more like Paul."

"What could be better than going out with two Beatles rolled into one," Pam said dreamily.

"For me there's no one better than my lovely Rob - I think he's really adorable, and his looks remind me of Rod the Mod."

"Yeah I suppose so," Pam said, "same nose but a tidier hair style. I'm really pleased things have worked out so well for us with Rob and Jim."

"You know Tibs; maybe we could have a double wedding."

"Oh I don't know about that, Bat. I'm quite happy being single right now. Can you imagine what my mother would say if I told her me and Jim were engaged to be married?"

"She ought to be pleased you've found someone so nice to settle down with."

"Huh, chance'd be a fine thing!" Pam said derisively.

Next day Rob phoned Amy sending her into paroxysms of happiness by making arrangements for her to come and stay with him at the weekend.

"There's going to be a bit of a family reunion at our house. Pam's mum will be there but we can avoid most of that as we're playing at that wedding reception."

Amy didn't much like the idea of a house full of Rob's relatives but she would put up with anything if it meant being with him.

On the way home she met Coral at the station. Coral waited with her usual expression of disapproval as Amy paused at the station kiosk to buy twenty Pall Mall for the weekend, then they walked up the hill to the Crescent catching up with each other's news. Amy happily raved on once again about her Rob, no doubt boring Coral in the process but she didn't care. At number one by the phone box Coral said goodbye and walked up her garden path. Amy hurried on round the Crescent, arriving home just in time to watch Ready Steady Go.

Saturday afternoon Amy's train pulled into Pam's station and Amy waved to her friend. Pam had a holdall she used as her weekend case. She threw it up into the rack then sank onto the seat beside Amy.

"My mother's been having another go at me," she moaned, "she expects me to spend the evening at Rob's because of the family reunion. At least dad and Ronnie won't be there. I told her we're going to a wedding reception with the group but she wasn't happy about it. I told her we'd try and leave early just to shut her up."

"Rob said he wants to stay at the reception as long as possible to avoid all his boring relatives," Amy said.

"Yeah, and so do I!"

The girls split up at the East End and Pam headed for Jim's while Amy walked round to Rob's house. She was disappointed to find him out when she arrived.

"He's gone to watch West Ham with his dad," Rob's mum told her. "Come in the kitchen and give me a hand with the food for tonight dear."

Amy didn't mind as it helped to pass the time. She sat at the kitchen table, which was heaped with loaves of sliced bread and various fillings. Rob's mum gave her a large plate, a knife and the butter dish. She spread the butter on the slices of bread while Rob's mum added the filling and made them into sandwiches. She sipped a cup of tea between buttering and listened to the list of aunts, uncles and cousins coming that evening.

"It's a pity you're going off with Rob and the others. By the time you get back here I expect most of them will have gone."

Amy tried to sound disappointed.

"Of course Pam's mum will still be here 'cos she's staying overnight. It'll mean a bit of a squeeze for all three of us in my bed!" She chuckled but Amy found the thought of being squashed in a bed with Pam's mum and aunt far from amusing.

The front door opened and closed and then Rob appeared in the kitchen doorway wearing a West Ham scarf and a broad grin.

"We won!" he exclaimed pulling off his scarf.

"I think we could have guessed just by looking at your face," his mum said. "Fancy going off when you knew Amy was coming," she added reprovingly.

Rob looked a little sheepish. "Sorry Amy, but it was an important match - I didn't want to miss it."

Amy said she didn't mind even though deep down she really did. 'If Rob had been coming to see me, wild horses couldn't have dragged me out of the house,' she thought, but she smiled and kept her thoughts to herself.

After an early tea the van arrived with Dave and John. They drove over to Jim's to load up the gear and soon the van was packed with Amy and Pam squashed in the back yet again on Rob and Jim's laps.

At the reception the girls helped to carry the equipment through the hall to the stage at the far end. Some of the wedding guests were already staggering slightly and shouting at one another as tables were moved to the sides of the room ready for an evening of dancing.

"Looks like we could be in for a bit of a rough night tonight," Jim observed glancing around the crowded room from the stage.

"We'll just keep our heads down and play whatever they want - hopefully that'll please 'em," Rob said, and began tapping his cymbals to test them out.

Soon the group were ready and launched into a lively rendition of 'Good Golly Miss Molly'. Pam and Amy sat at a table next to the stage. Suddenly there was the sound of glasses smashing over the music.

"I think a fight has broken out in the kitchen," Pam said craning her neck to see what was going on. There was a lot of shouting and chairs got knocked over but by the time the group were into their second number the fight appeared to be under control.

During the interval records were played while the boys sat at the table with the girls and enjoyed a cold beer.

Rob pulled his chair close to Amy and whispered in her ear: "How would you like a skirt for Christmas?" Amy's heart melted. Rob could be so sweet.

"Sounds lovely," she said, "and what would you like me to get you?"

Rob thought for a moment then whispered, "some cuff links would be nice." Amy had been worrying over what to get Rob for Christmas but now he had solved the problem for her.

At the end of a rowdy evening the gear was carefully loaded back into the van and returned to Jim's basement.

"Are you coming over to this family reunion?" Rob asked Pam.

She wrinkled her nose. "I really don't fancy it - especially as my mother will be there," she said.

"D'you realise I've got to spend the night sandwiched between your mum and your aunt," Amy said to Pam looking none too pleased, "I'm dreading it. It'll be worse than sharing a bed with you and your smelly mutt."

"Oh, poor you," Pam said trying to sound sympathetic and suppressed a giggle.

"Humph!" Amy retorted and walked out to the van.

Dave and John dropped Rob and Amy off at his maisonette. They were greeted by the sound of much chatting and laughter as they entered the front door. Most of Rob's relatives had waited to see him and his girlfriend before leaving. Amy felt herself flushing as she was introduced and everyone turned to stare at her. Mrs Tibton winked at Amy and patted the settee next to her so Amy went over and sat down. She had a plate of sandwiches thrust under her nose so she took one to be polite even though she didn't want it. She quietly nibbled at the sandwich while Rob chatted on the far side of the dining room table. After a while people began to leave and then it was time for bed.

Sharing a bed with Rob and Pam's mums was every bit as bad as Amy had imagined. She was pinned down in the middle of the bed, flat on her back all night not daring to turn onto her side in case she came face to face with Mrs Tibton or Rob's mum, both looking ghoulish in their curlers and face cream.

Amy got up late Sunday morning. She hadn't slept well. Pam's mum and aunt had already had breakfast and were just finishing the washing up when Amy put in an appearance in the kitchen. There was no sign of Rob. His dad was reading the Sunday paper in his favourite chair by the fireside in the lounge.

"John, Carol's husband, called round for Rob," his mum told Amy, "wanted him to give a hand with some painting before the baby arrives – it's a week overdue now." Amy's heart sank.

"He should have called me, I wouldn't have minded doing a bit of painting."

"He didn't want to disturb you, love."

Amy would much preferred to have been disturbed than spend the morning with his parents and Pam's mum. Mrs Tibton poured her a coffee. Amy didn't want any breakfast so she spent the rest of the morning browsing through the Sunday paper after Rob's dad had finished reading it.

Rob arrived home in time for lunch wearing scruffy overalls splattered with paint. He went and changed to emerge looking his usual smart self just as everyone was sitting at the table.

No sooner was dinner over than Pam and Jim arrived. They weren't keen on going out when Rob suggested it, so everyone settled down to listen to records. It wasn't much fun though with the parents sharing the same room and trying to talk over the music.

"I'll be leaving to catch the five o'clock train home," Mrs Tibton announced as Rob's mum brought in a tray of tea things at around four o'clock. "You two girls can come with me to keep me company," she added in a tone that would brook no argument. Pam and Amy exchanged glances that said it all. Amy felt she hadn't had Rob to herself at all this weekend.

Rob and Pam's Uncle Charlie popped in to say how much he had enjoyed the previous evening. He stayed for a cup of tea and then offered to give his sister-in-law and the two girls a lift to the station.

Pam and Amy only managed the briefest of goodbye kisses with the boys before Mrs Tibton was bustling them into the waiting car. They turned to wave out of the rear window as the car whisked them swiftly out of sight.

'Bugger!' Amy thought savagely, glaring at the back of Mrs Tibton's tightly curled head. She had told Rob she would ring him in the week and Jim had arranged to ring Pam.

"Not one of our better weekends," Amy muttered to Pam, and she nodded in agreement.

Next day Amy had the Monday morning blues at work. She decided to do a bit of Christmas shopping in her dinner hour to cheer herself up. She went across the road to a jeweller's where she had seen a lovely wall clock. She wanted to get it for her parents and could just picture it on the bare wall above the mantelpiece in the lounge where a large mirror used to hang. The shop assistant put a new battery in it and set it going at the correct time. While he carefully put it in a box and gift-wrapped it for her, she had a look at the cuff links on display in a glass case but couldn't see any she really liked for Rob.

That evening, unable to wait for Christmas, Amy gave her parents the present there and then. They were thrilled with the wood and gold coloured clock decorated with the signs of the zodiac around the edge of the face. Amy was right; it did look smart hanging on the wall where the mirror had been.

The next evening Amy arrived home from work to be handed a Christmas present from Ray. It seemed he couldn't wait for Christmas either. He had bought her 'Gin House' by Paul Williams. She had been dropping broad hints that she wanted this record and was glad her brother had cottoned on.

After tea she took the record over to Pam's house. Pam needed cheering up because Jim hadn't phoned her as promised, though she had doubts whether the doleful dirge of 'Gin House' would help much. They sat up in Pam's bedroom and played the record anyway.

"I thought Rob was the unreliable one," Amy said flopping down on the bed.

"I know - Jim has never let me down like this before."

"Maybe he's got a good reason; perhaps something has happened," Amy suggested hopefully.

"Well, he'd just better have a really good excuse," Pam said crossly. Amy knew Pam wouldn't tolerate being messed around the way that Rob let her down repeatedly. Perhaps she should be more like Pam and not let him off the hook so easily when he came out with his lame excuses. The trouble was she loved him too much to stay cross with him and she suspected that he knew it.

Wednesday lunchtime Amy hurried down to the phone booths in the basement to tap a phone call through to Rob. She tried several times but couldn't get through.

"Bugger it!" she exclaimed and slammed the receiver down in a fit of frustration. She went to join Mary and Jeanette in the canteen as they were serving Christmas dinner. Sitting down to turkey, roast potatoes and all the trimmings soon put Amy in a good mood again. The cafeteria was festooned with garlands around every pillar and across the ceiling giving it a festive air. There was no such festivity allowed in the drab Draconian offices. Christmas appeared to be taboo up there.

"I saw Eric down the Scene last night," Mary said getting her cigarettes out, "he invited me to his party on Boxing Day but I can't go as I'm already going to my mate Pat's party."

"Did you see Mick or Dick?" Amy asked without any real interest.

Mary shook her head. "Haven't seen that pair for a while now."

That evening Pam came round to Amy's looking a bit happier than the previous evening. They walked round to their school friend Vie's house to pay her a visit. "Jim phoned me at last today," Pam said as they walked up the road arm in arm.

"And what was his excuse for not ringing you yesterday?" Amy asked.

"He's been in bed with the flu," Pam said, "poor love, he did sound poorly. I'm going up to his house Friday evening after work to mollycoddle him."

"Mind you don't catch his bugs," Amy warned, adding, "I haven't managed to get through to Rob yet but I'll try again tomorrow."

Vie and her husband Rick were living in Vie's bedroom at her parents' house. They had eloped to Gretna Green the previous year causing a school scandal. The police had intervened to stop them before they tied the nuptial knot and Vie's mum had finally agreed to their marriage providing they returned to Kent.

Petite Vie looked her usual chirpy self. Rick was no bigger than Vie; with his slim build, black hair and blue eyes he was good looking in a Rocker sort of way, but then Vie had always been more interested in leather-clad Rockers on motorbikes than Mods on scooters.

He obviously felt a bit outnumbered because he soon excused himself. "I'll just pop down to the pub for a quick pint and leave you girls to have a good natter together," he said grabbing his jacket and escaping out the bedroom door.

There was a lot of catching up to do and Vie seemed genuinely interested in hearing all about Rob and Jim which was just as well because they were the main topic of conversation.

Next day in the lunch hour found Amy in one of the Pru's phone booths tapping furiously on the receiver rest. All she got for her trouble was the unobtainable signal. She dialled the operator and asked her to check the line. After a minute of silence the operator came back on the line to report that the phone was out of order. Amy was dejected. She couldn't get in touch with Rob. Why didn't he ring her instead from another phone?

After work she met Pam and they went up to Oxford Street to do some late night Christmas shopping. Then they decided to go down the 100 Club. The Artwoods were playing on stage and Amy spotted two of the Birds lounging in the shadows by the side of the stage. Ronnie Wood with his unmistakable long black hair looking as dishy as ever and the diminutive singer with his wild unruly mop. Ronnie had the same blonde model-type girl hanging on his arm but the singer seemed to be on his own. He glanced around and noticed Amy looking over at them. He grinned at her but she quickly looked away feeling awkward. The next thing she knew he was standing beside her asking her for a dance. She was thrilled to be smooching with the singer of the Birds even though she didn't really fancy him. 'If only it was Ronnie,' she thought longingly.

By the time Pam and Amy were on the train home, Amy realised she hadn't given much thought to Rob all evening.

"You were definitely flavour of the evening," Pam said, "non-stop blokes coming to ask you to dance."

"Eight all together," Amy said with a smile, "I counted."

"Good job Rob didn't come down there and find you smooching with eight blokes."

"It would serve him right for not ringing me," Amy said feeling a slight depression beginning to weigh her down. Maybe he would phone her tomorrow to make arrangements for the weekend.

Amy felt agitated all the next morning as she waited for Rob's call, but it didn't come. She tried ringing his work at lunchtime and this time she got through. Rob sounded fed up as he explained that he would be working over the weekend and wouldn't be able to see her. Then he cheered up a little when he announced that he was now an uncle. Carol had given birth to a daughter so there would probably be no playing footie with his niece. Amy congratulated him trying to hide her feelings of devastation at not seeing him. He promised to ring her on Monday.

Amy sat slumped at her desk after lunch feeling dejected and then the phone rang. It was Rob! She brightened up at the sound of his voice but he was only ringing to get her address. He didn't say why he needed it and Amy didn't ask. She assumed he was going to send her a Christmas card. Yet there was something about the tenseness she could detect in his voice that niggled at her.

That evening she stayed in and watched T.V. trying to take her mind off Pam spending the weekend with Jim but it didn't work and deep depression set in. All she could look forward to was the promised call from Rob on Monday and maybe a Christmas card.

Amy tried to keep busy when she finally dragged herself out of bed at lunchtime on Saturday. She walked into town and finished her Christmas shopping - all except Rob's cuff links and a present for Mary. She treated herself to a pretty silk petticoat as a consolation before walking home again.

Later that afternoon she sat in the lounge playing records and writing her Christmas cards including a special one for Rob which she had carefully picked out for the wording. Then she walked to the post box at the opposite end of the Crescent and posted them all, pausing to give Rob's card a kiss before slipping it tenderly through the red slot. As she walked back home she did some mental calculations and realised she had been going out with Rob for exactly six weeks. 'It must be a record,' she thought, 'Mick was about five weeks and five days.'

Amy spent Sunday morning in bed trying not to think of Pam enjoying herself with Jim. She finally got up at 2p.m. and pulled on her housecoat, as dressing was too much effort. She picked at her dinner, her appetite having deserted her, and then lounged on the settee until three o'clock when she spotted Aunt Margaret and Kathleen arriving at the front gate for a visit. Although she wasn't actually related, Amy had always called her aunt. Mum went into panic mode and ordered Amy to go and get dressed which Amy ignored, much to her mother's annoyance. Margaret's looks and demeanour were so similar to the Queen's that mum almost bobbed a curtsey and put on her posh telephone voice when she arrived.

After an hour of embarrassing her mother by continuing to loll on the settee in her housecoat and only speaking when she absolutely had to, Amy got bored by all the small talk and wandered off upstairs to finally get dressed.

She didn't want to sit through a stuffy high tea with Kathleen spouting off about her public school and watching her mother fawning over Margaret so she slipped out the back door to take the Christmas presents round to Aunt Ruth and Uncle Henry. She stayed for a couple of hours watching their T.V. They gave Amy presents to bring home with her and when she got back she was relieved to find Margaret and Kathleen had left.

She was greeted by the expected ear bashing from her mother for being so rude in front of guests. "You mope around the house all day and then swan off out when Kathleen is here to see you."

"She's not my type," Amy said defensively.

"Just because you're not seeing that boyfriend of yours this weekend, you take it out on poor Kathleen."

Amy gave a huff and stomped off to bed. She definitely didn't need reminding about Rob - he had been on her mind constantly.

At her desk next morning, Amy looked despondently at the usual Monday pile of agents' accounts heaped in her in-tray waiting to be ticked off in the ledger. Her heart wasn't in it as she plucked one off the top of the pile and heaved the heavy leather-bound ledger open. Why didn't Rob ring?

At lunchtime Amy headed off to the little jewellers shop off Leather Lane at the back of the Pru and picked out a lovely pair of rolled gold cuff links with a maroon stone that were prominently displayed in the window. She thought they looked beautiful and was certain Rob would love them. They were quite expensive but it didn't matter because they were for her beloved.

That evening she went over to Pam's. She didn't really want to hear about the great weekend she had spent with Jim and Pam guessed as much so she kept the details to a minimum.

"Let's go round and see Chris," Pam suggested, "I haven't seen her for some time." Chris was a short chubby girl who lived near Pam. They used to go to school together when they were in the juniors and had remained friends.

Chris was a bubbly, giggly girl and she soon had Amy smiling at her jokes. She brought out a bottle of gin as her parents were out and the girls sipped gin and orange as they listened to records and chatted until it was time for Amy to catch her bus home.

The next day Rob still hadn't phoned. Amy couldn't concentrate on her work and by the afternoon she was worried sick. At tea break she slipped down to the basement and rang his office only to be told he was out. She rang Pam who wanted to meet her after work in the city.

They met up at the entrance to the underground. "Yvonne rang me," Pam said, "she asked me to meet her at the Guardian where she's working."

Scatty Yvonne was another of their gang from school who had fallen out with them. The reason why was a mystery. Consequently she hadn't been in touch for a very long time. They walked into the foyer of the Guardian Assurance to be greeted with a yell of "Hiya Bat, hiya Tibs!" Yvonne clattered down the main stairs looking the same dishevelled, rosy-cheeked girl they knew at school. She seemed genuinely pleased to see them and grabbed each one by the arm and started back up the stairs.

"I must show you where I work," she said in her broad Scottish accent pushing open a heavy door on the first floor. Inside was a large, almost empty office, full of desks piled with papers. She weaved between the desks until she reached one over by the window, which was far untidier than all the others.

"This is my desk." She said proudly giving the phone a flick with her finger. "My boss sits in his office over there." She nodded in the direction of a glass-panelled booth in the corner. "He's ever so nice - even takes me out to lunch sometimes. Of course he's married," she added matter-of-factly.

"This makes the Pru feel like something out of a Dickens novel," Amy said looking round the bright office, which she could easily visualise as a hive of activity during the day. "We've got rows of solid wooden desks and huge dusty ledgers to update."

"My office is positively poky compared to this," Pam commented somewhat enviously.

"Anyway let's go and have a bite to eat and catch up on our news," Yvonne said picking up her handbag from under her desk and grabbing her coat, which was draped across her chair.

Yvonne took them across the road to a Wimpy Bar. "Just like old times eh Bat?" she said with a grin. They went in and sat down at a table by the window. Yvonne had dragged Amy into numerous Wimpy Bars when they had been best mates at school. Yvonne had always been very fond of her food and consequently had struggled to keep control of her weight.

This evening they all tucked into egg and chips though Yvonne couldn't resist having double egg, burger and chips followed by a rum baba and coffee. They told Yvonne all about their wonderful romances with Jim and Rob. Yvonne described her latest boyfriend as the love of her life. Amy recalled that most of Yvonne's many boyfriends were usually described in similar terms.

"By the way, Bat, I know a handsome young man who works at the Pru - I think he's in the policies department. He told me he fancies a girl in accounts with long blonde hair. I think he must mean you, unless you know of anyone else who matches your description."

Amy frowned trying to place who he might be. She sometimes had to walk through the policy department and had noticed a really dishy boy who worked in there. "Does he have black hair, vivid blue eyes and wear a mohair suit?"

"Well, he's got brown hair and I think his eyes are greeny brown," Yvonne said.

"Can't be the one I'm thinking of then," Amy said disappointed.

"I'll tell him to go up to your office and introduce himself," Yvonne said, "though I think he's a bit on the shy side."

The sheer number of blokes Yvonne knew constantly amazed Amy, including the ones she went out with. At school she had often tried to arrange blind dates for her and Pam with some of her male acquaintances.

The girls came out of the Wimpy Bar and said goodbye to Yvonne who was off to meet her boyfriend while Pam and Amy caught the train home.

Amy walked into the lounge to find World War Three threatening to break out. Dad was putting up the Christmas decorations according to his carefully drawn out plan of the ceiling. It was strictly adhered to, year in, year out. He and mum were arguing over which was the longest paper chain as it had to form a diamond shape around the entire room. Amy offered to help and mum was diplomatically despatched to put the kettle on for a cup of tea.

"Sometimes your mother will argue that black is white," dad grumbled from the top of the step ladder, "I've put these up ever since you were little so I ought to know how they go by now."

By the time mum reappeared with a tray of tea, most of the chains were in place and the four enormous balloons were inflated for hanging in the four corners. Amy glanced at the empty bay window as she sipped her tea. Every year she yearned for a tree to be there decorated with lights and ornaments. She could just picture it shining out through the windows. 'Maybe now I'm working I'll fork out and get one for next year. That'll show my tight-fisted parents,' she thought taking an extra-large swig of tea, which she promptly choked on.

At lunchtime next day Amy hurried down to the phone booths in the basement to ring Rob. His boss answered the phone and told her that Rob was at dinner. He promised to tell Rob to phone her back. Amy had no appetite for food in the canteen; she was so worried about not hearing from her beloved Rob. She sipped a coffee and puffed nervously on a cigarette while Jeanette tucked into cottage pie and chips. There was no Mary today as she was absent.

With lunch over she galloped back upstairs to be by the phone at her desk waiting for Rob's call. She didn't have to wait long.

His voice sounded odd, distant. "I've written you a letter," he said.

"Oh, what about?" Amy asked, surprised and a little puzzled.

"I've been feeling very mixed up lately and don't think I'll be seeing you any more." His words took a few moments to sink in. The colour drained from Amy's face as the truth hit her: 'He's packing me up,' she thought and a lump stuck in her throat. She could hear Rob apologising at the other end of the phone but her mind was in turmoil.

"Are you still there?" he asked. All Amy could manage was a grunt. She knew if she tried to speak, begged him to change his mind, she would dissolve into floods of tears. She could not allow that to happen - she still had some pride left.

Rob hung up leaving a heartbroken Amy still holding the receiver, hot tears now falling down her cheeks. She slowly replaced the phone feeling numb and tried to concentrate on her ledger, her hair falling around her face concealed her tears but behind her she could hear Vera whispering to Audrey: "What's up with Amy? Is she crying?"

Amy couldn't take the eyes burning into her back any longer. She pushed back her chair and ran up the office dabbing at her eyes. She dashed down the stairs to the ladies in the basement where, after locking herself in a cubicle, she gave vent to her emotions. Loud sobs wracked her body. She wanted to curl up and die. Life was no longer worth living now that she had lost the love of her life. How could she possibly carry on? Tomorrow would be Christmas Eve and Pam would be spending Christmas with Jim. As far as Amy was concerned, Christmas had been cancelled. It didn't mean a thing any more. Everything had become totally meaningless to her.

After crying for half an hour, she emerged from the cubicle and splashed cold water on her face to try and soothe her red, sore eyes. Feeling a little more composed, she returned upstairs to her desk.

"Are you all right, Amy?" A concerned-looking Sue asked as she sat down. Amy could only shake her head miserably. Sue came over and put an arm around her shoulders. She had guessed what had happened.

"Boys!" she said scornfully, "they're not worth upsetting yourself over."

"You're all right 'cos you've been engaged to Peter for nearly a year now," Amy said.

"Yes, but sometimes he drives me up the wall with his irritating little habits and I wonder why I put up with him." She smiled. "You're young - you'll soon bounce back. Plenty of fish in the sea."

"But it's Rob I want," Amy said stifling a sob.

"If he can't see what he's losing then he's not worth bothering with. You should show him that you couldn't care less by going to loads of parties over Christmas and New Year. Enjoy yourself, get a little tipsy and you'll be surprised how quickly you'll get over him. Promise me you'll give it a try."

Amy nodded but she lacked conviction. Unable to focus on her work she went back down to the basement. She was surprised not to get a ticking off from Vera for leaving her desk again but Vera had stayed tactfully silent for once.

She phoned Pam and poured out her woes to her between sobs. Pam was at a loss how to console her friend. She felt guilty that her cousin had caused so much grief.

"Tell you what, Bat, meet me at my office tomorrow lunchtime and we'll go out for a drink."

Amy agreed. Maybe a drink and cheerful company would help. She went into the ladies and splashed more cold water on her face. Every minute of every hour was now an ordeal for her to endure. Back in the office she waited for the closing bell to ring so she could escape home.

Up in her bedroom that evening the violent sobs returned. She couldn't eat and that night sleep refused to come and ease her tortured mind.

Next day she only had to get through until 12 noon as it was Christmas Eve. There were presents to open and Vera had brought in a bottle of sherry. The smoking ban had been lifted for the morning so Amy smoked heavily and drank the sweet sherry. It went to her head, as she hadn't eaten for two whole days.

At midday she caught a bus to New Zealand house, a gloomy Victorian building, where she met Pam and they went to the nearby Ship and Compass pub for the next three hours. Amy stuck to the sweet sherries - not that she particularly liked sherry but didn't want to mix her drinks. Pam tactfully tried to steer the conversation away from boyfriends, but it was the only thing on Amy's mind.

"Rob said he was mixed up," she said, "do you think once he's sorted himself out he might have a change of heart?" She knew she was clutching at straws but it was all she had left.

"I don't know, Bat, I wouldn't get your hopes up if I were you."

"Well, he's your cousin. I thought you might have an idea how his mind works."

"We've never been that close. I've seen more of him lately than all the previous years put together."

A black unthinkable thought suddenly crossed Amy's mind. "He hasn't found someone else has he?" she asked looking desperately at Pam. "Maybe that's why he didn't ring me. Perhaps that's why he's feeling mixed up."

"I'm sure Jim would have told me if Rob was seeing someone else," Pam said firmly though she secretly wondered if he would.

At 4.30 they returned to Pam's firm where a colleague of hers, a pleasant young man with curly dark hair called Mick, insisted they go on a pub-crawl with him.

"We'll head for Trafalgar Square and stop at every pub along the way," he said, "how does that sound?"

"Great," said Amy staggering to her feet, "just what I need."

"Er - are you sure you should be drinking on an empty stomach?" Pam asked looking worried, "maybe you should eat some food first."

"I'm absolutely fine," Amy assured her friend and walked off after Mick feeling a little light-headed and trying not to sway.

The atmosphere in the pubs was euphoric with everyone getting in the Christmas spirit. At one time Amy found nine sherries lined up for her and she had no idea who had bought them. She found she could knock them back easier now and even liked the taste of them. With each one she raised her glass and called out a loud "Cheers!" to the crowd in general. A blonde German boy came over and sat next to her and started talking about Christmas back in Germany. Amy was attracted to his turquoise blue eyes and she suddenly had an overwhelming desire to fling her arms around his neck and kiss him.

'I must be drunk,' she thought, quickly followed by, 'Oh, Oh - I'm going to be sick.' She jumped up and staggered to the ladies, just making it in time to throw up down the loo. Afterwards she felt slightly better and returned to find more sherries on the table for her. There was no sign of the blonde German though.

Pam and Mick decided that Amy had had enough. Instead of going on to Trafalgar Square, they each took one of Amy's arms and put it around their neck before half carrying her to the station. The fresh air nearly knocked Amy out. She couldn't remember getting to the station and being sick again on the platform before being bundled into a seat on the train. Pam thanked Mick for his help and she sat opposite Amy on the way home wondering how she would cope with her at the other end. But after a while Amy roused out of her drunken stupor. The drink had given her Dutch courage.

"Promise me, Tibs, that you will tell Rob how upset I am; how much I miss him and still want to go out with him."

Pam looked a little uneasy. "I'm not sure I'll be seeing him," she said evasively.

Amy started getting agitated and more insistent as she pleaded with her friend. "And most important of all," she said raising her voice, "please tell him how much I love him." Other passengers were glancing across at Amy as her pleas got louder and more desperate.

Pam assured Amy she would do her best and tell Rob if she saw him. This was what Amy wanted to hear. She quietened down and insisted Pam get off at her own station. "I'll be O.K. to get home on my own," she said, "I'll grab a taxi at the station."

"Well so long as you do," Pam said dubiously, "don't forget Eric's having a party on Boxing Day. Why don't you go? There'll be quite a few people there you know – it should be fun."

"Yes, maybe I'll go, but if Mick or Dick shows up I'll be off straight away."

"Oh I'm sure they won't be there," Pam said confidently hoping to convince Amy.

The girls wished each other a happy Christmas as Pam got out at her station and Amy called after her a reminder to tell Rob what she had said.

She made it safely home in a taxi and slumped straight into bed. At least the drink enabled her to have a good night's sleep.

Amy made the effort to get up in time for Christmas dinner next day. She felt dreadful and the hangover made her head throb as if it was going to explode. She could only manage to force down a few mouthfuls of chicken before leaving the table to lie down on the settee in the lounge. She had no interest in the festivities and only half-heartedly opened her presents. Nothing could cheer her up. She watched T.V. but her mind kept wandering. She tried hard not to think of Rob and what he might be doing.

Boxing Day arrived and Amy resolved to make the effort and go to Eric's party. She hoped it would take her mind off Rob.

The party was being held in a room above a pub on the other side of town. Amy walked the mile and a half to get there, feeling a bit nervous at going to a party alone. On arriving she soon recognised many familiar faces and relaxed a little. Ritchie, Ken and all their mates were there. One of them, called John, who Amy had always liked the look of, being tall, dark and very handsome, came over and chatted. He got her a drink and before long they were dancing together and she ended up sitting on his lap, giggling at his jokes, all thoughts of Rob banished to the far corners of her mind.

At 2.30 a.m. John brought her home in his car. It had started to snow heavily. As they sat in the car outside Amy's house, his kisses became more passionate until Amy pushed him away and fumbled for the door handle. "I must go, it's late," she said.

"Must you?" John said trying to hold on to her but Amy was determined so he reluctantly gave up. "O.K. I'll phone you in the week and we'll go for a drink."

Amy had given him her works phone number at the party. She waved as he drove away and then went indoors, her head in a whirl.

'Ooh, I think he's lovely,' she thought with a sigh as she climbed the stairs to bed, 'what a difference to Rob!'

Monday was a bank holiday so Amy took herself off up to London on the train and wandered around the sales in Oxford Street. She spotted Fred Bloggs browsing for a bargain in the men's department at C & A's but decided to avoid him. He was one of Pam's ex's who Amy had once had a crush on. She took the tube to Wardour Street where, in a small crowded record shop, she was thrilled to find Georgie Fame's E.P. 'Live at the Flamingo' and a great Blues L.P. She caught the train back home and enjoyed spending the evening listening to her new records played at full volume. She ignored the irritated looks she got from her parents and Aunt Ruth who had popped round for tea and a quiet chat. They failed to appreciate the amazing Georgie Fame belting out 'Night Train' on his Hammond organ.

The following evening after the first day back at work, Pam arrived at Amy's house to catch up with what she had been doing over Christmas.

Amy was in a good mood because John had rung her at work and invited her to a New Year's Eve Party.

She was impatient to tell Pam all about the gorgeous John she had met at Eric's party. They carried the record player up to Amy's bedroom so they could listen to Amy's new records.

"I wish I'd gone to Eric's party," Pam said wistfully slumping onto the bed.

"You look fed up," Amy observed glancing at her friend as she put a record on the turntable, "thought you'd be on cloud nine after spending Christmas with Jim."

"I got bored just sitting around with his family watching telly. We didn't go to any parties - in fact we didn't do anything. Much as I like being with Jim, he seemed perfectly happy doing nothing but eat and lounge around the house all day."

"Sounds as boring as my Christmas. I'm glad I made the effort to go to Eric's party else I wouldn't have met the gorgeous John. He's such a hunk - the classic tall, dark and handsome; nothing like Rob. Can't wait to see him again. Are you seeing Jim this coming weekend?"

"Yeah," Pam sighed, "I just hope he's going to take me out somewhere nice for a change. At least this John has helped to get you over Rob pretty quickly," she added.

"I'm not over him completely yet but meeting John has definitely helped. If you happen to see Rob be sure to mention that I've got a dishy new boyfriend won't you. I don't want him to think I'm pining away for him."

"Perhaps I shouldn't tell you, but Jim did mention that Rob has got a new girlfriend - he met her at a party."

Amy felt a sick pang in the pit of her stomach. She hadn't expected this to happen quite so soon and the unwelcome news hit her hard but she put on a brave face. "Oh well, we've both moved on then," she said offhandedly with a smile and quickly changed the subject. "By the way I nearly bumped into one of your ex's in Oxford Street on Monday - Fred Bloggs."

"You should have spoken to him and found out what he's up to these days. It must be almost exactly a year ago that I was going out with Fred 'cos I got him a wallet for Christmas and then packed him up before New Year. Fred is a really nice bloke - you used to fancy him once didn't you?"

"Yeah, back in our school days. Seems like ages since then. I only fancied him because he looked so much like John Lennon with his Beatle haircut and black leather jacket. Anyway I chickened out in Oxford Street and decided to cut and run. Talking of Oxford Street, I must go up there in my dinner hour tomorrow, as I need a new pair of shoes for the party on Thursday. Saw some nice ones in the sales on Monday."

The talk moved on to clothes they had bought and various presents received until it was time for Pam to catch her bus home.

Thursday evening Amy sat waiting impatiently for John. She passed the time by painting her nails and had just finished when there was a knock at the door. John had arrived early in his dad's car. In her excitement, Amy tugged on her gloves and then realised too late that her wet nails had stuck to the fluffy gloves.

The New Year's Eve dance was being held in a fairly large community hall. Eric was there with Ritchie and his mates. Amy decided to stick to gin and orange all night and found a never ending supply of drinks being bought for her, some by people she didn't even recognise. Her nails looked a mess as she tried to hide them and discreetly pick the fluff off, but after a few drinks she no longer cared who noticed her fluffy nails.

At midnight the lights flashed on and off and a huge net of balloons was released from the ceiling. Everyone crossed arms and sang 'Auld Lang Syne' followed by shouts and cheers. Amy found herself being hugged and kissed by all and sundry and was quite relieved when John dragged her away to a quiet corner for a celebratory snog.

The dancing and drinking continued until 2.00a.m. when the party ended and John steered a very unsteady Amy out to his car and drove her home. Amy's head felt fuzzy. She didn't remember the journey home and had the uneasy feeling that she must have fallen asleep.

The lights were still on at Amy's house, which meant her parents were waiting up for her so she quickly kissed John goodnight and staggered out of the car.

"I'll ring you at work tomorrow," he called after her as she tottered across the green towards her front gate. Amy just waved vaguely and hoped he would drive off before she threw up in the front garden.

Chapter Six

January - Joining The Scene

"I wish you could have been there last night, Bat. Georgie Fame was fantastic - more than could be said for Jim." Pam was telling Amy all about the previous evening spent at the Flamingo with Jim as the girls walked briskly arm in arm down to the town wrapped up in their suede coats and scarves against the biting cold of the early evening.

"Sounds as if you're not so keen on Jim any more," Amy observed trying to sound nonchalant. Ever since her split with Rob she had tried to hide her feelings of jealousy because Pam was still so involved with Jim.

"To tell the truth Bat, I'm getting a bit bored with him. It's not the same as when all four of us went around together. It's not much fun now."

"Well we can have some fun tonight, just the two of us at the Flamingo," Amy declared, "and with each of our parents thinking we are tucked up in bed at the other's house, hopefully we shouldn't get any aggro there."

The girls arrived in the High Street, which was fairly quiet for a Saturday evening. The Christmas decorations still twinkled merrily from the rooftops of the shops.

"Hey Pam, look who's crawled out of the woodwork," Amy whispered, giving her friend a nudge.

"Happy New Year girls," said Mick stopping in front of them so they couldn't just walk past. He grinned broadly. "Had a good Christmas?"

"Yeah, we've had a great time, haven't we Pam?" Amy said defensively, wondering if Mick had heard about her break-up with Rob and had stopped to gloat. Pam nodded in agreement.

"That's good," he said, then added, "by the way - Eric's up at the Railway. He's going on to a party tonight so if you're not doing anything and fancy a party why not go and see him?"

"Yeah, we might just do that," Amy said casually, "aren't you going to this party?"

"Me and Dick might pop in a bit later, so maybe we'll see you both then? Take care." He sidestepped around them and continued on his way.

"What do you think Pam? I'm not sure it's a good idea if Mick and Dick are going to be there."

"Well, we were going to hang around in the Wimpy to kill some time before heading up to the Flamingo so I suppose it wouldn't matter if we went to this party instead - it might be a laugh."

"OK," Amy said dubiously, "we don't have to hang around if the party's no good."

At the Railway Tavern they found Eric and a few of his mates enjoying a drink at the bar. He bought the girls a drink and pulled up a couple of bar stools for them to sit on.

"So, a little bird told us you're going to a party tonight," Pam said.

"Oh? Well, it's only a small party just round the corner from your house Amy, at Carol Turner's house - you probably know her. You're both welcome to come along."

"Oh yes, we know Carol don't we Pam - though not all that well."

"Drink up then and we'll get going," Eric said and drained his glass. He bought some bottles to take to the party and then they all piled into his big old convertible with its draughty soft top pulled up. They drove back up the hill that the girls had recently walked down and parked outside a small end of terrace house that had all its lights on and music blaring out of open windows. People spilled out of the front door into the front garden clutching glasses of drink. There was a lot of laughter and shouting as Amy and Pam followed Eric and the others through the door into the hallway. Carol came clattering down the stairs beaming at the newcomers.

"The more the merrier," she yelled, "especially if you come bearing booze. Here let me take your coats - I'll put them up in the bedroom." She pointed them towards the kitchen where the table and worktop were hidden under bottles, cans and glasses.

A friendly looking bloke in a black leather jacket who was leaning against the sink gave the girls a smile. "Here, let me get you two lovely ladies a drink - I'm Graham by the way." He found a pair of clean glasses and poured them out a gin and orange. "Maybe we can have a dance later?"

"Thanks," Amy said as they took the glasses from him and then pushed their way through to the lounge where the loud music blasted from a Dansette perched on a bookcase in the corner.

"Carol must have very understanding neighbours," Amy yelled in Pam's ear.

"Wonder where her parents are," Pam yelled back.

"Who cares, so long as they're not here. Isn't that Marilyn Cooper with that octopus?" Amy nodded towards a couple cuddling on the sofa. The girl's long blonde hair was dishevelled and covered most of her face.

"Can't really tell - it might be her. Let's find a space and have a dance, Bat." They put their glasses down as 'Heard it through the grapevine' started to throb out from the loud speaker. As they danced, others joined them including Graham until the centre of the room was a mass of writhing bodies.

Several dances later Amy spotted Dick in the doorway. He caught her eye and grinned. She smiled back at him, which gave him the courage to come over. Then Amy realised that Mick was behind him. They were wearing their leather coats.

"We've only just arrived," Mick said, "glad you both came after all. How about a dance?" He grabbed Amy round the waist before she had time to argue and started smooching while Dick asked Pam if she wanted to dance. Amy saw her nod and fall quite eagerly into his arms.

At 10.30pm. it was time for Amy and Pam to leave for the station to catch the last train up to London. Mick and Dick offered to walk to the station with them. As the girls hunted for their coats in the bedroom Pam giggled.

"It's just like old times again Bat. I think Dick wants to ask me out."

"But what about Jim?"

"Oh, I'm not bothered about seeing him any more - I prefer us going out in a foursome."

"Well I suppose if Dick asks you out then Mick will ask me since those two rarely do anything apart and it doesn't look like he's still going out with Jenny."

"Would you go back out with Mick? I thought you liked John."

"I do but I don't think we're getting anywhere so I wouldn't have any guilty feelings about two-timing him."

At the station the boys saw the girls onto their train and arranged to meet them Sunday afternoon at the local cinema.

"Makes a change for us to be going up West all night instead of them," Amy said spreading out on the seat as the train gathered speed.

"I'm surprised they didn't want to come with us," Pam said.

"Come off it," Amy scoffed, "they were probably afraid they would have to pay for us to get in the Flamingo."

Pam grinned. "Yeah of course - they haven't changed much in the last few months have they?"

The girls joined the throng of late night revellers in London's West End as they made their way to the Flamingo in Wardour Street. It was just opening as they arrived so they put their names down to become members.

"At least it'll be a bit cheaper to get in once our membership cards come through," Pam said as they threaded their way onto the dance floor. Tonight the music was by Ronnie Jones and the Nighttimers and John Mayall's Blues Breakers.

The girls enjoyed themselves dancing and listening to the R&B all night without flagging too much. Despite the stuffy hot atmosphere they kept their coats on but regretted it when they emerged into the cold early morning air at 6a.m. to head for home. At the station they shivered on the platform waiting for the first train to arrive.

"It wasn't quite as good as when Zoot Money was on," Amy said as they finally settled into their seats on the train.

"P'raps it was due to the lack of a boyfriend," Pam replied then wished she hadn't said that when a pained look flitted across her friend's face. She quickly changed the subject. "At least we managed to stay awake all night. I didn't feel tired at all."

"Yeah but you could tell the ones who had taken something - they were dancing and bouncing around non-stop with energy to spare."

"I think we should steer clear of drugs if we can manage to stay awake without them," Pam said. Amy just grunted noncommittally and gazed out of the window at the suburbs flashing past.

On reaching Amy's station they walked back up the hill.

"There's Eric's car still outside Carol's house," Amy said, "let's see if it's open." There was no sign of life at the house - all was quiet. They crept up to the car and tried the rear door handle. The door opened so the girls climbed in. They huddled together and tried to get some sleep but the cold was too intense in the draughty old car.

"It's no good, Bat, I can't sleep," Pam said through chattering teeth, "let's go round to your house and see if we can get in."

Amy agreed so they headed round the corner into the Crescent. "This place is like Fort Knox," Amy said crossly as she tried the back door and found it locked and bolted. All the windows were tightly shut. "It's useless – we might as well go over to your house, Tibs - p'raps the walk will warm us up."

Arm in arm they made the trek to the next town and arrived just as Pam's dad was letting the dog out into the garden.

"Where have you two been all night?" he asked looking stern, "didn't you say you were staying at Amy's house?" Amy thought she saw a twinkle in his eye. Pam could nearly always get round her dad.

"I told you I was going over to Amy's yesterday. Well, we went to a party which lasted most of the night and now we're really tired so we're off to bed." She added a loud yawn to emphasise the point.

"Your mum will give you all night party if she finds out," Mr Tibton said, adding, "better get upstairs quick before she wakes up."

"Thanks dad." Pam gave her dad a quick hug and then they hurried into the house and crept up the stairs to Pam's bedroom.

Crammed into Pam's single bed they managed to snatch a few hours sleep before it was time to get up and get ready to go and meet Mick and Dick.

Pam lent Amy a pair of jeans and a top and they hurried downstairs for a quick mug of coffee before leaving. Pam didn't fancy facing a third degree from her mother so she was relieved to discover she had gone to the newsagents for cigarettes.

"Your mum is very suspicious," her dad told her, "I don't think she believes your story."

"Well we're off out now," Pam said and gulped down the last mouthful of coffee, "maybe by tonight she'll have forgotten about it."

The girls hurried to catch the bus being careful to watch out in case they bumped into Mrs Tibton on her way back from the newsagents.

The bus took them to the main Broadway and stopped opposite the cinema. As they hopped off the bus they spotted Mick and Dick hovering in the entrance.

"I don't much fancy this film they're taking us to see. Sounds like a Western and I can't stand Westerns," Amy grumbled as they crossed the road.

"Well at least they're meeting us outside so they'll be paying for us to get in," Pam pointed out.

"Just trying to get back in our good books," Amy whispered cynically as Mick approached. He gave her a cautious hug and Dick did the same to Pam. With their arms round the girls shoulders they steered them through the heavy glass doors and the plush foyer to watch the matinee performance of Cheyenne Autumn.

The film was every bit as boring as Amy expected but she enjoyed being back in a familiar foursome again. She could almost kid herself that the last two months hadn't happened, that Rob was just a bad dream. At least Mick never broached the subject of what had gone wrong between her and the wonderful boyfriend she had bragged about, which relieved Amy greatly.

Afterwards they walked to the nearby Wimpy Bar and ordered coffees and chips because the girls confessed to being ravenous as they hadn't eaten all day.

"So now you go to the clubs up town, why not come down the Scene on Tuesday evening?" Mick suggested.

"Yeah, great idea," Dick chipped in.

The girls glanced at each other and a knowing smile passed between them. Little did Mick and Dick realise that they had been spied on by Mary and what they had been getting up to had been relayed back to Amy.

"We'll have to join I suppose else we can't get in," Amy said.

"That's easy enough," Mick said cheerfully adding, "so we'll see you down there then?"

"Yeah, I expect so," Amy responded unenthusiastically, noting that by meeting them inside, the boys were up to their old skinflint tricks again.

After an extra-long day at work on Tuesday due to volunteering for some overtime, Amy finally met up with Pam at the Wimpy Bar along the road. Pam was already waiting, sitting at a table in the window, sipping a coffee.

Amy dropped into the seat opposite. "Oh Tibs, why did I go and offer to do overtime?"

"'Cos you need the money, Bat," Pam replied matter-of-factly.

"Yeah, you're right - I do need the money but the time does drag so."

The waiter came over and the girls ordered egg and chips. "Let's go mad and have a rum baba for afters," Amy said studying the menu, "with all this overtime I'm feeling rich."

"We need to get to the Scene fairly early as we've got to mess around filling out forms to join," Pam reminded her friend and glanced at her watch.

At the end of their meal Amy scooped up her last mouthful of rum baba. "Let's pay for this and get going," she mumbled grabbing her bag, "it's quite a walk to the West End from here."

They arrived in Shaftesbury Avenue, which still looked very festive with its Christmas lights ablaze, and turned into Windmill Street, walking beneath the dazzling vanes of the windmill above the theatre bearing its name. The lights flickered to give the impression that the vanes were turning. After a short distance they turned into Ham Yard, which seemed very dark and dowdy after the bright lights. There was a rough area where some cars were parked and an illuminated entrance to a big multi-storey car park.

"Are you sure this is the right place?" Pam asked nervously peering into the gloomy shadows.

"Mary gave me the directions; this is definitely the place. Let's look round here." Amy grabbed Pam's arm and they walked round a corner into another part of the yard. In a far corner a dim light glowed and music could be heard drifting up from the bowels of the earth.

"That must be it," Amy said not sounding too sure.

"Doesn't look very promising," Pam observed. Just then a crowd of Mods came round the corner laughing and joking. They made straight for the entrance and vanished down a flight of steps. Pam and Amy followed them and looked in through the doorway. A long, steep flight of concrete steps led down to a small foyer where a couple of well-built bouncers sat at a table. The walls were covered with posters advertising events - some that had long since gone.

One of the bouncers spotted the girls hesitating in the doorway. "Come on in, girls," he said with a broad smile and beckoned, "don't be shy."

"Er - we'd like to join," Amy said as she and Pam clattered down the steps.

"No problem for two lovely girls like you," said the second bouncer, "George here will find the forms for you." George turned and rummaged in the top drawer of a small filing cabinet. He pulled out some papers and laid them on the table.

"Just fill in these and then next week you should get your membership cards." He gave the girls a pen each and they bent over the forms scribbling answers to all the questions.

More people were arriving, noisily stomping down the stairs and shouting greetings to the two bouncers who appeared to be called George and Harry. When the girls had completed the forms George took them and studied them.

"That looks OK to me," he said, "now we'll let you in tonight as members even though it's not yet official. Harry will stick a pass out on your hand and then you're free to come and go as you like."

Amy held out her hand and Harry made an invisible mark on the back with a special pen. Then he did the same to Pam. As they entered the dance hall through a set of double doors they passed under an ultra-violet light, which revealed the mark on their hands. Tonight's pass was a circle with a line through it.

Pam giggled. "It's like joining a secret society," she said. Inside it took a while for their eyes to get accustomed to the gloom. The walls, doors and ceiling were all painted black as was the norm. Along the nearest wall was a padded seat that stretched the length of the room and on the opposite wall there were alcoves with more padded seats set in them. In the corner next to the entrance was a glass cubicle where the DJ sat playing records and talking into a microphone. Amy looked at him as he jigged around to the music with a pair of headphones around his neck. His eyes wore a glazed expression and Amy concluded he was high on drugs.

On the other side of the entrance was a raised stage where people were lounging and at the far side of the stage a doorway with a sign above it led to the cloakroom. Pam nudged Amy.

"C'mon - let's go and hand our coats in."

They walked across the floor and into the cloakroom where they found a small Chinese lad sitting behind a counter.

He grinned at them. "Hello, my name is Chicko. You two are new here." Amy nodded and handed over her coat. Pam did the same. "You will like it here," he told them, "the Scene has a good atmosphere and great music. This is where Patrick Kerr used to come to discover the latest dances to demonstrate on Ready Steady Go."

Amy looked suitably impressed with this snippet of news about her neighbour who also lived in the Crescent, but right now there was a more pressing need. "Where is the ladies, Chicko?"

"Ah - you will find it at the far end of the dance floor. The doors are marked Boys and Girls so don't go wandering through the wrong door."

"We'll try not to," Pam said returning his smile and they walked back out into the main room. It was filling up fast now. The girls edged past groups of Mods dancing their intricate steps to a record that neither of them had heard before.

"I like the music," Amy yelled in Pam's ear, "don't recognise it though." Pam shook her head in agreement. They reached the far end and walked along the back wall past a door labelled 'Boys' and came to one marked 'Girls'. Amy pushed it open and they went in.

The room was slightly better lit and had just two cubicles. A chipped and scratched mirror hung on the wall above the two hand basins. A girl was cursing as she tugged and banged on the Tampax machine fixed to the wall.

"Flippin' machine never works," she said crossly. She gave it another thump, which did the trick, and the drawer flew open. She hurried into one of the cubicles so Amy dashed into the other while Pam freshened up her make-up.

"No sign of Mick or Dick yet Bat," Pam said when Amy joined her by the hand basins to wash her hands.

"No doubt they'll be late as usual," Amy said. She dried her hands and then brushed her hair.

"Let's go and get a drink - there's a bar next door," Pam said closing her handbag.

They emerged from the ladies and entered the small bar in the corner. There wasn't much of a selection so the girls opted for an orange squash each. They perched on the bar stools and gazed out at the figures moving around on the dance floor. Amy nearly choked on her drink when she suddenly spotted a familiar face.

"There's Mary!" she shouted. "Mary, Mary!"

Mary turned when she heard her name being called and walked over to the bar. A petite blonde girl wearing expensive looking Mod clothes followed her. "Hi ya. You found this old dive then," she said with a grin, "by the way this is my friend Pat."

The girls all nodded and Amy introduced Pam.

"Me and Pat are old friends; we used to go to school together," Mary told them.

"Same as me and Pam," Amy said.

"Let's go and get Blocker Tony to put some decent music on," Pat said tugging Mary's arm.

"OK, See you later," Mary said and they headed off towards the record booth.

The girls finished their drinks and decided to try out their Mod dance as James Brown's 'Out of Sight' started up. Amy caught Mary's eye as she stood over by the booth and gave her a thumbs up.

As they danced, Amy noticed that Mary and Pat had wandered over and stood nearby puffing on cigarettes while they watched them dance. As the music ended they joined Pam and Amy.

"Why don't you two have a dance?" Amy asked accepting a cigarette from the packet Mary was offering.

"Oh, we don't dance very often, do we Pat?" Mary said somewhat disdainfully and Pat nodded in agreement. "We prefer to watch everyone else making a fool of themselves - present company excepted of course," she added hastily. "I like the dance you ones do."

"Thanks," Pam said, "it took us long enough to perfect it."

"Oh good, he's playing the record I asked for at last," Pat said as 'La la la la la' by the Blendells started to blare out of the speakers.

Amy and Pam danced while Mary and Pat went over to the side and sat on the bench. Two numbers later in walked Mick and Dick. They saw Amy and Pam on the dance floor and walked over grinning broadly.

"Hi ya babe," Mick said putting an arm around Amy's shoulder and giving her a quick kiss. "How d'you like it down here?"

"Yeah, seems OK," Amy said casually. Mary and Pat suddenly appeared beside them. "Oh by the way, Mick, I believe you know our friends Mary and Pat," Amy said innocently as the two girls greeted Mick and Dick noisily. Mick and Dick seemed at a loss for words as the full impact of this revelation gradually dawned on them.

"So you two have been telling Pam and Amy what we get up to down here then?" Dick said, "not that we've done anything to be ashamed of," he added hastily. Apparently Eric hadn't mentioned to Mick and Dick that Mary knew Pam and Amy.

"Let's go and get a drink," Mick suggested grabbing Amy's hand. Amy thought he seemed keen to get away from Mary and Pat. They headed out through the doors and up the stairs with Dick and Pam following.

The cold night air made them shiver, as the girls didn't have their coats.

"We'll go to the Pic - it's just round the corner," Mick said and hurried Amy across the yard and down a slope into the brightly lit entrance to the multi-storey car park. As they walked across to another exit hot air blasted out of a large vent accompanied by a sickly smell.

"Ugh! What's that horrid pong?" Amy asked holding her nose.

"It's coming from a restaurant vent," Mick told her.

"Well I definitely wouldn't want to eat in that place then," Amy mumbled through her hand. She glanced round and saw Pam holding her nose too. Over by the vent a couple of old tramps had settled down on a tatty old quilt for the night; their worldly goods in a few carrier bags beside them.

"At least they've got a warm, dry place to sleep," Amy observed.

"They're here every night. The owners of the car park turn a blind eye and let them be," Mick explained, "they don't seem to mind the pong - maybe it smells good to them."

They emerged from the second exit into a dark back street. Light streamed out from the windows of the Piccadilly cafe. They hurried inside and sat at a table near the window. It was a sparsely furnished, very basic cafe. Mick and Dick went over to the counter and bought four coffees.

"This place stays open as long as the Scene is open. They get most of their business from the Mods during the evening," Mick said putting two cups of coffee in front of the girls, "and Saturday nights it's open all night."

"Not many in here tonight," Pam remarked glancing around.

Amy picked up the menu which had been wedged between the sugar bowl and salt-shaker. She studied it for a few moments. "Nothing very exciting on offer here," she said wedging it back into its previous position, "just fry-ups and chips."

Pam took a sip of coffee and pulled a face. "Even the coffee's pretty naff," she said.

"Try some more sugar lumps," Amy suggested, "it might help."

Pam reached over to the sugar bowl. Just then a loud shout stopped her in mid grab.

"Yoo-hoo, thought we'd find you hanging out in this dive!" It was Mary yelling across the cafe as she came in followed by Pat. The cafe owner scowled as they threw themselves into chairs at the next table. Mick and Dick shuffled uncomfortably in their seats.

"Hey, Garçon, two cappuccinos," Pat said loudly snapping her fingers.

"There's no waiter service here," the cafe owner said coldly, "if you want coffees come and get them and we don't do cappuccinos."

"Told you this was a dive," Mary said in a loud whisper handing round her Benson and Hedges.

"I'll get you some coffee," Dick offered.

"Oh you're a brick, Dick," said Mary and then started giggling.

"Mary, you're a poet," Pat said, "but don't know it!" The two girls fell about laughing.

Amy and Pam finished their coffee and when Dick returned they suggested going back to the Scene. A look of relief flashed momentarily across Dick's face.

"Good idea," Mick said jumping up eagerly and leaving half his coffee undrunk.

"We'll see you later," Amy said to Mary as they left. Mary just waved. She was still giggling and once outside Amy glanced back to see Mary throwing sugar cubes across the cafe trying to attract the attention of two youths sitting with their backs to her.

"Don't know what's got into Mary tonight," Amy said apologetically, "she's not as loud as that at work."

"Her and Pat did show us up a bit in there," Pam said as she snuggled up to Dick. He opened his loose fitting tan leather coat and pulled it around her shoulders so they were sharing it. Mick didn't offer Amy his leather coat so she hugged herself to keep warm and hurried into the smelly car park basement.

Back down the Scene they had a few more dances and then it was time to get to Charing Cross station to catch the last train home. They waved to Pat and Mary who were dancing with a couple of boys.

"I bet they're the two they were chucking sugar at," Amy said to Pam as they climbed up the stairs.

Mick and Dick accompanied the girls as far as Woolwich where they got off the train to catch a bus.

"See you down the Scene on Thursday," Mick called out to the girls, who were leaning out of the window as the train started to move off, "it should be good as there's going to be a live group playing."

"Well don't be late then," Amy yelled as the train gathered speed.

"Some hopes," Pam muttered as they sat down, "those two are always late."

"Did you notice how edgy they were in Mary's company?" Amy said and giggled, "a definite sign of a guilty conscience."

Amy was having a trying day on Thursday. John rang in the morning but she had to cut their chat short when she saw Fanny Rogers glaring across the room at her. She was summoned to her desk for a reprimand on having private calls during working hours. This irritated Amy and her grotty mood became exacerbated when she went to get her coat from her locker at lunchtime only to find she had lost her locker key. She had to go to personnel and sign for a duplicate key, which left her with little time to hurry down Leather Lane to the record shop and buy her R&B L.P. She dashed in only to be told they were out of stock.

"Oh bugger!" she blurted out in frustration and returned to the Pru in a thoroughly bad mood.

After work while she waited for Pam to arrive, she went down to the basement to ring John back but he wasn't home from work. His dad answered the phone and sounded very friendly. He chatted to her for a while and invited her to come to tea one day soon.

"I shall nag John to bring you home," he said, "I like to meet his girlfriends and you sound like a very nice girl." Amy flushed, pleased with the compliment. She liked to hit it off with boyfriends' parents.

She emerged from the phone booth as Pam came out of a nearby lift. They went into the ladies to freshen up and then caught up with each other's news over toast and coffee in Lyons before making the trek over to Wardour Street in the West End. A record shop there was still open and Amy was thrilled to find they had the R&B L.P. she wanted. They went into the Macabre for coffee and then walked to Piccadilly tube station so that Amy could put her LP in the left luggage for safekeeping, as she didn't want to risk losing it down the Scene. Round the corner in Ham Yard they found Mick and Dick lounging on the railings.

"Wow, you two are actually here on time!" Pam exclaimed.

"Don't sound so surprised," said Dick trying to look hurt.

Mick greeted Amy with a sneeze. "I've been and caught a rotten cold," he mumbled through a large handkerchief.

"Great, you can keep it to yourself," Amy said backing away. They went down the steps and Mick and Dick paid for the girls to get in. Amy and Pam exchanged grins behind their backs at this novel turn of events. Once inside the girls made their way to the ladies to brush their hair and adjust their make-up.

"What came over those two?" Amy said as she tugged a comb through her hair, "I couldn't believe it when they offered to pay for us."

"Maybe they're turning over a new leaf," Pam suggested.

"Or maybe they don't want to risk losing us again having got back with us a second time." Amy said and giggled, "after all, they are obviously completely besotted with us."

They re-joined the boys as the group on stage finished tuning up their instruments and suddenly let rip with their first R&B number.

"That's Ronnie Jones and the Nighttimers," Mick yelled in Amy's ear, "it should be a good night." She nodded in agreement. They were the group who had played down the Flamingo the previous Saturday. The room was packed with little room for dancing but Amy and Pam managed to do a restricted version of their Mod dance to a couple of numbers and then smooched with Mick and Dick.

They all came out of the Scene at the end of a great evening and collected Amy's record from the left luggage before heading for Charing Cross and home on the train. The girls said goodbye to the boys at Woolwich Arsenal and arranged to meet them at Lewisham on Saturday evening so the girls could take them to the El Partido as Mick and Dick had never been there.

"Ring me tomorrow," Mick called to Amy as the train departed.

"Hope I don't catch his cold," Amy said slumping down beside Pam.

"Bound to after snogging him just now," Pam remarked with a grin.

Friday mid-morning, as Amy returned to her seat on A division with a cup of coffee from the trolley, the phone rang. It was John wanting to see her Saturday night.

"Er, sorry John but I've arranged to go out with my mate Pam," Amy said, thinking on her feet.

"Can't you put her off and come out with me instead?" he asked sounding a little peeved.

"No I can't," Amy said indignantly, "that's not the way I treat my friends."

"OK, I'm sorry, so how about we go to the flicks Sunday night instead then?" Amy agreed. She was quite enjoying doing a bit of two-timing. She put the phone down and Sue caught her eye.

"Was that your Mick ringing you?" she asked in a hushed voice so Vera wouldn't hear.

"Er, no - it was John actually. I'm seeing him Sunday and Mick Saturday."

"Oh, I could never do that to my Peter," she said emphatically.

"Well I wouldn't do it to a boy I was engaged to. I don't think me and John will last much longer and as for Mick - he annoys me too often for us to ever reach the engagement stage."

During the lunch hour Amy went down to the basement to ring Mick at work.

"Jenny rang me yesterday," he told her.

"Sounds like she still fancies you."

"I think she suspects that I'm going back out with you."

"Why did she ring you?"

"Dunno. Maybe she was just checking what I'm doing,"

"It's none of her business," Amy said feeling a pang of jealousy, "why didn't you just tell her that you're going out with me again? I think you enjoy stringing her along."

"Well you needn't worry because I wouldn't two-time you - I don't sink that low."

Amy had an attack of conscience and quickly changed the subject. "I'll ring tomorrow to arrange when and where we all meet up at Lewisham."

She rolled out of bed at lunchtime next day and strolled round the Crescent to the phone box to ring Mick at home.

"I haven't heard from Dick about arrangements for meeting up tonight," he told Amy, "why don't you ring me back later this afternoon and maybe by then I'll have spoken to Dick."

"D'you think I've got nothing better to do than wander backwards and forwards around the street just to phone you?" Amy said crossly. "Unlike you, I don't have a convenient phone in my hallway, in case you've forgotten."

"Well I can't say for sure what time we'll be meeting you and Pam 'cause I don't know what time Dick is picking me up."

"You're pathetic!" Amy said contemptuously, "you can forget about tonight - me and Pam will go on our own without you two." She slammed the phone down and stomped back home in a bad mood. Indoors she played her R&B record at full volume to try and cheer herself up. She sat in a chair gazing out of the bay window at a group of children playing hopscotch on the pavement. She didn't notice her dad coming in until the music stopped abruptly. He had switched her record player off.

"You can't do that," she yelled indignantly.

"Oh yes I can, my girl. Have a bit of consideration for others. I don't mind you playing your music but not so loud that you deafen the neighbours through the walls."

"It wasn't that bad," Amy said defensively knowing full well that she had been pushing her luck.

"Oh and I've been down to Macfisheries to have a chat with Pam's dad," he added. Amy felt her stomach tighten and tried to look unconcerned.

"Checking up on me were you?" she said accusingly.

"Just making sure your story tallied for last Saturday night about going to a party and sleeping over at Pam's."

"What did Pam's dad say?" Amy asked casually while desperately hoping he hadn't mentioned about the girls coming home Sunday morning.

"Oh, he confirmed your story all right so I suppose I'll have to believe it."

"Well it's the truth!" Amy said indignantly adding, "I wouldn't lie about it."

Her dad just shrugged and gave a non-committal grunt as he left the room. Amy had the uneasy feeling that her dad could read her like a book and always knew when she was lying.

She went upstairs to have a bath and get ready for the evening.

After tea she caught a bus over to Pam's and confronted her with the news that they wouldn't be seeing Mick and Dick that night.

"Maybe they'll come over there anyway," Pam said hopefully. She had been looking forward to seeing Dick and felt somewhat let down by Amy.

"I doubt it," Amy said as they left to walk to the station and catch the train to Lewisham, "I don't think they like going to new places. Haven't you noticed that they always frequent the same old haunts?"

"Now you come to mention it, Bat, they are a couple of stick-in-the-muds."

The girls enjoyed their evening at the El Partido. There was no-one there they recognised and no sign of Mick and Dick either.

Back at Pam's they crammed into Pam's bed once again with Monty insisting on squeezing in between them on top of the covers.

"That was good of your dad to cover for me last weekend, Tibs, when my dad checked up with him,"

Amy said trying to push Monty's wet-nosed muzzle away from her face.

"Yeah, thank goodness he did else you'd have probably been banned from staying over here."

"I'm not sure that he believed it though, so we'd better be a bit careful - I don't want to end up grounded indefinitely. If that happened then I would have to leave home."

"If you did, then I'd come with you, Bat."

"We could have a terrific laugh in a flat of our own, Tibs."

"Mm, but would we be able to afford it?"

"Well, let's hope it doesn't come to that just yet, eh?"

For an answer all Amy got was a doggy lick on the face from Monty because Pam had dozed off.

Amy arrived home in time for Sunday lunch next day and spent a lazy afternoon listening to records and getting ready to go out with John. She kept the volume at a reasonable level so as not to antagonise her parents any more; she didn't want to invite another row. She washed her hair and varnished her nails, this time making sure they were thoroughly dry before doing anything else.

John arrived at 8pm looking very smart as usual in a dark navy suit. Amy liked to be seen out with him, as he was so good looking. He was everything that Mick wasn't and yet Amy didn't feel she was falling in love with him. She didn't know why this was and it puzzled her slightly.

He drove her over to Erith where they saw 'Topkapi' at the Odeon. Amy enjoyed the film and when he brought her home she wondered whether she dared invite him in for a coffee. Then she had a mental picture of her dad coming downstairs in his pyjamas minus his teeth and decided not to risk it - it would be far too embarrassing. He promised to ring her at work during the week.

After a busy Monday at work, Amy met Pam in the basement of the Pru where they freshened up before heading across Holborn to the Wimpy Bar for egg and chips. It was a chilly evening but the brisk walk across town to the West End soon warmed them up. They went into the Macabre for a coffee and then it was time to make for the 100 Club in Oxford Street where the Birds were topping the bill. The girls enjoyed themselves dancing and watching their favourite group performing. Amy kept a wary eye on the exit just in case Rob or Jim showed up, but she needn't have worried.

Tuesday after work was a repeat of Monday for the girls as they had their usual egg and chips in the Wimpy Bar followed by coffee in the Macabre while they waited for the Scene to open. At eight o'clock they clattered down the stone steps at the entrance to the Scene Club and collected their membership cards.

The girls carried on dancing and ignored Mick and Dick when they walked in. The boys came over anyway looking sheepish and made their apologies about Saturday night. Amy had a sulk and didn't forgive Mick as readily as Pam forgave Dick. But she was in a good mood and couldn't keep up the pretence of sulking for very long. By the end of the evening they were back to normal again and smooching around on the dance floor. They all caught the same train home, the boys alighting at Woolwich. Amy promised to ring Mick later in the week.

"We're far too easy on those two, Tibs," Amy declared as the train pulled away, gathering speed.

Pam nodded, "I just can't stay cross with Dick when he gives me that sad 'little boy sorry' look."

Amy went up Oxford Street in her lunch hour on Thursday to get a pattern for a suit and a length of beige woollen material.

John rang her in the afternoon and arranged to take her out on Saturday night so she promised to ring him at home on Saturday.

Back home that evening she shut herself in the dining room and set about cutting out the suit and putting in the tailor tacks. She had brought her record player in so she could listen to records as she worked. Ten minutes later her younger brother, Ray, came in brandishing a record.

"I bought the Moody Blues today - must listen to it." Without waiting for an answer from his sister, he took the arm off the record and put his new record on.

"You could have waited 'til mine had finished," Amy said crossly. Ray ignored her and turned the volume up as 'Go Now' blasted out. Before it was halfway through dad came out of the lounge holding his ears and turned the volume down.

"What have I told you my girl about playing your records too loud!" he yelled.

"It's Ray's record," Amy retorted, "and it was him who turned the volume up. Why do you always assume it's me?"

"Because it usually is," her dad countered and returned to the lounge.

"It's not fair, you didn't get told off - you never do. Go away and take your record with you."

Ray just gave an irritating smirk and strolled out leaving Amy to fume quietly to herself.

At lunchtime on Friday Amy rang Pam and arranged to meet her at the hairdressers Saturday morning in order to get their split ends singed.

At home, after tea she walked to the phone box and rang Mick. He wanted to take her bowling Saturday night so Amy agreed as she couldn't get round to telling him she wouldn't be seeing him.

Saturday morning found Pam and Amy in the hairdressers causing a right stink as each tightly twisted strand of hair had a lighted taper passed along its length burning off any split ends that stuck out.

"This two-timing can get a bit complicated," Amy said as she and Pam emerged from the hairdressers (to the relief of the remaining clientele) and walked along the High Street to the Wimpy Bar for a coffee, "I've arranged to see both John and Mick tonight."

"Who would you rather go out with?"

"Oh definitely John - he's so dishy."

"Well if you met Mick you'd be coming bowling with me and Dick as that's what we're doing tonight, but I don't mind going with just Dick if you want to see John."

"I suppose I'd better give Mick a ring and make some excuse," Amy said getting a twinge of conscience.

The girls sat at an empty table by the window in the Wimpy and ordered their coffees.

"So where's John taking you tonight?" Pam asked

"A dance I think. His mate has got some tickets but I don't know where it is."

"I'd rather go dancing than bowling," Pam said wistfully, "but Dick probably prefers bowling and I suppose it'll make a change."

"I expect you'll enjoy yourself once you're there, Tibs. I'll ring Mick and tell him I've caught his rotten cold and try to sound really rough on the phone."

"Yeah, make him feel guilty for giving you his cold," Pam said with a giggle.

"Don't forget if you happen to see him tonight, I'm stuck at home with a box of tissues."

"Maybe I'll send him round to cheer you up!" Pam said with a mischievous grin.

"Don't you dare! This two-timing lark is tricky enough to juggle without you putting your oar in," Amy said getting up. "I'll go and ring him now and then ring John to arrange a time for tonight." She left Pam finishing her coffee and headed for home and the phone box.

John arrived on time at 8pm to collect Amy and drove her into town where he had arranged to meet his mate Ritchie. Amy thought John looked extremely suave in his mohair suit and once again felt proud to be seen out with him.

"It's only a work's dance that I've got tickets for," John said sounding slightly apologetic, "but there'll be a live group on stage so it shouldn't be too bad."

Amy didn't mind, as the alternative would have been bowling which wasn't one of her favourite pastimes.

John turned into a spacious car park in front of a large square industrial looking building. Ritchie was waiting at the entrance with a blonde young-looking girl hanging on his arm.

"This is where Ritchie works," John explained as they walked across the car park towards the entrance, "they're holding the dance in the works canteen."

It didn't sound very promising but Amy was determined to enjoy herself regardless. They all headed up the stairs to the first floor guided by Ritchie and the canteen turned out to be a surprisingly large room with tables around the sides and plenty of space for dancing in the centre. The lighting was low and subtle which relieved Amy as she had visions of harsh strip lights glaring down from the ceiling. A group were pounding out a Searchers number down the far end on a temporary stage. The serving hatch in the canteen had been transformed into a bar for drinks and snacks. They sat at a table halfway down the room and John went to fetch a round of drinks.

Ritchie seemed to know everyone else in the room and was busy calling out a greeting or sharing a joke with fellow workmates. He introduced his girlfriend to Amy. Her name was Vera and she appeared to be completely besotted with Ritchie, giggling at every word he uttered regardless of whether or not it was funny.

John returned with a tray of drinks, but as soon as a slow number started up, Amy grabbed John and dragged him onto the dance floor for a smooch, desperate to escape from Vera, as she found her company tedious. She wondered what someone as nice as Ritchie saw in her.

Amy found the evening fairly enjoyable and even managed to extricate Ritchie from Vera's clutches for a couple of dances. At 12.30am John brought Amy home and promised to ring her at work during the week.

Sunday afternoon Pam arrived at Amy's to find out how her date with John went. "Dick turned up on his own for a change at the bowling alley," she said, "apparently Mick, Eric and the others had all gone up West."

"Huh, he's always got money to spend when he's not taking me out," Amy commented bitterly.

"Let's go to the Black Prince this evening, Bat. Tony Knight and the Chessmen are on stage and they're not a bad group."

Amy got changed and after tea the girls caught a bus to the Black Prince. The evening was quite good and they met one of their old schoolmates, Anita, nicknamed Nit, with her boyfriend Dave. They sat chatting to them for a while catching up on all the latest news and gossip.

Little Ray, who used to run the Inferno before it burnt down, was there with a crowd of his mates and one of them, called Mick, offered the girls a lift home at the end of the evening, which they gladly accepted.

Next morning Amy took a change of clothes to work with her as she and Pam were going to the 100 Club that evening.

Pam arrived at the Pru after work and the girls got ready down in the basement. After a wash and fresh application of make-up they changed into their ski pants, Hush Puppies and twin sets before heading to the Wimpy Bar in Holborn for egg and chips.

Down in the 100 Club their favourite group, the Birds, were performing on stage at their usual deafening decibels. As the girls danced Amy yelled in Pam's ear: "Have you noticed how the singer keeps staring at us?"

Pam nodded and smiled. "Great isn't it! I think he fancies you. I prefer Ronnie, the lead guitarist, with his long black hair."

So did Amy. He was definitely the dishiest bloke around but he only seemed to have eyes for his gorgeous blonde model girlfriend. Amy sighed and looked at the singer draped over the microphone, his wild hair completely hiding his face and wondered whether he might come and ask her for another dance during the break. But it didn't happen because the group vanished up the stairs when they took their mid-session break. Amy wasn't bothered since she didn't fancy the singer anyway.

Tuesday after work found the girls going through the same ritual as Monday down in the basement of the Pru. Tonight they were going to the Scene so they headed for the West End and went into the Wimpy Bar in Oxford Street for a change to have their egg and chips.

Down the Scene they found Mick and Dick lurking in the gloom by the stage. Mick looked pleased to see Amy and apologised for giving her his cold. Amy didn't need to pretend to snuffle because she really had developed a bad cold since the weekend.

Mary turned up and chatted briefly before leaving to go and find her friend Pat.

At the end of the evening, after catching the train and saying goodbye to the boys at Woolwich, Pam and Amy relaxed in a compartment they had all to themselves.

"Mick kept pestering for a photo of me tonight but he wouldn't tell me why he wants it," Amy said.

"He probably wants to put it on his bedside table and kiss it each night before he goes to sleep," Pam said with a giggle.

Amy laughed. "Somehow I don't think he's *that* smitten - or if he is, he hides it well!"

The next day it snowed heavily but the trains still ran on time so Amy decided to stay on after work and do some overtime as everyone else on her section was also staying.

Thursday Amy heroically struggled to work through the snow despite her cold getting worse because more overtime was available and the extra money would come in handy. She was annoyed that John hadn't rung her so she phoned Mick in her lunch hour and arranged to go to the flicks with him Friday evening. Afterwards she went into the canteen and spotted Jeanette and Mary sitting in a corner. Amy grabbed a pie and a coffee at the counter and went over to join them. As she sat down Mary produced a record from her handbag.

"Thought you might like to borrow this as you said you liked it when it was played down the Scene," she said pushing it across the table. Amy read the label - it was the Blendells singing 'La la la la la'.

"Wow! Thanks Mary. I shall have to try and get hold of a copy but the record shops don't seem to stock a lot of the records that are played down the Scene."

"I think they are imported from America. My brother got hold of this one for me, but I didn't ask how."

"Maybe I'll try the record shop down Leather Lane - they sometimes stock the more unusual records."

"Drink up you two, it's time we were getting back upstairs," Jeanette said looking at her watch, "don't want old ma Rogers breathing fire and brimstone down our necks for being late."

That evening at home Amy washed her hair and then worked on her suit setting in the pockets but her head throbbed and her throat felt raw so she decided to spend Friday at home nursing her cold in the hope that she would feel better by the time she met Mick in the evening.

Next morning she wrapped up and walked round to the phone box to ring work and tell them she wouldn't be coming in and then spent the rest of the day doing some more work on her suit.

After tea she caught the train to Woolwich and found Mick waiting outside the cinema. She was pleased to see Pam and Dick were also there. 'Father Goose' was being shown which they all enjoyed and afterwards the boys walked the girls to the station.

As the train pulled away Mick waved and called out: "See you down the Scene on Tuesday."

Amy flung herself down on the seat and scowled.

"What a sod!" she exclaimed crossly.

Pam looked just as peeved. "I'm fed up going out with such a cheapskate. I don't think we should see them any more."

Amy nodded. "Enough is enough. It's been three weeks now since we started going out with them again and they are back in their old bad habits."

"I bet they'll be up the West End tomorrow night enjoying themselves when they ought to be seeing us," Pam said resentfully. "My parents are going to stay at my aunts' for the weekend so why don't you come over tomorrow?"

"It's a pity we're flat broke and can't go out dancing tomorrow night."

"Never mind, Bat, we've only got to survive until pay day on Tuesday."

Amy walked over to Pam's the following afternoon only to find Mr and Mrs Tibton still at home. They had postponed their visit until the next weekend. Amy stayed for tea and then decided to walk home. Along the way she met Dennis the Menace, her next-door neighbour and an ardent Rocker who was also heading home and, unusually for him - especially on a Saturday night - he was still sober.

"I'm skint," he said by way of an explanation.

"Join the club," Amy said with a grin, "the end of the month is always a bit of a drag."

"It's a good job I get paid weekly else I'd be broke for three and a half weeks every month. I went and blew all me wages yesterday as soon as I got 'em."

"I've got no sympathy for you if you can't manage your money better than that," Amy said disdainfully.

"You can talk," Dennis retorted, "since you're skint too."

"I don't normally run out of money until just before the next pay day."

"No good asking you to lend me the money for a drink then," Dennis said resignedly as they arrived at their adjoining houses.

Amy entered the Pru on Monday morning feeling fed up. She had endured a boring weekend but at least her cold had almost gone. During her morning break Pam rang with the good news that her dad had lent her some money, which meant she and Amy, could afford to go to the 100 Club after work to see their beloved Birds. This cheered Amy immensely and gave her something to look forward to.

Down the 100 Club, once again the singer appeared to be staring at the girls from between a curtain of unruly hair.

"I'm sure he's madly in love with us!" Pam yelled in Amy's ear as they danced.

"Can't blame him - he's obviously got good taste!" Amy yelled back with a grin.

At last payday dawned and Amy became solvent once more. Pam arrived at the Pru after work and the girls went through their routine in the basement toilets followed by a walk to the West End and egg and chips in the Wimpy Bar in Oxford Street to pass the time until the Scene opened.

The girls hurried down the stone steps and flashed their membership cards at the bouncers on the door before plunging into the gloom of the club.

As they emerged from the cloakroom, Amy grabbed Pam's arm and tugged her towards the ladies at the far end.

"Don't look, but Mick and Dick are waving to us; they're sitting on the edge of the stage."

After tidying their hair and adjusting their make-up, the girls emerged from the ladies to find Mick and Dick hovering outside. Amy just glared at Mick and walked across to the benches along the side wall followed by Pam. As they sat down Mick and Dick walked past and went out.

"I think they've got the message at last," Pam said.

"Well what do they expect after not asking to see us at the weekend?" Amy demanded crossly.

"Watcha," said a cheery voice and Mary slumped down on the bench next to Pam, "you two look pretty fed up."

"We've just finished with Mick and Dick," Amy said, "and good riddance!"

Mary took out her cigarettes and offered them to Amy and Pam. She flicked her lighter and inhaled a deep lungful of smoke.

"I've just been chatting to Eric outside but I don't suppose it matters now that I let it slip about how you've been seeing John since Christmas."

"I'm sure Eric will pass on the news to Mick - not that I care. Serves him right for being such a skinflint," Amy said with a wry smile then added, "anyway that sod John hasn't rung me, so it doesn't look like I'll be seeing him any more." Nevertheless she enjoyed imagining how peeved Mick was going to be when he discovered he had been two-timed.

"I expect Dick will assume that I've been seeing someone else too," Pam said with a sigh, "not that it really matters."

"Where's Pat tonight?" Amy asked looking around to see if she could spot her.

"Washing her hair. She's coming along later to give me a lift home in her car. I don't think she's all that keen on spending much time down here."

Blocker Tony in the corner booth put the Blendells record on the turntable. As the music blasted out it reminded Amy. "I'll bring your record back tomorrow, Mary.".

"Oh, you needn't bother," Mary said offhandedly, "my brother has got hold of another copy, so you can keep it."

"That's great! Thanks - I'll buy you lunch in the canteen tomorrow."

The girls were relieved that neither Mick, Dick nor Eric returned to the Scene for the rest of the evening. After Pat arrived and took Mary home, they spent the rest of the evening dancing their Mod jive.

On the train home, Amy arranged to go over to Pam's house on Saturday as Mr and Mrs Tibton would be away for the weekend.

She spent the rest of the weekday evenings working on her suit and finally got it finished in time to wear on Saturday. She was pleased with the way it fitted with double vents in the back of the jacket and a tie belt.

By the time she arrived at Pam's it was 8.30pm. She walked in to find Pam's parents still there because they had postponed their visit to London yet again until the following Saturday. It was too late to go anywhere so Amy accepted the mug of tea Mrs Tibton offered her with a wink and then Pam took her up to her bedroom to show her the dress she was busy making in a thick blue woollen material.

They arranged to meet up at the station on Sunday to go up West to the afternoon session at the Flamingo Club. Then Amy headed back home feeling thoroughly fed up but consoled herself with the thought that at least tomorrow she would be going out again and could finally get to show off her new suit.

Next day as the train drew in at the station in Pam's town, Amy leaned out of the window and waved to Pam who was standing near the waiting room. She climbed on board and undid her coat to show off her newly finished dress.

"Looks great Tibs," Amy said admiringly as Pam did a twirl and then fell onto the seat as the train lurched off. She complemented Amy on her neatly fitted suit with its twin vents. They were looking forward to a good session that afternoon as John Mayall was on the bill with the Blues Breakers.

Downstairs at the club it didn't matter if it was day or night as the lighting - or lack of it - was always the same. It wasn't as packed out as the Saturday all night session. Amy nudged Pam and nodded towards the tables on the raised platform over to one side. There were several familiar faces from the Inferno and one or two of Eric's mates but no sign of Mick or Dick, much to the girls' relief.

Amy felt good in her new suit and by the end of the afternoon three dishy boys had asked her for a dance and Pam had danced with their mates.

They emerged from the Flamingo into the chilly early evening air of Wardour Street and quickly headed for the Macabre Coffee Bar to while away the time until the Scene opened. They played some records on the jukebox while they sipped cappuccinos and smoked cigarettes, flicking the ash into skeletal hands.

Their choice of records came to an end and someone else had selected Sandy Shaw. Amy didn't like her scratchy voice so it was time for them to leave and wander down to the Scene.

They hadn't been to the Scene on a Sunday evening before and were disappointed to find the club nearly empty. Blocker Tony sat slumped in the record booth going through the motion of playing records but he looked as though he was somewhere else entirely.

"I don't think Mick and Dick ever come down here on a Sunday so we don't run any risk of bumping into them," Pam remarked as they sat on the edge of the stage assessing the few groups of people hovering around the sides or down at the snack bar.

"They obviously know which nights to avoid," Amy said, "but now we're here we might as well have a dance."

The girls did their Mod jive to a couple of numbers before returning to lean on the stage for a rest. Amy noticed her handbag gaping open. She had left it in view on the stage with Pam's bag while they danced. She grabbed it and checked the contents, then gave a groan. "Oh no!" she gasped.

Pam was concerned to see her friend looking so aghast. "What's up, Bat?"

"My purse has been pinched!" Amy exclaimed in horror, "it held my season ticket and front door key."

"How much money did you have?"

Amy thought for a moment. "I'm pretty sure there was only about one pound, which was lucky," she said.

"And your season ticket expires today as it's the end of the month so that doesn't matter," Pam reasoned trying to console her distraught friend.

"So that just leaves my front door key and I can get a new one cut I suppose."

"Whoever stole it won't have a clue what door it unlocks. You might even find your purse gets handed in once the money has been taken."

"I'd better go and report the theft to the bouncers," Amy said, "just in case my purse should turn up."

The girls stayed in the club for a while longer but Amy no longer had any inclination to dance as the theft had put a sour note into the evening.

After checking to see if Amy's purse had been handed in and being told it hadn't, the girls decided to leave and make their way to the station to catch the train home. Pam lent Amy the train fare and Amy realised she would need to hurry home before her parents went to bed.

"They definitely won't appreciate being woken up by me banging on the front door," Amy said as she waved goodbye to Pam at her station.

Chapter Seven

February - Desperate Measures

Monday evening the girls met up after work and headed for the Marquee club in Wardour Street. Amy was feeling apprehensive; it was the first time she had been back there since splitting up with Rob. The Yardbirds were topping the bill and they were Rob's favourite group. The girls handed in their coats at the cloakroom and Amy scanned the faces in the crowd as they pushed their way through to the dance floor. She was relieved to see no familiar ones.

The Yardbirds eventually arrived on stage and launched into their repertoire starting with 'Over, Under, Sideways, Down.' There was no room to dance so the girls stood and watched. Amy wasn't overly impressed with them. She leaned across to Pam.

"They're definitely not as good as the Birds," she yelled and Pam nodded in agreement.

Towards the end of the session Amy heard a voice saying 'hello'. She turned to find Rob standing next to Pam. Amy's heart gave a lurch and her legs turned to jelly. There was a dolly-rocker girl at his side wearing a lot of make-up and heavily backcombed hair who he introduced as Shirley. Amy decided to ignore him and turned back to watch the Yardbirds on stage, her mind in a turmoil. She was relieved when Rob moved on with the dolly-rocker trailing behind him.

Once the Yardbirds left the stage to be replaced by some other lesser group, Amy gave Pam a nudge.

"I think we might as well go," she said and started to push her way through the crowd towards the cloakroom. Pam followed, realising that Amy wanted to avoid any further meetings with Rob.

Outside, as they walked to the station, Pam said, "I suppose we should have guessed Rob would show up tonight as the Yardbirds were appearing."

Amy had been very quiet, trying to calm down from seeing Rob with another girl. She realised she was still infatuated with him but wasn't going to admit as much to Pam. She accepted that it was going to take a long time to get over him. "Oh well, it was inevitable we'd bump into him sooner or later," she said, trying to sound as though it didn't matter, "especially as the Marquee is one of his favourite haunts."

Pam could tell Amy was trying to put on a brave front so she changed the subject. "Tomorrow night is Scene night so I expect Mick and Dick will be down there. I shall enjoy giving Dick the cold shoulder if he tries to chat to me."

"Yeah, we've given those two far too many chances. I'm really fed up with Mick now," Amy said, glad to be talking about someone other than Rob.

Before parting, as Pam alighted from the train at her station, they arranged to meet up at the Pru the following evening as usual.

As Pam and Amy turned into Ham Yard Tuesday evening making for the entrance to the Scene, they heard their names being yelled out. It was Mary hanging her head out of the window of Pat's Mini Countryman. They were parked up on the other side of the yard. Mary beckoned them over and got out so that Pam and Amy could climb into the back seat. Mary handed round her cigarettes.

"It's a bit too early to go down there - no-one's arrived yet," Mary said twisting round to flick her lighter under Amy's cigarette and then Pam's. As Pat wound her window down to allow the smoke to escape, Blocker Tony came wandering over and leaned in.

"Hiya girls, any chance of a fag?"

"I might have guessed you'd be on the cadge," Mary said with a grin and thrust her open cigarette packet towards him.

"Thanks," he said taking one, "come and see me inside and I'll play whatever records you want." Pat lit his cigarette with the end of hers and then he strolled off towards the Scene giving a wave.

After the girls had finished their cigarettes they all piled down the steps and into the gloom of the club. Pam and Amy made their way to the ladies at the far end to freshen up while Mary and Pat went over to the booth to chat to Tony and pick some records.

When Pam and Amy emerged from the ladies they were surprised at how quickly the place had filled up. Doby Gray was singing 'The In Crowd' as they threaded their way back through the dancers. Amy spotted Mary waving as she tried to attract her attention. A moment later Mary was next to Amy looking flushed with excitement. "Look who I've just found," she said triumphantly and moved to one side. Skulking in the background were Mick and Dick grinning sheepishly. Amy glanced at Pam. She was glaring at Dick and also at Mary for bringing them over. Amy had told Mary that they had finished with Mick and Dick but Mary obviously had other ideas and was enjoying trying to patch things up.

They said 'hello' and then Mick attempted a weak joke to try and relieve the tension. Mary, in her role as matchmaker, seemed determined to get them all back together again. A slow number came on so she thrust Amy towards Mick.

"Go on, have a dance you two," she said encouragingly. Mick took hold of Amy and guided her out into the crowd. Amy looked back to see Dick following with Pam. He looked nervous as Pam was still frowning at him.

After a couple of dances the tension lessened and they were chatting more easily so the boys suggested they walk round to the Pic for a coffee. Pam and Amy were quite enjoying giving them a hard time. Mick and Dick had to make all the effort to keep the conversation going while the girls just responded with monosyllabic answers.

Back at the Scene they danced some more and then Dick offered to accompany the girls to the train. They both seemed keen to get back together with the girls despite their obvious coolness towards them.

Mick and Dick accompanied them on the train but were hesitant when it came to saying goodbye as they alighted at their station so they left without making any arrangements for meeting up with the girls.

After they had gone and the train was speeding on its way, Pam let out a huge sigh of relief. "I wish Mary hadn't interfered tonight," she said crossly.

"She probably thought she was doing us a favour."

"Well I haven't changed my mind," Pam said decisively with a toss of her head, "I still don't want to go out with Dick any more."

"I'm surprised they played along with Mary. Perhaps they are really madly in love with us after all," Amy said and giggled.

Pam gave a derogatory snort. "Huh - if they are, they certainly hide it well!" She changed the subject. "I'm really fed up with my job at the New Zealand Insurance Company, Bat. It's so boring doing the same things day in and day out."

"They're always recruiting at the Pru. Why not arrange to come for an interview? It would be great if we both worked at the same place."

"It would definitely be a lot easier for going out together after work," Pam said after giving the idea some thought, "I think I'll ring up tomorrow and see if I can get an interview."

"I can't guarantee that the work will be any more interesting, though it probably depends on which department you end up in."

"At least it's a much bigger company with a canteen, a theatre and loads more people. At the New Zealand, I just see the same few faces every day and we have little in common."

"We'll be able to spend our lunch hours together, Tibs - it'll be fun - and the hours at the Pru are a bit less too."

The train drew into Pam's station and they arranged to meet up on Friday evening at Welling. They had heard about a club that had opened there called The Twisted Wheel and wanted to try it out.

"I doubt it's as good as the Inferno was but we might as well go and see," Pam said as she stepped down onto the platform. Amy hung out of the window to wave as the train pulled away.

Friday evening found the girls wandering along the High Street in Welling in search of the Twisted Wheel. They finally found it wedged in the middle of a row of shops. Inside it was brightly lit and looked more like a coffee bar than a nightclub. The girls walked in and gazed around.

"Well, I don't think much of this place," Amy remarked, "even the music is awful."

"Let's not bother hanging around, Bat. How about we head back to the Railway Tavern?"

Amy agreed, so they left and made their way back to the station.

As they walked through the bar at the Railway Tavern, Pam nudged Amy. "Look who's over there."

Amy glanced across the room and saw Mick and Dick propping up the bar. "Let's just ignore them," she said and continued through the crowd into the dance room.

"Hello girls," said a familiar voice.

Pam spun round and flushed as she recognised Fred Bloggs, her ex-boyfriend, standing behind her. They chatted for a while and he introduced his friend, Roger, to them. Amy had seen him down the Railway before.

"So, where have you girls been hiding? Haven't seen you around lately," Fred said.

"We've been going to the clubs up West," Pam told him.

"If you're clubbing all night and want a bit of help to keep going, I can probably get hold of some blues for you," Roger offered.

Pam looked at Amy and hesitated.

"Yeah, why not?" Amy said casually as though they were well used to popping pills.

"Give me your address and I'll bring them round tomorrow," Roger said. He produced a card and a pen for Amy to write on. She scrawled her address and then Pam dragged her off for a dance.

She looked agitated. "What are you doing - arranging to buy pills from that Roger," she demanded, "we've never taken any yet and I don't think we should start now."

"Look, your parents are going away this weekend and that means we can stay all night down the Flamingo. A few pills will stop us from flagging at around 2 o'clock in the morning. It'll be a laugh, Tibs, you'll see."

"I don't want to end up in a state like Blocker Tony," Pam said.

"You won't 'cause we'll be careful," Amy promised, "besides, according to Mary, he avoids the come downs by taking more pills which is a daft and probably dangerous thing to do."

Amy lazed in bed all Saturday morning finally getting up at midday to take a bath. Afterwards she came downstairs to hunt for something to eat as she was ravenous. Then there came a knock at the front door. She opened it and found Roger standing there.

"Thought I'd better let you know that I wasn't able to get hold of any blues for you," he said. Amy put her finger to her lips and came out onto the porch pulling the door close behind her. She didn't want her parents overhearing their conversation.

"I'll be seeing another mate but not 'til tomorrow so he might be able to score." Amy was disappointed at having nothing to keep her and Pam going down the Flamingo.

"Oh well, never mind, Roger, we've managed to keep awake all night before so I'm sure we can do it tonight."

"Er, you mentioned you're a member of the Scene club. I don't suppose you could lend me your membership card? I want to pop down there tonight and mine has expired."

"I'll get it for you but I'll need it back by Tuesday," Amy said and went back indoors to fetch it. She returned a minute later and handed it to Roger.

"Thanks," he said slipping it into the inside pocket of his jacket, "I'll be down the Railway tomorrow evening so if you're there I can return it then or else I'll drop it back to you Monday evening." He walked back down the front path and Amy returned to the kitchen in search of food.

Mid-afternoon she got ready and walked for over an hour to reach Pam's house, only to discover that yet again Pam's parents hadn't gone away for the weekend. Pam took Amy up to her bedroom and closed the door.

"What's going on!" Amy demanded crossly, "why haven't your parents bloody well gone?"

"Ssh!" Pam said trying to calm her friend down, "mum says she has got one of her heads and doesn't feel like travelling."

"So now we can't stay out all night. I think your mum suspects and has done this on purpose!" Amy said, tossing her handbag on the floor and flopping down on the bed.

"You might be right," Pam agreed, "she's been asking me a lot of questions about where we're going this evening. I've had to say we're going to a party 'cos she's getting very edgy about me frequenting nightclubs."

"What about the 100 Club on Monday evenings and the Scene on Tuesdays?" Amy asked, concern etched on her face.

"I think she's under the impression they're just dances that we go to."

"Your mum is getting to be a right pain."

"You don't have to tell me - I have to live with her!"

Mrs Tibton made egg and chips for tea and then the girls left to catch the train to London.

"Don't be too late home, you know your mother worries," Mr Tibton called out as they were closing the front door.

The girls arrived at the Flamingo and clattered down the stairs to the basement. The evening session was just getting under way with the compere on stage announcing Zoot Money and his Big Roll Band.

"At least there's a great R&B band on stage this evening," Pam said as they made their way to the front of the dance floor and found a couple of seats where they could relax and have a cigarette.

"It's not as packed tonight," Amy said looking around the gloomy smoke-laden room.

Zoot Money and his band came on stage to cheers and whistles and after a brief tuning up they launched into 'Little Girl', which had the girls on the dance floor in no time.

Two boys, who told the girls their names were John and David, came and joined in the dancing with them and soon got chatting. Every time Amy and Pam wanted to have a rest, they persuaded them to dance some more. Eventually they took the girls over to the bar and bought them cokes. Pam and Amy slumped onto two stools exhausted while John and David still jigged around between sips of coke. Amy suspected they had taken some pills to have so much energy. They enjoyed the boys company as they were continually joking and larking around. After more dancing it was soon time for the girls to leave and catch the last train home to Pam's. The boys tried to talk them into staying down there all night but Pam knew it was out of the question. They said goodbye and left the two boys still dancing as they headed for home in the chill night air.

Arriving back at Pam's house they found her dad waiting up. He made them a hot drink which they took up to Pam's bedroom.

"Pity we couldn't stay there all night," Amy said kicking off her shoes and sitting on the bed.

"Never mind, Bat, I'm sure we'll find a way one day. Maybe another visit to my Aunt Anne's?"

There was a scratching at the door. Pam opened it to let in Monty. Amy gave a groan. "Your bed isn't big enough for the three of us."

"Well just push Monty off. He can sleep on the rug beside the bed," Pam said climbing under the sheets. Amy finished undressing and squeezed into Pam's bed only to be joined by Monty determined to sleep between them and oblivious to Amy's attempts to push him down onto the rug. She eventually conceded defeat and tried to get some sleep but it wasn't easy with Monty's wet nose pressed into her neck.

Next morning after a hard-boiled egg for breakfast Pam accompanied Amy to the bus stop and they arranged to meet up that evening at the Railway Tavern.

Back at home, Amy walked in and received a barrage of questions from her mother who didn't believe that she had stayed over at Pam's house.

"You've been off at one of those clubs all night haven't you?" she said crossly giving Amy a hard stare.

"I've told you, I slept at Pam's," Amy said indignantly, "you can check with her parents if you don't believe me."

"I shall get your father to go down to Macfisheries and ask Mr Tibton. You had better be telling me the truth my girl!"

Amy turned on her heel and flounced out of the room. She stomped up the stairs to her bedroom feeling hard done by.

That evening she got ready and walked down the hill into town to the Railway where she found Pam waiting outside. They went through the bar and into the dance hall at the rear. After carefully looking around they were relieved to find no Mick or Dick in evidence.

"I hope Roger comes 'cause he's got my Scene membership card and I need it for Tuesday night," Amy said.

"I think I just spotted Fred over in the doorway," Pam said craning her neck to get a better look, "so I expect Roger will be with him."

"By the way, Tibs, I should warn you that my dad will be paying a visit to your dad at Macfisheries sometime soon to check that I really stayed at yours last night," Amy said as the band started up with a loud rendition of 'Jump Back'.

"It's just as well that we didn't stay up town all night like we wanted to," Pam yelled over the pounding rhythm of the drums.

The girls moved into the centre of the floor and danced their Mod jive for a couple of numbers and then made their way out to the bar for a drink. They were perched on bar stools sipping iced orange squash when Amy felt a tap on her shoulder. It was Roger with Fred behind him. He returned Amy's membership card - much to her relief.

"I might be able to get you some pills for next Friday," he said quietly in her ear. Amy just nodded.

Fred plucked up the courage to ask Pam for a dance so they all returned to the dance hall. A slow number had started so Pam smooched with Fred and Amy danced with Roger. At the end of the number Pam dragged Amy off to the ladies.

"I like Fred but I don't want to be lumbered dancing with him for the rest of the evening," she said powdering her nose.

"You don't seem to appreciate how lucky you were to have been his girlfriend," Amy said recalling the enormous crush she had once had on Fred with his striking resemblance to John Lennon. She had been devastated when he asked Pam out.

"Looks aren't everything, Bat. Fred is a nice bloke but dates with him became monotonously boring. He was never much of a dancer and his idea of a good night was watching the telly. Let's go down to the far end of the dance hall next to the stage. We should be OK there as Fred likes to stay close to the bar."

The girls made their way back through the throng to the stage and managed to avoid Fred and Roger for the rest of the evening.

Pam arrived at the Pru Monday evening and found Amy freshening up in the basement ladies cloakroom. After a snack in the Wimpy Bar, the girls trekked over to the 100 Club in Oxford Street to see the Birds.

Once again they thought the group were the best they had ever heard. A dark-haired girl was loitering around near the stage and appeared to be on her own. She finally smiled at Pam and Amy and came over to introduce herself. Her name was Ye-ye and she was a French student staying in Battersea. She explained that she was supposed to be meeting a friend there but he hadn't turned up.

"You can hang out with us until he arrives," Pam offered and Ye-ye looked relieved.

The three of them danced until the Birds disappeared upstairs for their mid-evening break and then they went to the snack bar at the back of the club for a coffee. Ye-ye was very friendly and chatty. She spoke English well and admitted to feeling a bit lonely in London, as she didn't know many people.

She took a sip of coffee and then asked, "do you come down here often?"

"We're normally here on Mondays to see the Birds," Amy told her.

"If I give you my phone number, would you please ring me in the week and then if you like we can arrange to meet up." Ye-ye rummaged in her handbag and produced a piece of paper and a pen. She scribbled her phone number down and passed the paper over to Amy who promised to ring her and carefully put the piece of paper in her purse.

After another ten minutes, the Birds returned on stage so it was time to get back on the dance floor and enjoy being deafened once again by their earthy R&B sound.

The following evening Pam and Amy arrived at the Scene Club having spent some time in the Wimpy Bar at Holborn and the Macabre coffee house in Wardour Street while they waited for the club to open.

They danced for almost an hour until Mary and Pat arrived and suggested they all go to the Red Lion Pub across the road.

Mary's boyfriend, Trevor, was in there with a couple of mates and Mary wanted to introduce him to Amy and Pam. Trevor was tall, slim and passably good looking with unruly fair hair. He insisted on buying the girls a drink so they opted for a vodka and lime each. Mary enjoyed bossing him around and he didn't seem to mind, having a very laid back, casual attitude. He didn't have a membership card for the Scene so preferred to stay in the pub.

Amy noticed him giving appreciative glances in Pam's direction when Mary wasn't looking. She finished her drink and then told Pam they had better go back down the Scene.

"I think Mary's Trevor fancies you," she said as they descended the stone stairs and showed their fluorescent passing out mark of a cross in a circle on their wrist to Harry at the door.

"Well I hope he doesn't cause trouble because I'd hate to get on the wrong side of Mary. I bet she can be a right spitfire if someone upsets her."

"Did you like Trevor though?" Amy asked with a mischievous grin.

"He's OK but I wasn't aware of him eyeing me."

The girls squeezed through the crowd on their way to the ladies when who should they bump into but Mick and Dick. There was no avoiding them so they said a brief 'hello' and then quickly continued into the ladies.

"They looked pleased to see us - I think," Pam said taking out a comb and raking it through her hair. Amy did likewise.

"It'll soon be Valentine's Day - d'you think we'll get a card from them Tibs?"

"Huh, you must be joking, Bat - they're too tight-fisted!"

The girls emerged from the ladies and made their way to the opposite side of the dance floor knowing that Mick and Dick tended to stay near the record booth. They could dance in peace there with little fear of bumping into them again.

On their way home at Charing Cross station the girls were in time to catch a fast train which was just as well because they spotted Mick and Dick waiting on the platform but they needed a slow train that stopped at all the stations including theirs. Pam and Amy hopped onto the train as it began to pull away and gave a wave to the boys as their carriage drew level with them. They waved back half-heartedly but didn't smile.

Pam and Amy sat discussing the evening and made arrangements for meeting up the next day after work ready for the evening session at the Flamingo.

"I can hardly wait, Tibs. With Georgie Fame playing the Hammond organ it should be fantastic down there.

"Perhaps we'd better get there early to be sure of getting in - just in case it gets full," Pam suggested.

"Yeah, good thinking. He's very popular with all the wogs that go there."

"By the way, Bat, I've had a letter from the Pru and I've got an interview this Friday."

"That's great! I'm sure you'll pass with flying colours. I've got to go to the staff department on Thursday for an interview as I'll have been there six months and if I pass I'll be placed on the permanent staff - not that I'll notice any difference. I don't think I'll even get a pay rise," Amy said despondently.

Wednesday evening the girls made sure they arrived early at the Flamingo. Even so they still had to join a long queue in Wardour Street. They finally got inside and found the low-ceilinged room crammed with people. Music was playing through loud speakers on the stage until it was time for the compere to announce Georgie Fame on stage with his Blue Flames to raucous applause, shouts and whistles. There was no room to dance and the seats were all taken so Pam and Amy found a place to stand behind the seats down the front where they had a good view of the stage. Georgie introduced the members of his band, including Speedy, wearing a multi-coloured woollen hat, who was renowned for frantically playing the bongos; then he launched into 'Night Train' making his distinctive Hammond organ sound more like a pounding steam train at times. During his next number a scuffle broke out down by the side of the stage so Georgie incorporated 'easy boys, easy' into his lyrics to defuse the situation. It worked because they stopped fighting, preferring to listen to the music instead.

After several more numbers they took a short break and the room emptied out slightly giving the girls room for a bit of dancing. A fair-haired Mod boy came over and asked Amy to dance. His name was John but as they smooched around the floor he kept trying to kiss her. She got fed up with him and after finally pushing him away, she went over to the snack bar where Pam was trying to get the waiter's attention. She eventually got served and the girls shared a coke before pushing their way back across the smoky crowded room to their vantage point behind the seats ready for the return of Georgie Fame.

"What was wrong with that Mod who asked you to dance?" Pam asked.

"Too flippin' amorous!" Amy declared, "I wouldn't have minded but I didn't really fancy him."

"If it had been me I'd have shoved him flat on his back!" Pam said with a laugh.

"Yes, I know you would," Amy said recalling the time at the Inferno when Pam had shoved a boy away from her and caused a domino effect as several people in the crowd all fell down, and Amy had tried to disown her friend.

Just then the compere appeared to bring Georgie Fame back on stage to tumultuous applause. He opened the second half of the session with 'Parchment Farm' to appreciative cheers. He had a way of getting the audience involved to the point where the atmosphere was absolutely electric. The pulsating bluesy rhythm of the organ bounced around the walls and low ceiling. With nowhere to go, it seemed to just get louder. The girls were completely enthralled by the music. Speedy did a long solo on the bongos to noisy cheering and whistling mainly from the large crowd of Jamaicans down by the stage. Over an hour later he closed with 'Baby Please don't Go'.

"He's even better tonight than when I came to see him here with Jim," Pam said in Amy's ear.

Amy's heart gave an involuntary skip. The mention of Jim's name automatically made her think of Rob and she would prefer not to. The evening drew to a close and the girls made their way home feeling on top of the world after listening to some terrific sounds.

Amy headed for Leather Lane during her lunch hour next day. She needed to buy a birthday card for Coral, her ex-school friend. As she browsed through the cards she spotted a whole stand of Valentine cards so she had a look through them too and found one that she considered to be nasty enough to send to Mick.

Friday evening Amy hurried home from work as she had arranged to meet Pam at the Railway Tavern. She dashed up the approach road and found Pam waiting outside the station booking office.

"How did your interview go today?" Amy asked as they queued to get into the dance room at the rear of the bar.

"It was pretty horrendous," Pam said with a shudder, "they kept asking me questions about insurance policies that I didn't know the answers to. I tried a bit of bluffing but I don't think I fooled them."

"Oh, don't worry, Tibs, with your qualifications they'd be daft not to offer you a job," Amy said blithely adding, "besides, they're desperate for more staff."

"Huh, thanks," Pam said peevishly.

"You'll be fine, Tibs." Amy tried to sound reassuring. "Talking of qualifications, I fancy learning to touch type. I'm sure it will come in useful if I decide to get a different office job one day because I definitely don't intend staying at the Pru forever or I'll end up like the two old sourpusses, Vera and Audrey, on my section. Why don't we book some evening classes?"

"It could be handy to be able to type," Pam agreed, "I remember seeing some evening classes advertised in the local paper - I'll check it out and see if they include typing. By the way did you ring Ye-ye like she asked?"

Amy looked a little guilty. "No - I forgot. Besides, I think I've lost her phone number. Maybe we'll see her down the 100 Club again."

Inside the dance room a group were thumping out 'Johnny B Good' down on the stage and the place was packed with writhing bodies gyrating to the music. The girls were soon joining in with the dancing and enjoying themselves. The group gave a good performance and even managed some Motown numbers. During the break the girls went to get a drink at the bar and found Roger there with a few mates but there was no sign of Fred, much to Pam's relief. He came over and pulled Amy to one side.

"Sorry love, but I haven't been able to get in touch with this bloke I know in order to score."

"Never mind," Amy whispered, "but keep trying won't you." She returned to Pam who eyed her friend suspiciously.

"What was all that about?" she demanded.

"Roger couldn't get hold of any pills for us," Amy said.

Pam grimaced. "I still think we'd probably be better off without them."

"Oh, it'll just be a laugh, Tibs - you'll see." Amy felt a tap on her shoulder. It was Roger back again.

"Me and my mates will be at the all-nighter down the 'Mingo tomorrow so why don't you girls meet us there?" he suggested.

"It all depends on whether I'll be able to stay out all night," Pam said, and then a thought occurred to her. "Er, will Fred be down there with you?"

"No, he's got a date with some girl," Roger said, and then left to re-join his mates.

After a few more dances Pam had to leave to catch her train home. Amy accompanied her across the road to the station and just had time to make arrangements for meeting up at Pam's house next day as the train pulled in to the platform.

"There's still a chance my parents might be away tomorrow night staying with Aunt Anne," Pam said leaning out of the carriage window.

"Huh, I'm not counting on it," Amy said.

Saturday afternoon Amy walked over to Pam's house and found her looking fed up. Her parents were still at home yet again.

"Never mind, Tibs," Amy said as the girls sat in Pam's bedroom putting on their make-up, "we'll just have to make the most of an evening down the Scene."

After tea they caught the train up to town and headed for the Scene. They were surprised at how crowded it was for so early in the evening.

"Probably because there's going to be a live group on stage later on," Pam surmised squeezing through the dancers to reach the ladies.

"I think the poster on the wall by the entrance said 'Unit Four Plus Two'," Amy said, "not one of my favourite groups but maybe they're better live."

Five minutes later the girls were back on the dance floor and spotted Mick and Dick standing over by the record booth.

"Let's go and chat to them and make their day," Pam said, "they're looking pretty fed up."

"Perhaps Mick's fed up because he's got my Valentine's card," Amy said with a grin.

"You didn't sign it did you?"

"'Course I didn't - it wasn't a very nice card."

Mick and Dick brightened up as Amy and Pam approached smiling at them for a change. The girls ended up staying with them all evening and even got treated to coffees round at the Piccadilly cafe.

The group finally put in a brief appearance on the stage and managed a passable performance ending with their hit of 'Concrete and Clay'.

Mick and Dick were staying there all night but Pam and Amy had to catch the last train home to keep Pam's parents happy but before leaving they agreed to meet the boys down the Scene on Tuesday.

Sunday morning Amy caught a bus home so she could change her clothes before dashing back to meet up with Pam and catch the train back up to town again. They were going to the afternoon session down the Flamingo where John Mayall's Blues Breakers were appearing.

They had just got their eyes accustomed to the gloomy interior of the club when a good looking boy in a smart mohair suit asked Amy for a dance and his tall skinny mate danced with Pam. Amy liked his dark Beatle haircut and the scent of his aftershave. He introduced himself as Nick Benson and his mate's name was Charlie.

John Mayall was great and played some terrific R&B. During the interval Nick suggested they all go down the Coffee An at Leicester Square. The girls hadn't been down there before and were surprised to discover it was accessed by steep wooden steps from an open hatch in the pavement. Strip lights starkly lit the cramped underground room and the tables were squashed in with leatherette-covered benches. The coffee was pretty awful instant coffee served up in chipped china cups with a saucer if you were lucky.

"A complete contrast to the Macabre," Pam whispered to Amy after giving the room a deprecating perusal.

"We often come here for a quick break from the Flamingo," Nick said putting the cups of coffee down on an empty table. They squeezed onto the benches and chatted as they sipped the grotty coffee.

Amy nudged Pam and looked across to a far corner. Pam followed Amy's gaze and saw a youth with a needle busy injecting into his arm. Pam looked away, shocked at what he was doing so casually and publicly.

Amy didn't much like the place so she finished her coffee and hurried the others up so they could return to the Flamingo.

After the session finished Nick suggested they move on to the Discotheque a short distance from the Flamingo, also in Wardour Street.

Amy glanced at Pam and she pulled a face.

"Isn't it always full of teenyboppers?" she asked.

"It's not that bad," Nick said, "there's no live groups but they play some pretty good music."

Nick and Charlie insisted on paying for the girls to get in. They had to go upstairs to the first floor for a change. Amy had heard rumours about the club being a bit sleazy so she entered with a certain amount of trepidation. It was just as gloomy as the Flamingo with coloured disco lights flashing around the room. Then Amy noticed alcoves along the sides of the room with mattresses on the floor. People lounged on the mattresses and Amy could see how the place had acquired its sleazy reputation.

Pam took one look and grimaced. "I don't think I want to stay here," she whispered to Amy, "I'll just have a couple of dances and then I'm going home."

"What about Charlie?" Amy asked.

"I'm not too keen," she replied pulling a face.

After a few dances Pam made an excuse about having to get home so Charlie offered to walk her to the station. Amy could tell Pam would have preferred to go alone but she accepted his offer anyway.

Amy stayed on in the club with Nick and eventually caught a later train home. Nick took her to Charing Cross station and arranged to meet her on Wednesday evening to take her round to his house which Amy didn't object to as she quite fancied him.

Tuesday evening Pam and Amy went down the Scene and before long met up with Mick and Dick.

"I received a very badly typed Valentine's card," Mick said, giving Amy a meaningful stare.

"Don't know why you're looking at me like that," she said crossly, "it's got nothing to do with me. I wouldn't waste my time or money sending you a Valentine's card. You must have a secret admirer."

"I don't think a secret admirer would send a nasty card. It's more like the sort of card I'd get from you," Mick said searching Amy's face for a tell-tale sign. Amy wasn't good at lying and was sure her face would give her away so she quickly grabbed Pam and pulled her onto the dance floor in order to escape Mick's suspicious gaze.

"Mick's annoying me," Amy said as she and Pam danced, "he thinks I sent him that nasty Valentine's card."

"Well, you did," Pam said with a grin, "and what's more he knows it was you."

"I don't know why we're still bothering with those two after finishing with them," Amy said.

"I suppose they're better than nothing," Pam replied with a shrug.

"That's debatable," Amy said scornfully."

"By the way, Bat, I've managed to book us some typing lessons and they start next Wednesday."

"That's great, Tibs," Amy said smiling, "it'll be another string to our bows."

Despite feeling very fed up with Mick and Dick, the girls still agreed to meet up with them on Friday evening at the Railway Tavern.

Amy rushed home from work the next evening in time to change, then dashed back to the station to catch the train for the twenty minute journey back up the line to meet Nick as arranged.

He was waiting on the platform in a black leather jacket and jeans. Amy thought how good he looked as she linked arms with him. They chatted easily during the brief five minute walk to his house which was in a fairly large unprepossessing Victorian terrace. He ushered Amy into the front room, which was in darkness so he switched on a couple of sidelights that kept the room only dimly lit. Amy could hear a television in the back room and guessed that his parents were probably out there.

Nick gave Amy a pile of albums to sort through and finding one by Georgie Fame, she handed it to Nick for him to put on the record player.

They had just settled down on the settee with Nick's arm around Amy's shoulders when the front door bell rang. Nick gave a groan and jumped up to answer it. Charlie came sauntering in oblivious to the fact that he might be surplus to requirements. He flopped down in a chair and made himself comfortable.

"I like your mate, Pam," he observed, "but she seemed a bit aloof." Amy smiled to herself. She knew just how cold Pam could be towards anyone she didn't fancy very much.

"She's OK when you get to know her," Amy said defensively, "besides she's got a boyfriend at the moment." She hoped this bit of information would deter him from chasing after Pam.

It took nearly an hour before Charlie finally got the message that he was intruding on an intimate evening. He got up and made some excuse about having to go and see someone, before letting himself out.

"Thought he'd never leave," Nick said drawing Amy towards him for a kiss. Amy enjoyed snuggling up with Nick while listening to the music but their privacy was short lived as the sliding door that divided the front and back rooms was suddenly pushed open and a dark-haired middle-aged lady poked her head in to ask if they would like some coffee. Nick introduced Amy to his mother and then she went off to the kitchen to fetch the drinks. She returned with a tray containing two mugs, a sugar bowl and a plate of biscuits.

"Help yourselves," she said with a beaming smile putting the tray down on the glass topped coffee table, "I'll leave you both in peace now," she added giving Amy a wink as she closed the sliding door.

"I like your mum," Amy said spooning sugar into her mug and stirring.

"She's OK but can be a bit nosy about what I'm doing," Nick said taking a biscuit, "Charlie keeps nagging me to move into a flat with him but I don't much fancy doing all my own cooking and washing."

"It'd give you a lot more freedom though," Amy pointed out, "especially if it was up West."

"But that would cost an arm and a leg. If I can't afford a decent flat in the right area then I would prefer to stay put with all the home comforts. I know mum spoils me but then being an only child I suppose that's natural."

"Me and Pam often talk about getting a pad together. We both get a bit fed up with parents imposing their restrictions on us - treating us like kids instead of responsible adults."

"Are you a responsible adult?" Nick asked with a grin giving Amy's waist a playful pinch. She squealed and wriggled as Nick tickled her until she begged him to stop.

"Well I like to try and kid my parents that I am, but if we did get a place up town I know we'd have a right laugh."

"You could have as many parties as you liked and stay out all night without worrying about what parents might say," Nick said.

"Yeah, it'd be great," Amy said with a sigh.

"Talking of staying out all night - how about coming down the Flamingo Saturday night?"

"I'd love to but I'll have to do it without my parents finding out which won't be easy."

"I'm sure you can manage it," Nick said encouragingly and gave her a kiss.

He walked Amy back to the station and put her on the train home. They arranged to meet on Charing Cross station Saturday evening. Amy spent the journey home deep in thought trying to come up with a way of staying out all night.

She met Pam at the station Friday evening and they crossed the road to the Railway Tavern where they had arranged to meet Mick and Dick.

The group playing on stage in the dance hall didn't sound too promising so the girls stayed in the bar perched on bar stools and ordered a gin and orange each. Suddenly Roger appeared at Amy's side grinning.

"I've got something for you," he said, "let's go outside."

"I shan't be long, Tibs," Amy said and slid off the stool to follow Roger. Outside he drew Amy round the corner of the Tavern, produced a small packet and thrust it into her hand.

"My mate came up trumps so I managed to get some blues. There's twenty for you."

"That's terrific, Roger," Amy said and rummaged in her bag for her purse to pay him.

"So, will you be going up West tomorrow night now?" Roger asked as he pocketed the money.

"I'm determined to try and get out for the all-night session at the Flamingo, but parents are a problem. Anyway, I'd better get back to Pam - thanks for these," Amy said patting her handbag. She hurried back into the bar and retook her seat.

"Well?" Pam asked meaningfully. She'd guessed what had been going on.

"I've got some blues," Amy whispered excitedly, "and I might have thought up a way for us to stay out all tomorrow night without our parents knowing."

"How do we manage that?" Pam demanded dubiously.

Amy took a sip of her drink. "Well, you tell your parents that you're staying at my house - they won't object to that will they? I'll tell my parents that you're staying over and we'll be cramming into my bed. You arrive early in the evening and we sit around for a while maybe watching telly and looking bored. Then we do a bit of yawning and decide on an early night. Now comes the tricky bit. We go up to my bedroom and lock the door. Then we get out of the window onto the porch roof and climb down the side panels. We dash to the station in time to catch the last train up to town. Next morning we return and quietly sneak back in through the window, unlock the door and get into bed. Our parents will think we are safely tucked up in bed all night and be none the wiser!"

"It could so easily go horribly wrong," Pam said after giving the plan some thought.

"It's worth a try though, Tibs - especially as we've got these blues to see us through the night. It'll be a laugh."

"What'll be a laugh?" asked a familiar voice and Amy turned her head to find Mick and Dick standing behind them.

"Oh, er, nothing," Amy said evasively and drained her glass. Dick bought a round of drinks and then Mick suggested they drive to the next town, as there wasn't much happening at the Railway.

"I've got my car outside," he informed them, "so it won't take very long." It had been a while since Mick's car was in working order so they all went outside and climbed inside.

After a twenty minute drive Mick drew up outside the Wimpy Bar in the High Street.

"Anyone for chips? he asked, "my treat."

They all went in and ordered chips and coffee. Pam and Amy were busy selecting some music from the jukebox when Eric's car pulled up outside and he came in.

"Thought I recognised your old banger outside," he said to Mick and sat down. The waiter brought over the chips and coffees and Eric ordered the same.

"Not much going on around here tonight," he said sounding a bit fed up, "the others have all gone up West but I didn't really feel like going."

"We're still going down the Scene tomorrow night though aren't we?" Mick asked through a mouthful of chips. Then he turned to Amy. "Will you girls be there?"

"Our parents are getting very stroppy about us going out clubbing so we'll probably have to stay in - dead boring," Amy said giving Pam a discreet nudge.

"Well you could come up to town for just the evening," Dick suggested.

"Mm, maybe," Pam said doubtfully.

With the chips finished and the coffee drunk, they returned to the cars outside and said goodbye to Eric. Mick drove to Pam's house and Dick walked her to her door. They stood chatting for a while before Dick came back to the car and then Mick drove Amy home. She got out and then leaned in through the open car window.

"If we don't manage to see you tomorrow night then I suppose it'll be Tuesday evening down the Scene," she said and gave Mick a quick goodnight kiss aware that Dick was waiting to move into the front passenger seat.

She waved them off with only a slight feeling of guilt at deceiving Mick. If her plans worked out then she would be spending Saturday night with Nick.

Pam arrived at Amy's house the next evening carrying an overnight bag. Mr and Mrs Brown were sitting in the lounge watching the telly.

"Mum and dad don't mind me staying here tonight," she told Mrs Brown, "so I've packed my night things."

"Amy mentioned that you would be sharing her bed," Mrs Brown said, "I hope you'll be comfortable squashed into her single bed."

"Oh, I'll be fine – it won't be the first time we've shared," Pam said cheerfully as Amy beckoned her out of the room. They went upstairs to Amy's bedroom and closed the door.

"I've brought the clothes I want to wear tonight in this," Pam said tossing the bag onto the bed. "I've arranged to meet Dick at Charing Cross at the same time as you meet up with Nick."

"The only trouble is - Dick will probably tell Mick I'm two-timing him - not that I really care."

"I'm looking forward to tonight, Bat. Show me the pills you've got," Pam said kicking off her shoes and lying back on the bed. Amy opened her wardrobe and rummaged in the bottom amongst her shoes until she straightened up holding a small packet.

"I've kept them hidden in the toe of a boot. Can't be too careful with my mother nosing around."

Amy opened the packet and carefully shook the contents onto the bedspread. "Ten blues each," she said, "that should keep us going all night."

"I still owe you half the cost of them," Pam said pulling her purse out of her bag, "let me sort it out with you."

Amy replaced the pills in the packet and returned it to the boot in her wardrobe.

"We'd better go downstairs and watch a bit of telly until it's time to get ready and leave," Amy said, "only my parents might get a bit suspicious if we seem to be too keen to get to bed so early."

The girls returned to the lounge and sat watching telly for almost an hour. Then, to the girls' consternation, dad announced that he felt tired and was off to bed. He got up and left the room. Amy glanced at Pam and pulled a face. This was going to make it more difficult. Amy waited another half an hour in the hope that her father would now be sound asleep and then gave a yawn.

"I'm feeling tired - how about you, Tibs?"

"Yes, I think I'm ready for bed." They got up and said goodnight to mum before creeping quietly upstairs. Amy paused to listen at her parents' bedroom door, which was adjacent to her room. She thought she could hear a gentle snore.

In Amy's room they quickly changed and put on their make-up. Amy grabbed an armful of clothes from the wardrobe and pushed them down the bed to look roughly like two bodies under the covers.

"That's just in case someone should climb up and peer through the skylight above the door. They will only be able to see the end of the bed."

When they were ready, Amy tiptoed across the landing to the bathroom and returned with a beaker of water so that they could take the pills. Amy hadn't had any experience of swallowing tablets so she found it very difficult but finally managed to get them down her throat. Pam swallowed hers with no trouble at all and then they had the tricky job of getting out of the window.

With dad in the next bedroom they had to be very careful not to make a noise. After locking the bedroom door, Amy opened the window and pushed it right back against the wall. Then she and Pam clambered out onto the porch roof, trying hard not to giggle. Amy closed the window and then they climbed down the side of the porch and jumped onto the front doorstep. They waited and listened with baited breath to see if they had been heard but no-one appeared at the windows so they quickly crept up the path and hurried off up the street to catch the fast train to London.

By the time they were on the train the pills started to take effect. Amy kept bouncing up and down on the seat because she couldn't keep still.

"I can't wait to get to the Flamingo and start dancing," she said excitedly, "I feel like I'm bursting with energy."

"Yeah, me too," Pam said and gazed into Amy's eyes. "Hey Bat, your pupils are getting all dilated."

"Yeah, so are yours," Amy said and then fumbled in her handbag. She produced some sticks of chewing gum. "We'd better chew these else we'll be chewing the insides of our mouths all night," she said passing a stick to Pam.

At Charing Cross they found Nick waiting beneath the clock. Amy could tell by his dilated pupils that he had also been popping some pills. There was no sign of Dick.

"I'll give him ten minutes to show and no more," Pam said gazing around amongst the crowd for a glimpse of him. After ten minutes and no Dick, Pam had waited long enough.

"C'mon," she said, "we'll go down the Flamingo without him." Pam walked off with Amy and Nick following behind through the Saturday night crush of revellers. At the Flamingo Nick insisted on paying for everyone.

They kept their suede coats on and Nick wore his leather jacket. Tony Cotton was playing on stage and despite the room being packed, hot and smoky, Amy, Nick and Pam couldn't keep still. They danced through the night without feeling tired or in need of a break.

Later in the night Chris Farlow took over on stage and still they danced wearing their coats in the stuffy heat, the sweat pouring from them.

"I bet we will lose a good few pounds in weight tonight," Amy said pausing to light up a cigarette.

"I feel really great. I'm quite glad not to be stuck with Dick all night," Pam said and puffed on her cigarette. The next number thumped out through the speakers so the girls and Nick began dancing again.

At six in the morning the club closed and they emerged into the grey dawn light, their hair plastered to their heads and faces, mascara smudged under their eyes.

"Christ we look a mess!" Pam exclaimed looking at Amy. Amy pulled her hair forward around her face in an attempt to conceal it. Nick still looked pretty smart. He suggested they go and get a cup of tea. He took them to a scruffy cafe in a back street that was packed out, as it was one of the few cafes open at that time on a Sunday morning. It served up strong stewed tea from a tea urn and didn't appear to have coffee on the menu. The tea was welcome and refreshing, as they hadn't stopped for a drink all night. Then they walked back to Charing Cross to catch the train home. Nick came with them and got out at his station. He kissed Amy goodbye and promised to ring her at work next day.

"Now we've just got to creep back into my bedroom without waking my parents," Amy said, handing Pam another stick of chewing gum.

"I'm not looking forward to that," Pam said apprehensively, "what if your parents have discovered that we are missing? We might be in for it when we get to your house."

"Well, it's just too bad," Amy said, "it was worth it - we had a really great time didn't we Tibs?"

"Yeah, taking those pills made all the difference. If we hadn't taken them we'd have been flagging by two in the morning."

The girls arrived at Amy's house at quarter to eight and tiptoed up the path. Amy carefully climbed up the side of the porch with Pam following behind.

"Ooh, Bat, I'm dying for a pee - must be this cold morning air," Pam whispered and then began giggling.

"Sssh," hissed Amy, "hang on 'til we're inside."

Up on the porch roof Amy pulled her bedroom window open and heaved herself up onto the sill with Pam pushing from behind. Pam was trying hard to control her giggles.

Just then a voice called out: "Morning Amy. What are you up to?"

Amy glanced round to find her neighbour, Mr Denton, leaving for his morning shift at work. She quickly put her finger to her lips and waved him past. Knowing he was a good sport, she hoped he wouldn't say anything to her parents.

It was Pam's turn to scramble in through the window, but as she jumped up onto the sill, she hit the window causing it to crash back against the bedroom wall where Amy's parents were asleep. The girls froze and listened for any sign of movement but there was just silence.

"Phew!" Pam gasped and then burst into another fit of giggles as Amy tried to pull her into the bedroom. "Oh Bat, I've peed me breecks, as Yvonne would say," Pam whispered sobering up, "I feel all cold and wet."

Once inside Pam made a beeline for the bathroom to rinse out her tights and knickers and wash her face.

Amy closed the window and removed the clothes from under the covers. After Pam returned, Amy went and washed her face too. Then they squeezed into Amy's bed but found it uncomfortable as they both kept rolling into the dent in the middle. The last thing they felt like doing was sleeping so they lay chatting non-stop until they heard Amy's parents stirring and getting up.

Pam gave a giggle. "All your neighbour could see of you was your backside sticking out of the window, yet he still recognised you."

"Well who else would be climbing in at my bedroom window?"

"D'you think he'll spill the beans to your mum or dad?"

"No, I doubt it, but if I get a chance to speak to him - I'll ask him to keep it secret."

About an hour later there was a tap on the bedroom door and dad appeared carrying a tray. "I've brought you up some coffee," he said, "did you sleep all right?"

Amy gave a smile, relieved that their escapade had gone unnoticed. "Yeah, we slept fine," she said reaching out to take a mug of coffee. Then she noticed with horror, her nicotine-stained fingers. They hadn't been stained before she went to bed the previous evening. Worried that her father might notice she quickly stuffed her hand back under the covers. "Er, just leave the tray on the chair, thanks dad."

Mr Brown left the room and the girls looked at each other and burst out laughing.

"We did it, Bat," Pam said gleefully, "we actually got away with it."

"Now we can stay out all night on Saturday nights whenever we want," Amy declared triumphantly.

"But if we do it too often, we're bound to get caught," Pam remarked sounding a little worried. "It could so easily have gone wrong."

When the girls finally put in an appearance downstairs Amy was shocked to receive an unexpected interrogation from her mother.

"You two must have gone out like a light last night," she said eyeing Amy suspiciously, "I came up and knocked on your door but you didn't answer. I wanted to know if you had the cat in there with you as I couldn't find him."

"Er, yeah we were really tired and fell asleep in no time," Amy said trying not to give a tell-tale flush. "C'mon Pam, let's get ready and go over to your house."

She quickly hustled Pam out of the room before her mother could ask any more awkward questions.

Only after the girls had arrived at the Black Prince that evening did they notice the effect of the pills beginning to wear off. The Graham Bond Organisation were playing and despite feeling dead tired and lousy, they couldn't resist dancing to the marvellous music.

At the end of the evening they caught their separate buses home. As Amy began the twenty minute uphill slog home from the bus stop a minivan bibbed on its horn and pulled up next to her. It was Tim offering her a lift. Amy gratefully accepted as she was beginning to doubt whether her legs had the strength to carry her home.

Amy told Tim all about the previous evening's escapade when the girls climbed out of the window.

"You must've been really desperate to go up town all night if you were prepared to go to those lengths," he said chuckling.

"When you're stuck with stuffy parents like we've got then there's not much choice," Amy said as he drew up outside her house. She thanked him for the lift and hurried indoors.

Nick rang Amy next day as promised and they arranged to meet up in Oxford Street because Amy wanted him to see the Birds performing.

Pam arrived at the Pru after work and they got themselves ready before going to the Wimpy Bar for a snack. Then they walked to Oxford Street and found Nick waiting outside the 100 Club. He insisted once again on paying for all three of them to get in. Amy found this such a refreshing change after Mick's tight-fisted ways. Pam was hoping Ye-ye would be there so she wouldn't have to play gooseberry all evening. The Birds came on stage and announced that it was their last time at the club as in future they would be appearing at the Ealing Club on Ealing Broadway. The girls were devastated at this news.

Amy gave a groan. "That means we'll have to travel right to the end of the central line on a Monday evening to see them now."

"I think that was where the Stones used to play before they moved to Richmond so it must be pretty good there," Pam said trying to look on the bright side.

"The Pretty Things and Alexis Korner have also played there," Nick added, and then the Birds kicked in with a terrific final performance which instantly converted Nick into a raving Bird fan.

During the interval the drummer fell down the stairs and sprained his ankle so his drumming in the second half was with drumsticks only but didn't spoil the music one jot. Pam was getting a bit fed up as there was no sign of Ye-ye so she decided to leave shortly after the start of the second session despite Amy begging her to stay.

"I'll see you tomorrow evening," she said to Amy and walked off to the exit.

"It's a pity she's not keen on Charlie," Nick said, "else he could have come down here with her."

"Well she's supposed to be going out with Dick, but after he let her down on Saturday night I'm not so sure."

Tuesday evening the girls headed for the Scene. Dick was there with Eric but there was no sign of Mick. When Dick didn't offer Pam an excuse for not turning up on Saturday she stormed off to the ladies to find Amy.

"Why do we bother with those two?" she yelled throwing her handbag into the washbasin.

"Well I've definitely had enough of Mick and don't want anything more to do with him," Amy said tugging a comb through her hair, "they are both as bad as each other - a pair of unreliable skinflints!"

When Pam had calmed down they returned to the dance floor and after an hour of non-stop dancing, Amy spotted Mary over by the stage so they went to chat with her and tell her of their latest split with Mick and Dick.

"Sounds as if you're better off with this Nick anyway," Mary observed handing round her Benson and Hedges, "and talking of boyfriends, I've got to go and meet Trevor in the Red Lion in ten minutes. Why don't you two come over there?"

"Er, no thanks, Mary. We'll stay here a bit longer," Amy said, "I'm sure Trevor would prefer to see you on your own."

Mary grinned. "The way he kept talking about you last week," she said looking at Pam, "I think he must have a bit of a crush on you."

"Oh come off it," Pam scoffed and then quickly dragged Amy back to the dance floor again.

"I told you he fancies you," Amy hissed in her ear.

"At least Mary doesn't seem very bothered about it," Pam said stubbing out her cigarette under her toe. She sighed. "Men! Why do we bother?" she said, sounding exasperated.

Their first typing lesson was booked for the following evening. It was being held in a large room above a pub in Pam's town. Amy met Pam outside where a door led through to a steep staircase. There were about twenty other girls in the class of varying ages. The tables were arranged in a U shape so Pam and Amy opted to sit midway at the far end. The teacher was pleasant though fairly strict. Each student had a portable typewriter in front of them. The rental cost of the typewriter was included in the course with an option to buy it at a reduced price at the end of the course. The keys had been covered with plastic caps to hide the letters. The caps were colour coded for the correct fingers to encourage proper touch-typing.

"This looks difficult," Pam whispered, "I wish we could see what the letters are."

They spent the lesson trying to memorise and type certain letters without looking at their finger positions.

Amy found it slow going. "I'll never remember where all the letters are," she said as they emerged from the pub lugging their typewriters.

"No cheating, Bat," Pam said grinning, "you mustn't remove the caps when you practise what we learnt tonight."

"She wants us to do a lot of practising at home before the next lesson, but I can't see me ever getting very proficient at it," Amy said despondently.

"Give it time, Bat, after all that was just the first lesson."

"Yeah, I suppose you're right," Amy agreed stopping at the bus stop just as her bus appeared from around a nearby corner. Then she brightened up. "At least it's payday on Friday - can't come soon enough!"

"You're seeing Nick Friday aren't you?" Pam said as Amy stepped onto the platform at the rear of the bus, "I'll try and pop over to yours on Saturday," she added as the bus pulled away.

Friday evening Amy met Nick outside the Railway Tavern. They went into the bar and Nick bought some drinks. Amy noticed him glancing around the room.

"Are you looking for someone?" she asked.

"A mate of mine said he might be here this evening, but if not then I'd find him over at the Twisted Wheel. He's getting me some pills for tomorrow night."

They finished their drinks and with no sign of Nick's mate, he suggested they catch a train to Welling, as it wouldn't take very long.

The Twisted Wheel was only half full. They found a couple of seats at the side and Nick bought two drinks. Then he spotted his mate across the room.

"I shan't be long," he said and dashed off through the dancers. Amy could see him talking earnestly with a small group of blokes then he returned to Amy.

"No luck," he said, "pills are scarce today - no-one seems to have any."

"Never mind," Amy said draining her glass, "drink up and lets go back to the Railway - it's better than this place."

The group playing in the back room at the Railway were pretty good and they spent the remainder of the evening smooching on the dance floor.

At the end of the evening they crossed the road to the station where Nick caught his train home.

"You'll still come up West tomorrow night won't you?" he asked leaning out of the carriage window, "I'll meet you under the clock same as last week."

Amy hesitated. "Actually Nick, I think I might give tomorrow night a miss. Escaping out of my bedroom window two weekends on the trot might be pushing my luck a bit." Amy didn't mention that the thought of trying to stay awake all night without the help of some pills no longer seemed so attractive to her.

He looked a little disappointed as Amy kissed him goodbye, so she agreed to meet him at his station on Sunday afternoon instead.

Amy got up Saturday afternoon and played some records waiting for Pam to show up but she never arrived which was very unlike Pam so Amy spent the evening practising her typing and then washed her hair.

Pam was surprised to find Amy on her doorstep Sunday afternoon.

"I think Nick was peeved with me for not going up to London with him last night," she said walking in and flopping down in an armchair.

"Why, what's happened?" Pam asked.

"I got to his station only to find Charlie waiting there for me. He told me Nick couldn't make it and that he'll ring me at work tomorrow - the sod!"

"Didn't Charlie give any explanation?"

"No, and I didn't bother asking as the train in the opposite direction was coming in on the other platform so I just thanked him for letting me know and dashed over the footbridge."

"Oh well, we can go up the Scene tonight - I think there may be a live band playing," Pam said, and then took Amy upstairs to her bedroom to show her the handbag she had bought.

"Wow, Tibs, that's a really great bag - and such soft leather," Amy said appreciatively caressing the supple black handbag.

"It was quite a bargain - I got it up Petticoat Lane in my lunch hour on Friday. They've got quite a few on the stall if you want one."

"Yeah, I think I will, Tibs - and it's a good size so it'll hold quite a lot of stuff. By the way, I thought you were coming over yesterday."

"Oh, that's right, but Chris popped round with a skirt that she wanted me to help her alter. She's pretty useless when it comes to sewing."

That evening at the Scene they enjoyed dancing to Gino Washington and the Ram Jam Band. They met up with the crowd who had been at Carol's party back in January. Graham, still wearing his black leather jacket, asked Amy to dance. She liked his friendly manner and felt totally at ease with him. At the end of the evening they all caught the train home together with plenty of rowdy laughing and joking on the journey.

After Pam had alighted at her station, everyone else continued on the train for two more stops before heading off home in different directions, yelling their goodbyes. Since Carol and Margaret lived just round the corner from Amy, they accompanied her home up the hill.

Chapter Eight

March - More Mick and Dick

How Amy hated Mondays at work, slogging through the extra-large pile of accounts from agents, marking them off in the ledger while Joan whizzed through her pile in half the time. By twelve o'clock Amy was wilting as Joan, with an empty tray, went off to lunch.

Then the phone rang. It was Nick full of apologies for letting her down on Sunday. He said he'd been sick so had stayed in bed. Amy could feel eyes boring into her back. She glanced round to see Miss Rogers glaring at her so she told Nick she would have to go and hung up.

She decided to cheer herself up by going to the record shop down Leather Lane in her lunch hour for a browse. After rummaging through the collection she bought a record that was a favourite down the Scene: Bo Diddley's 'Hey Momma Keep Your Big Mouth Shut'.

When she returned to her desk Nick rang again. This time Miss Rogers was still out at lunch so Amy could talk for a while and they arranged to meet that evening at the Railway Tavern.

At 8pm Amy hurried up Station Approach to find Nick waiting outside the Railway. They stopped in the bar for a drink before going through to the dance room where a local group was playing. Towards the end of the evening a fight broke out in the bar but it was quickly brought under control. Amy knew if her dad got to hear about it, being an ambulance driver, he would try and ban her from going there as he had from previous places when he had heard of ructions taking place.

Nick caught his train home after arranging to see Amy at the Railway on Friday. As she walked home Amy felt annoyed with Nick's casual attitude. 'He ought to be seeing me home, the sod, instead of me seeing him onto his train,' she thought irritably as she stomped up the steep hill, 'and come to think of it, why didn't he ask to see me on Wednesday - it's a long time 'til Friday.'

Tuesday evening found Amy and Pam down the Scene again. Mary and Pat arrived and tonight they also had Trevor with them. They all stood in a group chatting next to the record booth when in walked Dick with some of his mates, but there was no sign of Mick.

Mary thought Trevor was chatting to Pam far too much so she dragged him off for a dance. Just then a sheepish looking Dick came over and asked Pam for a dance. She gave him a smile and went off with him, much to Amy's surprise after the way Pam had ranted on about him the previous week.

"I think Pam must like Dick a lot more than she lets on," Amy said to Pat as she watched them smooching on the dance floor with arms wrapped round each other.

"Just as well else Mary might start getting worried in case Trevor asks Pam out," Pat said and puffed on her cigarette.

"Oh, Mary needn't worry about Pam," Amy said adamantly, "she would never dream of taking someone else's boyfriend."

Their dance over, Pam came back to tell Amy that she and Dick were going round to the Pic for a coffee. After they had left, Mary and Trevor returned and Trevor invited the girls over to the pub for a drink.

They stayed in the pub for over an hour and returned to the Scene for a few dances before it was time to catch the train home. Dick accompanied Pam on the train as far as his station and arranged to see her down the Scene on Saturday.

"I thought you had finished with Dick," Amy said once they were alone in the compartment.

Pam smiled. "I must be mad, but when he gives me that sorry little boy look I just can't stay cross with him. By the way he told me that Mick is seeing some girl - that's why he wasn't down the Scene."

"Poor cow! I pity her having to put up with him," Amy said scornfully. "I see Trevor didn't waste any time chatting you up this evening. You'd better be careful."

"I think it made Dick a bit jealous - that's probably why he took me off for a coffee."

Amy took out her compact from her make-up bag and started powdering her nose. "That reminds me, I found a posh-looking powder compact in the bogs at work today so I handed it in to the staff department - very honest of me wasn't it?"

"Speaking of the Pru - I got a letter this morning offering me a job there - I start in three weeks' time."

"That's great, Tibs. D'you know which department you'll be in?"

"No, they just said to report to the assembly point in the main rest room."

"That's where I had to go on my first day. You just follow the arrows from the foyer."

By the time Friday arrived Amy had decided not to bother going to meet Nick at the Railway. She was still feeling irritated with him so she stayed in and washed her hair instead.

Afterwards she took her record player into the kitchen and put on her new Bo Diddley record. Suddenly her father burst into the room looking furious and started shouting. "Don't you dare let me hear you speak like that to your mother else you'll get the thrashing of your life my girl!"

Amy looked puzzled for a moment and then the penny dropped. He had heard the lyrics of the Bo Diddley record - 'Hey Momma Keep your Big Mouth Shut.' She giggled, which infuriated her father even more. "Dad, for goodness sake calm down, it's only a song."

"Well I don't like it, so I don't want to hear it played again in this house," he said crossly as he turned and stomped out. Amy shrugged. 'I'll play it whenever I want,' she thought defiantly.

She met up with Pam on the train to London Saturday evening and told her she wasn't seeing Nick any more.

"I thought you quite liked him, Bat."

"He's getting too much like Mick - never seeing me home and sending Charlie to give me a message when he can't come himself."

"At least he's a lot more generous than Mick - he always offered to pay for us," Pam pointed out.

Amy sighed. "Maybe I was just getting fed up."

They went down the Scene and found Pat in the Ladies brushing her hair. "Mary's over at the Red Lion with Trevor," she said in answer to Amy's enquiry. As they all emerged onto the dance floor, they bumped into Dick coming out of the Gents next door. He took Pam off for a dance so Amy and Pat danced for a couple of records and then Carol, Margaret, Graham and several others joined them. They stood by the stage laughing and joking together until Pat announced it was time for her to leave. "I've promised to give Mary and Trevor a lift home."

After she had left, Amy danced with the two girls and Graham until it was time to leave. She caught the train home with them, as there was no sign of Pam and Dick. She presumed they must have already left.

After work on Monday Pam and Amy caught the tube to Ealing Broadway. It was a long journey that led to disappointment when they arrived at the Ealing Club on the Broadway. It didn't have as good an atmosphere as the 100 Club and it was nearly empty. To make matters worse, the Birds weren't appearing. A group played Tamla Motown songs all evening but Pam and Amy refused to stay fed up and decided to enjoy themselves regardless since they had made the effort to get there. Amy had spent Sunday fitting a lining into her new suit and tonight she felt good wearing it as she and Pam danced around the floor under the flashing coloured lights.

They made enquiries as they were leaving and were told the Birds would be appearing in two weeks' time on the Thursday.

Tuesday evening down the Scene, Pam went off with Dick again so Amy hung around with Mary, Pat and Trevor. Halfway through the evening a worried looking girl came dashing over and tapped Pat on the shoulder. "Do you own a Mini Countryman?" she asked breathlessly.

"Yes, what of it?" Pat said sharply.

"Well, someone has just crashed into the back of it!"

"What!" Pat shrieked and hurried out of the club and up the stairs followed by Mary, Trevor and Amy. Up in Ham Yard a crowd had gathered to examine the damage.

"Let me through!" Pat yelled shoving people aside. They parted and there stood Pat's little car looking rather sorry for itself with a large dent in its boot and a buckled rear bumper.

"Who did this?" Pat demanded looking round at the faces behind her.

"I heard a crash and when I came over to see what had happened, I saw a black car driving off," said a Mod wearing a parka and beret. "The car sped up Great Windmill Street really fast," he added.

Trevor bent down to examine the damage. "It's only superficial, Pat, you'll still be able to drive it OK," he said.

"Will your insurance pay for the repairs, Pat?" Amy asked.

"Mm, maybe," Pat said vaguely, "if not then I'll just have to sweet talk daddy into forking out. This has spoilt my evening so I'm going home." She unlocked the driver's door and got in. "Coming Mary?"

Mary quickly kissed Trevor goodbye and got into the passenger seat with a wave to Amy out of the window as Pat thrust the gear stick into first and roared off.

Trevor offered to buy Amy a coffee so they walked round to the Piccadilly cafe.

"That Pat has been thoroughly spoilt by her parents," he said dropping sugar lumps into his cup, "just because she's an only child, she has always had everything she wants. I don't think she appreciates how lucky she is to have her own car."

"I get the impression that both Pat and Mary have always had whatever they wanted," Amy said, "I think Mary gets spoilt by her older brothers judging by what she has told me."

Trevor grinned. "Yeah, she can be quite demanding at times - used to getting her own way. She's got Pat to drive her around else I'm sure she'd have her own car too if she asked for one. Must be great to have rich parents," he added a little wistfully.

"Money's not everything," Amy said reflectively and sipped her coffee, "as you said, if you get things too easily then you don't really appreciate them. I had to save my pocket money for three years in order to buy my record player and when I finally got it, it was a terrific sense of achievement and I've cherished it ever since."

"My family's OK - we're not rich, but we're not too badly off. Dad works at Scotland Yard so we live in a large block of maisonettes that's owned by the Yard. It's full of policemen's families." Trevor paused and gave a chuckle. "A right thieving bunch some of them are too. Mum complains to dad when her milk gets pinched from the doorstep."

Amy laughed. "Whereabouts do you live?" she asked.

"Just behind Sloane Square in Chelsea. It's a nice area - I like it there. Dad keeps on about us all emigrating to Canada once he retires at forty eight."

"That's young to retire isn't it?" Amy said in surprise.

"That's normal for the police. They only want you while you're young and fit. Dad wants to do carpentry out in Canada as a second career."

"It's a long way to go - why Canada?"

Trevor shrugged. "I don't really know. I think he's read books about the lifestyle out there and it's caught his imagination. But if he does go, I don't think I'll be going too. I like London - can't beat its nightlife. I think Canada would be too cold and provincial for my liking."

"Mm, I think you're right. This country takes some beating," Amy agreed. Their coffee finished, they walked back to the Scene just as Pam emerged with Dick.

"Time we were leaving," Pam said and gave Trevor a warm smile. "Where's Mary?"

Trevor quickly explained what had happened, then Amy said goodbye to Trevor and accompanied Pam and Dick to the station to catch their train home.

Saturday night Pam met up with Dick to go to the flicks so Amy met Mary down the Scene as they had arranged at work. Pat was still too upset about her car so didn't come but Trevor was there and he had brought a mate along with him. He introduced him as Len, a fairly innocuous Mod wearing a long orange leather coat. He danced with Amy for most of the evening and took her round to the Piccadilly for a coffee with Trevor and Mary. Amy didn't mind Len though she preferred his coat. He walked her to the station and made a date with her for Tuesday at the Scene.

After work on Monday Amy had to dash home because it was her typing lesson that evening. She was late as she hurried to the bus stop lugging the heavy typewriter when who should pull up beside her but Tim in his Minivan. He gave her a lift all the way to the pub in the next town where Pam was waiting for her. Grateful for the lift, she thanked him and waved as he drove off giving a bib on his horn to Pam as he went.

They found the typing getting a little easier as they had been practising and memorising where the keys were. The teacher gave them tests to assess their progress. Pam and Amy were pleased and a little surprised that they managed to pass.

At the end of the lesson they went downstairs into the pub for a quick drink. "How was the film on Saturday?" Amy asked offering Pam a cigarette.

She gave a groan. "Not much cop, and Dick was late so we missed the beginning."

Amy told Pam about Len.

"You'll have to introduce me to him tomorrow," Pam said, "I've got to give my approval you know," she added with a grin.

"Well he's not much to write home about but I love his coat."

"Can't be all that bad if he's got good dress sense," Pam conceded. Their drinks finished, they went outside to wait for Amy's bus home.

The next evening down the Scene, Pam and Amy met up with Dick and then Len arrived followed by Trevor and Mary. They all stayed together in a group dancing and chatting. Halfway through the evening they walked round to the Piccadilly cafe. Len and Trevor were in a boisterous mood cracking jokes that made the girls laugh. Back at the Scene Mary decided it was time for her to leave so she said her goodbyes and left with Trevor.

Len drew Amy to the benches along the side wall where they sat kissing and cuddling while Pam smooched around the floor with Dick.

At the end of the evening Len walked to the station with Amy and he gave her his works phone number.

"Ring me on Friday for a chat," he said as she boarded the train with Pam and Dick. Amy promised she would. After Dick got out at his station, the girls spread out along the seat as they had the compartment to themselves.

"He seems pretty keen on you, judging by your neck," Pam commented with a smile.

"Oh, does it notice?" Amy pulled up the collar of her coat; "I'll cop it from mum if she spots it."

"Just wear a polo neck for a couple of days," Pam suggested.

Next day at work Amy's polo neck sweater didn't fool Mary. During their lunch in the canteen she paused after a spoonful of yoghurt and asked, "what are you trying to hide then?" pointing accusingly at Amy's neck with her spoon.

"Is it that obvious?" Amy asked looking a little worried, "I'm hoping it'll stop mum from asking awkward questions."

"Oh, it's pretty easy to fool parents," Mary said offhandedly, "I reckon Len must be in love with you because he doesn't usually offer to take girls out."

"Well I don't think meeting me down the Scene really counts as taking me out," Amy said dismissively.

"I bet it does in Len's book," Mary said and gave a chuckle.

Jeanette joined them at their table. She had just bought a strawberry yoghurt at the counter.

"What's so funny?" she asked Mary tugging at the lid of her yoghurt pot.

"Oh nothing really. By the way - do you like Amy's polo neck sweater?"

Jeanette glanced up. "Yes, it's fine - why?"

"Pack it in Mary," Amy hissed.

Mary grinned. "Just testing."

Jeanette gave a shrug and tucked into her yoghurt.

Friday lunchtime Amy went down to the basement to ring Len. They chatted briefly and she arranged to see him down the Scene Saturday evening. Then she gave Pam a call, as it was her last day at the New Zealand Insurance Company. She was about to go out for a leaving drink with her workmates so Amy quickly arranged to meet up with her the following evening and then hung up as Sue was banging impatiently on the booth. They were going up Oxford Street shopping and didn't have much time.

Sue bought a twin set in Marks and Amy treated herself to a jumper. They paused for a brief spot of lunch in Lyons before returning to the Pru.

Saturday evening found the two friends back at the Scene. Dick was already there hovering by the record booth waiting for Pam, and Amy was relieved that Mick was still absent. According to Dick he was at the flicks with his new girlfriend. Len turned up on his own so the four of them spent the evening together dancing with a break for coffee at the Piccadilly cafe around 9.30pm.

As they sat at a table by the window Amy mentioned to Pam that her parents were going away next day to visit relatives.

"They'll be gone all day so why don't you come over?"

"Yeah, we could play records as loud as we want."

Len pricked up his ears. "How about I come down and spend the afternoon with you?" he suggested, "I'll bring some of my records." Amy glanced at Pam and shrugged.

"Yeah, why not. I can meet you at the station."

"Well in that case, I'll come over too," Dick chimed in, not wanting to be left out. Pam smiled, relieved that she wouldn't be left playing gooseberry. They all arranged to meet up at the station Sunday afternoon.

Amy stood on the platform next day waiting for the train from London to arrive. When it did pull in, only Pam and Dick alighted. There was no sign of Len. They waited for two more trains to come and go before they gave up and walked up the hill to Amy's house. She was none too pleased to be the one left playing gooseberry. She put the records on and made the coffee while Pam and Dick snuggled up together on the settee.

"Wait 'til I see Len," Amy said putting down the tray of mugs on the coffee table, "the sod had better have a good excuse for not turning up else he'll be getting the elbow."

"Maybe he caught the wrong train," Dick suggested.

"I told him what train to get - it's not like he had to make any changes," Amy said crossly.

"He could be hanging around the station right now," Pam said, "he wouldn't know where to come 'cause he doesn't have your address."

"It'd serve him right," Amy said grimly and took a swig of coffee.

Pam started work at the Pru next day and met Amy in the canteen at lunchtime to tell her how she was getting on.

"They've put me in a small department that handles lapsed policies," she said as they tucked into cottage pie, "I'm working with a nice friendly girl called Diane who is showing me what to do."

Jeanette came over to join them and Amy introduced her to Pam.

"Whereabouts is your office?" Jeanette asked.

"I think it's on the mezzanine floor," Pam replied, "it's going to take a while to find my way around this huge building."

"Oh you'll soon get used to it, Tibs," Amy said, "it didn't take me as long as I thought it would."

That evening, after going home on the same train, they met up again later at the Railway Tavern. There was a group playing they hadn't seen before who were quite good so the girls spent most of the evening dancing with just a couple of breaks for drinks in the bar.

"It's unusual not to find anyone we know here tonight, Bat," Pam said glancing round the bar as they were finishing their drinks.

"You spoke too soon, Tibs," Amy said giving a wave to someone across the bar behind Pam, "there's Tim over there from the Black Prince - he's coming over."

"Hello girls," he said leaning against the bar, "can I buy you a drink?"

"No thanks, Tim," Amy said with a smile, "we're about to go back into the dance hall."

"I've got my Minivan outside so if you two want a lift home in about half an hour's time just come and get me," he offered, and then returned to his mates.

The girls were happy to take Tim up on his offer of a lift. They squeezed into the front seat next to him and he drove Pam home first as she lived furthest away, and then he took Amy to her house.

"Been climbing out of any more windows lately?" he asked with a grin as he pulled up by the green outside her house.

"No - not yet. We might not get away with it a second time," Amy said as she opened the door. After thanking him for the lift she waved to him as he drove off. She liked Tim and wished he would ask her out. 'Maybe I'm just not his type,' she thought resignedly as she walked over the green to her house.

After work on Tuesday Amy and Pam dawdled over their egg and chips in the Wimpy Bar until it was time to head for the Scene once again.

Inside they found Dick and his mates huddled by the stage but no Mick. Dick came over and put his arm around Pam's shoulders and gave her a peck on the cheek. Amy felt a tap on her shoulder and turned round to find a sheepish-looking Len standing behind her. "Where did you get to on Sunday?" she demanded crossly.

"I'm sorry, but I caught the wrong train. By the time I realised and changed onto the right one I was so late that I didn't reach your station until six thirty."

"I'd long since given you up and gone home," Amy said.

"I didn't really expect you to still be there so I caught the next train back up to London," he said.

Amy remained cool with him for the rest of the evening. She couldn't forgive him that easily. He took her for a coffee and tried hard to get her smiling by cracking a few jokes and by the time they said goodbye at the station, Amy was feeling a little more forgiving.

Dick and Pam caught the train with Amy and on the journey Dick casually mentioned that he had tickets for a firm's dance in Welling on Friday evening.

"Why don't you both come," he offered, "it should be a good bash."

Amy didn't much fancy playing gooseberry to Pam and Dick again. Dick could tell she wasn't keen.

"I forgot to mention," he said with a smile, "Mick isn't going out with that girl any more. He's got tickets too and asked me to ask if you'd like to go with him."

"Oh Bat do come - it'll be a laugh," Pam cajoled, "the four of us again."

Amy didn't think it was such a good idea. She had been so fed up with Mick but Dick and Pam both wanted her to go so eventually she allowed herself to be persuaded. After Dick got out at his station the girls fell about giggling.

"We must be mad, Tibs," Amy said, "the number of times we finish with those two only to end up going out with them again."

"What will you do about Len?" Pam asked.

"Shan't tell him. What he doesn't know won't hurt him."

"I think you quite enjoy two-timing fellas," Pam said with a grin.

Thursday evening the girls were excited about seeing the Birds again despite having to take the long tube ride to the end of the Central Line once more. But it was all worthwhile when their favourite group struck up their raunchy sound on stage deafening everyone in the club, which was packed out compared to the previous Monday. Amy felt sure the singer recognised her and smiled from under his long mop of unruly hair, making her evening.

Next day during her lunch hour, Amy phoned Len and agreed to meet him down the Scene Saturday night. He tried persuading her to stay down there all night.

"I'll see what I can organise but I'm not promising," she said. She needed to check with Pam to see what she was doing Saturday night. She found her in the canteen with Diane. They were giggling together as Amy sat down with a roll and a coffee. She was surprised to feel a twinge of jealousy, which wasn't helped when Diane gave her a cold look as Pam introduced them. But then she smiled and Amy told herself it was simply her imagination.

"Will you be seeing Dick at the Scene tomorrow night, Tibs?" Amy asked before taking a bite of her roll.

"He mentioned on Tuesday that there's a film he wants to see so I suppose we'll be going to the flicks," she said.

"You should stand up for yourself and tell him if you don't fancy going to see a film," Diane cut in.

"Pam would definitely tell Dick if she didn't want to go," Amy said curtly, irritated by Diane's uncalled for opinion.

"Yeah, I would," Pam agreed.

"Well, Len wants me to stay down the Scene all night so I'll have to tell my parents that I'm staying over at yours," Amy said.

"That should be OK so long as your dad doesn't check up with my dad," Pam said after thinking about it briefly.

Amy made up her mind. "I think it's a risk worth taking," she declared with a toss of her head.

Then a problem occurred to Pam. "What if Mick decides to go down there and spots you with Len?"

"I'll try and find out from him tonight where he intends going tomorrow night, and if it's the Scene then I shall have to persuade him not to bother going, else I'll have no alternative but to stand Len up."

Diane stood up and tutted. "You lead such a complicated life," she said, "rather you than me." She turned to Pam. "It's time we were getting back to our desks."

"I'll be along in a couple of minutes," Pam told her. Diane turned on her heel and walked off.

"I get the feeling she doesn't really approve of me," Amy said offering Pam a cigarette and then striking a match.

"She hardly knows you so she can't have formed an opinion of you already," Pam said.

Amy shrugged. "I'm probably imagining it."

"Hey, guess what, Bat - I rang Dick a little while ago and, wonders will never cease, Dick told me he and Mick are going to collect us tonight in Mick's car. They are picking us up from my house at 8 o'clock."

"I can't believe they are finally turning over a new leaf," Amy said in amazement.

Pam grinned. "Maybe Mick has missed you and wants to give a good impression."

"Better late than never I suppose."

Amy caught the bus over to Pam's that evening and arrived just minutes before Mick's car pulled up outside. He and Dick both looked very smart in their best suits and the girls felt quite proud to be seen out with them. The dance was being held in a large room above a pub at Welling. It was Dick's firm who had organised it and the four of them had a great evening though the band weren't particularly modern. Nevertheless they danced the night away and enjoyed a cold buffet and drinks all laid on.

At the end of the evening they piled into Mick's car and he drove Amy home first. He stopped by the green and walked her across to her gate.

"Do you fancy coming down the coast on Sunday?" he asked pulling her towards him.

"Er, yeah, why not." Amy hesitated then asked casually: "What are you doing tomorrow night?"

"I've promised to give a mate a hand 'cause he's moving to a new flat," Mick replied stroking Amy's hair then added: "I really enjoyed being with you again tonight. I think the four of us make a good team."

Amy was surprised he hadn't asked her about Len. Maybe Dick hadn't mentioned that she was seeing someone else, though it seemed unlikely. She smiled and kissed him goodnight relieved to hear that he wouldn't be appearing down the Scene.

"I'll pick you up Sunday around 2 o'clock," Mick called out as he returned to his car.

On Saturday evening, after convincing her parents that she was off to stay at Pam's overnight, Amy hurried down to the station to catch the train to London. On the platform she was pleased to meet up with Carol, Margaret, Graham and several others.

They all clambered aboard the train and had a compartment to themselves for the journey.

"Are you staying down the Scene all night?" Graham asked sitting down next to Amy.

"Yeah, my boyfriend Len wants me to stay there with him," Amy told him.

Graham leaned towards Amy and whispered, "If you need any pills, I've got some blues I can let you have."

"I was going to try and manage without taking anything," Amy said, "but since you're offering, I'll buy twenty from you." She dug out her purse from her handbag and gave Graham a pound note. He discreetly slid a small packet into her bag.

"If Len doesn't object, I'll come and have a dance with you later on."

"Oh don't worry about him - I'll dance with whoever I like," Amy said defiantly.

Once down the Scene Amy hung around with Carol and Margaret until Len finally arrived wearing his orange leather. He was pleased to learn that Amy could stay all night. She mentioned that she had twenty blues in her bag.

"They're just in case I get really tired," she told him.

"I wouldn't mind some pills to help me through the night," Len said, "how about I buy some from you?" Amy hesitated. It would be better for them to either both take pills or both manage without, and since she felt fine, she preferred to go without but Len persisted until Amy relented and let him have ten. Only after swallowing them did he admit that he had never taken any before. During the evening Amy got more and more annoyed with Len as he became blocked out of his head and danced madly around the floor making a spectacle of himself. She was relieved when Graham appeared and took her to the opposite side of the club for several dances. Then she danced with Carol and Margaret for a while before searching out Len. She found him, still dancing frantically, unaware that Amy had been missing for some time. She regretted letting him take the tablets but it was too late now to do anything about it.

By six o'clock he had calmed down and was acting more normal when they left the Scene and walked round to the Last Chance in the Strand with Graham and the others. This club didn't close until 9 in the morning so they could dance for a while longer.

Just before nine o'clock they emerged onto the Strand and everyone headed for a coffee bar nearby. It was packed with all-night revellers queuing for coffee. A small area upstairs had tables and chairs with a shelf and bar stools along one wall.

Amy and Len managed to find a couple of stools to sit on. A rowdy mob behind Len seemed to want to pick a fight with him. One yob smashed the neck of an empty coke bottle and threatening to slash Len in the face with the broken glass. Len, still under the influence of drugs, didn't appear to be at all worried whereas Amy was quickly becoming panicky at the dangerous situation unfolding. There was no easy escape down the stairs as they were blocked with people queuing to get upstairs as well as down.

The yob thrust the jagged glass at Len catching him on the chin. It left a nasty gash that dripped blood. Amy gave a scream of horror while Len fumbled for a handkerchief to staunch the flow. Suddenly a familiar face appeared next to Len. It was Graham. Amy didn't know where he had come from but she was very relieved to see him. He quickly defused the situation by grabbing the yob's wrist and forcing him to drop the broken bottle. Graham was bigger than the yob and gave him a shove towards the stairs.

"Clear off now before I let you have it," he snarled threateningly clenching his fists. The yob and his mates obviously didn't fancy taking on Graham who was much taller than them so they retreated down the stairs, hurling abuse back at him as they squeezed past the queue.

"Thanks for coming to our rescue, Graham," Amy said, aware that she was shaking like a leaf. She took out her fags and handed them round, needing something to calm her nerves.

"They were just kids trying to cause trouble," Graham said casually, then turning to Len, "you OK?"

"Yeah, I'm fine," Len said dabbing at his chin. Amy took the handkerchief away and examined his wound.

"It's not a deep cut so you won't need any stitches," she pronounced, "you were lucky - he could have done a lot of damage with that bottle."

Len shrugged. "Yeah, I suppose so. Don't know why he started picking on me though."

"Maybe he was jealous of your leather," Graham suggested with a grin then he went to re-join his friends.

"Drink up Len, I've got to catch my train home," Amy said and drained her cup.

She arrived home and hoped she looked bright eyed and bushy tailed as though she had just got up from a good night's sleep at Pam's. She didn't dare have a kip on her bed in case her mother came in. Amy knew she would easily guess that she had been out all night. There wasn't much time anyway as she had to wash and change ready for Mick who would be arriving after lunch.

Mick turned up on time, but driving a Mini that Amy didn't recognise.

"I've borrowed my mate's car as mine's playing up again," he explained as they headed for the Thanet Way to Margate.

It was the end of March and spring was bursting out beneath a clear blue sky. They arrived at the seafront, parked up and strolled along the beach. The fresh crisp breeze blowing in from the sea helped to keep Amy awake. She was relieved that Mick didn't ask her any awkward questions about what she had been doing Saturday night.

They sat on a bench on the promenade, but as the afternoon wore on, Amy began to feel more and more ill. She tried to hide how bad she was feeling from Mick. He suggested they go into a photo booth on the promenade and have their photos taken. Amy smiled bravely for the camera but thought she looked pretty awful when the developed pictures appeared. Mick was pleased with them and carefully tore two off for Amy and kept two for himself.

"Let's go and find a cafe for something to eat," he suggested. The very thought of food made Amy's stomach heave. While Mick tucked into burger and chips, Amy just sipped a coffee, telling Mick she didn't feel hungry. She gazed out the window to avoid looking at Mick eating.

"Watcha Mick," said a voice. Amy looked round at two Mods who had just come in and sat down at the next table. Mick looked up and grinned.

"Dell! Fancy seeing you here," he exclaimed in surprise, "and Jeff." He introduced Amy to them.

"We know Mick and his mates from down the 'Mingo," Dell explained to Amy, adding, "I think I recognise you too."

"Yeah, I've been down there a few times," Amy admitted managing a weak smile. She thought Dell looked vaguely familiar and they were both quite dishy. She could see they were smartly dressed, wearing mohair suits under their parkas.

"We were down there last night - it was fantastic - as usual," Jeff said.

Amy was glad she had stayed down the Scene all night. If she had been down the Flamingo and these two had spotted her, things could now be getting very awkward.

Amy needed some fresh air before the journey home so she hurried Mick up and cut short his conversation with Dell and Jeff.

Outside she finally admitted that she was feeling poorly and wanted to get home as quickly as possible. Mick appeared to be quite concerned and put his arm around her. Amy didn't want to be fussed over. She preferred to be left alone when she felt ill.

In the car she wound down the window so that she had the wind in her face all the way home, which helped dispel the rising nausea. The last thing she wanted was to embarrass herself by throwing up in Mick's mate's Mini.

She made it home and promised to ring Mick in the week when she hoped she would be feeling better. "Sorry I spoilt our trip to Margate," she added.

"Rubbish - I enjoyed it even if you didn't," Mick said and kissed her goodbye. Amy assumed it was probably just a lack of sleep that was making her feel so ill.

Monday she felt a little better so headed into work and in the evening met Pam for their typing lesson above the pub. But as the evening wore on Amy began feeling worse again.

"I don't think I'll be going to work tomorrow," she told Pam as they stood waiting at the bus stop.

"I'll tell Vera if you like," Pam volunteered, "she's your section leader isn't she?"

"Yeah - you'd better make it sound as if I'm at death's door else she probably won't believe you." Amy's bus pulled up and she climbed on board.

"Just make sure you're well again in time for your birthday," Pam called out as the bus began to drive away.

Amy languished in bed all the next day feeling very sorry for herself. Her stomach ached and she couldn't bring herself to eat anything. By Wednesday she felt a little brighter so made the effort to get up and take a walk round to the phone box to ring Mick. She arranged to meet him Saturday evening down the Scene. He sounded concerned that she was still feeling ill.

"I'll be OK by then," she assured him. She had deliberately not mentioned that the next day was her birthday as she knew she would get teased by him something rotten for having a birthday on April Fool's Day. The fewer people that knew, the better, as far as she was concerned.

She returned home and washed her hair as she had heroically decided to return to work.

Chapter Nine

April - Easter at Brighton

Amy awoke to the realisation that she was now eighteen, leaving her only two more years as a teenager. Over a hurried breakfast she received a pendant watch from her parents and the promise of a record from Ray.

She arrived at work to find a pile of cards on her desk. Somehow her fellow workers had found out that today was her birthday. She also received a couple of record vouchers and then Sue whispered in her ear reminding her that it was the custom for the birthday girl to buy cakes for afternoon tea. She was none too keen on that arrangement.

At lunchtime Amy just had soup and a roll while Pam enjoyed a large plate of fish and chips. As they ate, they made plans to go to the Marquee after work to celebrate Amy's birthday.

"I saw Len down the Scene on Tuesday", Pam said, vigorously shaking salt over her chips, "I told him you weren't very well so he said he'd give you a ring at work."

"As far as I know he hasn't rung yet," Amy said, "I'll ask Sue if anyone phoned me while I was away."

"Dick was being really irritating all evening - kept poking and tickling me but I wasn't in the mood to be prodded or tickled. Maybe I'm getting fed up with him."

By afternoon tea break when Amy had passed around a box of assorted cakes from the nearby bakery, she was feeling decidedly queasy again and couldn't face eating a cake herself. She checked with Sue and was told there had been no phone calls for her while she was away. She rang Pam in her department and cancelled their arrangement for the Marquee, as she was feeling too ill.

"I always seem to get ill on my birthday," she moaned to Pam, "it's just not fair."

"Never mind, Bat, we'll have to celebrate your birthday when you're feeling better."

Amy staggered home after work and collapsed into bed. After a night of sickness, the next morning her mother brought her experience as an ex-nurse to the fore and took Amy's temperature. Finding it high, she diagnosed a probable case of grumbling appendicitis. "I'll go and phone for the doctor," she said, "this has gone on long enough."

Amy felt too ill to argue. The doctor arrived late morning, examined her and told her she had gastric flu. He gave her some medicine that tasted dire but she had no choice other than to persevered with it.

"That's never gastric flu," Mum observed as she tidied Amy's bed. "You've always been prone to bouts of grumbling appendicitis." She was unconvinced that the doctor's diagnosis was correct and felt sure she knew best. She left the room with a final "Pah!" of contempt.

Saturday morning, feeling a little better, Amy rose from her sick bed. Pam arrived late morning and gave her the Tamla Motown LP that she wanted which cheered Amy up immensely. "Let's play it now," she said excitedly fumbling with the arm of the record player. Then she had an idea. "How about we stay up town all night tonight?" After being cooped up in bed she desperately wanted to get out again.

"Are you sure you're feeling up to it?" Pam asked doubtfully. "You've been pretty ill."

"I'll be OK. I'll tell my parents that I'm staying at your house tonight."

"In that case I'd better head back home soon to convince my suspicious mother that I'll be staying here tonight," Pam said with a sigh adding, "parents do make life difficult."

"If only we had our own flat in London, Tibs, we would be able to do exactly as we like."

"Yeah, but I can't see my parents ever agreeing to that!" Pam said emphatically.

After Pam had left, Amy made a point of telling her mother how well she felt. "I'm absolutely fine - back to normal in fact," she insisted, "so I've arranged to go to a dance with Tibs this evening not far from her house so I'll be staying at hers tonight."

Her mother eyed her dubiously. "It's far too soon for you to be going out dancing. Besides you've still got medicine to take."

"I'll take it with me," Amy said and dashed off upstairs to get ready before her mother had time to put her foot down.

She met Pam on the train to London. Pam grinned as she climbed into the compartment.

"It's all organised. My mother thinks I'll be at yours tonight."

"Great! We'll have a terrific time. I've still got some blues left from last weekend."

"Er, I'm not too keen on taking anything, Bat."

"Oh, come on Tibs, if I take some then I'll want you to do the same else I'll be dancing all night and you'll be flaking out."

"I'll see. What'll you do if Len puts in an appearance tonight and you're with Mick?"

Amy shrugged. "I don't really care what Len thinks - he can like it or lump it."

"Sounds as if you've gone off him," Pam said taking out a comb and tugging it through her long hair.

"I was never all that keen in the first place."

When they arrived at the Scene they found the club still fairly empty so they went into the ladies, which was also empty, and Amy produced the small packet of pills from her handbag. "Let's take a few each," she said running the cold tap over the sink.

"I suppose a few won't do any harm," Pam said reluctantly.

"We'll enjoy ourselves a lot more, especially in the early hours," Amy said carefully dividing them into two lots next to the sink.

Back in the club they had a couple of dances and then Mick, Dick and several others including Eric came in. Mick and Dick were both in a mad mood and Amy suspected they had been taking pills by the way they kept messing around. Mick whirled Amy onto the dance floor and tried to do a tango but she quickly subdued him into a slow smooch instead. She could see Pam getting irritated with Dick. He was once again trying to tickle her and she kept hitting him.

Amy found the pills were having no effect so she asked Pam in a whisper how she was feeling.

"No different to normal," Pam whispered back, "maybe we need some more."

Amy noticed Graham with a group of his mates down near the snack bar. "I'll go and see if I can score," she hissed in Pam's ear.

The club was filling up now. She made her way through the dancers and tapped Graham on the arm. He turned round and smiled at her.

"Watcha Graham. By the way, thanks for rescuing Len from those yobs last Sunday morning."

"That's OK - glad I could help," Graham said diffidently.

"Er - any chance you can get hold of some more blues for me?"

Graham shook his head. "Sorry love, but I haven't seen my mate who gets them. He might show up later - if he does I'll come and find you."

"OK - thanks," Amy said and then squeezed between the dancers back to where the others were chatting in a huddle. Pam looked meaningfully at Amy who just shook her head. They danced with the boys for the rest of the evening and Amy was relieved that Len didn't put in an appearance to complicate things. Later the girls decided they would prefer to go down the Flamingo on their own.

When the Flamingo was due to open, they told Mick and Dick they were going home and insisted they would be fine walking to the station without them. Amy got the impression that Mick was relieved at not having to turn out and take her to catch her train.

They walked round to Wardour Street and joined the queue waiting to get in the all-nighter.

"They didn't seem to realise how late it is," Pam remarked, "our last train home left nearly an hour ago."

"I'm sure they're both blocked tonight," Amy said, "so there's no way they'd bother to try and calculate train times."

The girls were pleased to see Chris Farlow topping the bill and they found some space on the crowded floor to dance.

At around 2a.m. Amy suggested they pop back to the Scene. "We can surprise Mick and Dick and see what they are up to when they think we are safely tucked up in our beds at home."

"Maybe that's not a good idea, knowing those two," Pam said as she followed Amy up the stairs and out into the cool night air, which struck chilly after the stuffy, heat downstairs.

They walked into the Scene and scanned the dancing crowd; then Pam gave a gasp and nudged Amy. "Look over there. It's Dick and the two-timing swine is dancing with some blonde girl," she hissed.

"You were right, Tibs," Amy said, "maybe this wasn't such a good idea. I wonder what Mick is up to?" She studied the figures huddled in the shadows along the walls; some sitting on benches in the alcoves, others standing around in groups. She finally recognised Mick in an alcove. He was chatting to Eric, which relieved Amy. She knew Dick was going to cop it from Pam. She threaded her way over to the alcove and tapped Mick on the shoulder.

"Surprise!" she yelled. He turned round and his mouth fell open. "At least I haven't caught you with your arms around some floozy," she said with a grin.

"As if I would," Mick said trying to look hurt.

"Unlike Dick!" Amy added meaningfully turning to check what Dick was up to. She saw him heading in their direction with the blonde following behind him.

Pam had followed Amy over but now she had cold feet and couldn't face a confrontation with Dick and this girl. She grabbed Amy's arm. "C'mon, let's get out of here," she said and dragged Amy off to the exit.

As they reached the top of the stairs Amy heard her name being called. It was Mick hurrying to catch her up. Eric was behind him.

"Don't go getting the wrong idea about Dick," Mick said earnestly, "just because he was dancing with some girl - it didn't mean anything."

"They looked pretty cosy to me, the way they were smooching around together," Pam said bitterly. She turned to Amy. "C'mon Bat, let's go."

"Hang on a minute," Mick said putting an arm around Amy, "not so quick. Why don't we go and sit in Eric's car and have a chat?"

"I've got some gear if you're interested," Eric offered. Amy glanced at Pam and then agreed as

Eric's big old convertible was only parked a few yards away. The four of them climbed in. Mick and Amy in the back seat with Eric and Pam in the front. Amy handed round her fags.

"I've got some dubes," Eric said, "they're supposed to be for some kid but I can let you have them if you like."

"I think we should," Pam said decisively, surprising Amy, "I'll give you the money for them Eric, 'cause Amy bought the last lot."

Amy suspected Pam just wanted something to cheer herself up for the rest of the night. Eric handed over a small packet to Pam. She opencd it and counted out ten pills.

"There's five each, Bat," she said passing half of them back to Amy.

"I shall need a drink to swallow these," Amy said peering at the blue pills in her hand.

"I'll pop down to the snack bar and get you one," Mick volunteered and dived out of the car.

"Dick's not himself tonight," Eric said sounding slightly apologetic, "I haven't seen him so blocked before. I think he's taken more pills than usual."

"I thought he was being more irritating than normal earlier this evening," Pam said coldly.

"Don't be too tough on him - I know he's very fond of you."

"Well he's really blown it now. Can't care all that much for me if he's canoodling with someone else the moment my back is turned!"

Just then the door opened and Mick got in holding a bottle of coke.

"Here you are," he said handing the bottle to Amy. "I bumped into Dick - he was wondering where we were, so I told him that you'd seen him with the blonde girl. He looked a bit sheepish and slunk away to the gents."

"Serves him right!" Pam said turning to take the coke bottle from Amy after she had taken her pills.

"She's welcome to him 'cause I've definitely finished with him." She tossed the pills into her mouth and took a swig from the bottle.

"What's going on outside?" Mick asked pointing to a group of Mods hovering near the front of the car.

"Looks like they're busy rolling joints on my bonnet," Eric said with a chuckle, "good job there's no police around to raid the place tonight."

"It's time we were getting back to the 'Mingo," Pam said opening the door and stepping out.

"Why not stay here at the Scene with me?" Mick whispered in Amy's ear.

"'Cos Pam doesn't want to meet up with Dick," Amy whispered back, "and besides we've paid for the all-night session and Chris Farlow still has another turn to do on stage."

Amy gave Mick a quick kiss goodbye and he arranged to pick her up from her house Sunday afternoon at three o'clock.

She and Pam returned to the humid smoky darkness of the Flamingo to enjoy Chris Farlow's gravelly voice singing more R&B numbers. After he had left the stage, the girls decided to pop along to the Coffee An for a drink.

They took their cups of instant muddy-looking coffee to a table round the corner beneath the low-arched ceiling. The place was packed and they had just sat down when a boy with a posh accent asked if he might share their table. He sat opposite Amy and was joined by a friend carrying two cups of coffee who sounded equally posh. They seemed somewhat incongruous sitting in this scruffy basement coffee bar chatting about their maters and paters. Amy glanced at Pam and could tell she was having difficulty keeping a straight face. The boys included the girls in their conversation and it transpired that they both lived in mansion flats in Chelsea. One of them went over to the jukebox and selected a couple of Bob Dylan tracks.

"I've got all his records - he's fantastic," he said as the jukebox started playing 'Blowin' in the Wind'. He proceeded to treat Pam and Amy to a monologue on the wonders of Bob Dylan and his unique style of music.

Amy could feel the pills starting to take effect and needed to get back to the Flamingo for some serious dancing. "Er, I'm sorry but we have to leave now," she said getting up and pushing Pam towards the wooden steps at the entrance round the corner. They were relieved to escape up and out into the cool night air. "Thought we'd never get away from that Bob Dylan fanatic," Amy said taking two sticks of chewing gum out of her cigarette packet and giving one to Pam, "how are you feeling?"

"Great!" Pam exclaimed and stuffed the chewing gum into her mouth, "let's go and dance the rest of the night away."

At 6 a.m. the Flamingo closed so Pam and Amy walked to the Last Chance in the Strand to continue dancing until 9 o'clock. On their way they bumped into Dell and his mate from Margate. Amy introduced them to Pam and they chatted briefly. The boys said they had enjoyed a great night over at the Marquee where T Bone Walker had topped the bill.

The girls found the Last Chance packed as most of the clubs closed at 6 a.m. so nearly everyone headed for there. Pam and Amy were soon dancing again though only to records now. Then Amy made the devastating discovery that her handbag had been stolen.

"Let's go and tell the bouncers on the door," Pam said dragging Amy by the arm.

When they explained what had happened the bouncers immediately went into action. They called over the manager and he instructed two of them to guard the exit while he went and found a couple of flash lights.

"There's been a spate of handbag thefts tonight," he told the girls and then he and another bouncer started a thorough search with Amy and Pam tagging along behind. Eventually the manager pulled a bag out from behind a bench in a corner with a yell of triumph.

"Is this your bag, love?" he asked holding it up. Amy recognised it straight away and was thrilled to get it back.

"Thought I'd never see it again!" she exclaimed with relief and quickly checked the contents to see what was missing. She was surprised to find everything appeared to be there.

"Just my money has been nicked, as expected," she said examining her purse, "but I think there was only about a shilling in it so they didn't get much." Amy thanked the manager and the bouncers for all their help and then the girls resumed their dancing, being sure to keep a very close hold on their handbags.

Some boys came over and joined them. They chatted between the records and introduced themselves as John and Curly. They were there with a couple of other mates. When the Last Chance finally closed they offered to buy the girls some tea and took them to the same tatty cafe that Nick had taken them to previously.

Over mugs of tea, the boys asked where the girls lived and offered to give them a lift home in their van which they gladly accepted.

The van was parked in a back street not far away. It didn't take long to find and they all piled in. It was pretty old and grotty but the boys were good company so Pam and Amy were prepared to put up with a bit of discomfort in the messy interior.

The van reached Holborn and then got a puncture. The girls stood huddled together on the pavement watching the boys trying to jack up the van and change the wheel. As they waited in the chilly morning air, Amy began to feel decidedly nauseous. "I hope my gastric flu isn't coming back again," she said anxiously and gave a shiver.

"You do look deathly pale," Pam observed peering at Amy's face.

"I don't think I'll be able to go all the way home in that van - I'm not a good passenger at the best of times."

With the wheel successfully changed, Amy asked the boys to drop them off at New Cross station where they could catch a train home. The van drew up outside the station and Amy was relieved to stumble out into the fresh air.

"Maybe we'll see you at Brighton in two weeks' time - that's if you're going," John said leaning out of the driver's window, "everyone will be there so it should be fantastic."

"We haven't decided yet," Pam said, "but if we do go, we'll look out for you."

As Pam and Amy arrived on the platform a train steamed past on the opposite side heading for the coast. A yell from one of its carriages made Amy look up and she caught sight of Dell waving to her from a window. She managed a brief wave back and then the train was gone. Their train pulled in a few minutes later and they climbed into an empty compartment.

"I think we should definitely go to Brighton," Amy declared, "the boys were right - it'll be great and being Easter, we'll have extra time to spend there."

"That's if I can think up a convincing lie to tell my parents because I know they will never let me go there," Pam said disconsolately, "and also if you're OK by then - you really do look ill, Bat."

"Thanks," Amy said mustering a weak smile, "I'm sure I'll be fine. We've just got to come up with a good cover story to keep our flippin' parents happy."

Amy arrived home at midday and tried to give the impression of being fit and healthy as she breezed in and dashed up to her room. She still had some medicine left so she took a dose of it and lay on her bed - its comforting dip hugging her and making her feel drowsy as the effect of the pills gradually wore off.

After dozing for a couple of hours she felt a little brighter so got washed and changed ready for Mick who arrived in his car just after 3 p.m. He drove Amy over to his house where they played records. His mum arrived home at teatime and made them some beans on toast. Amy liked Mick's mum. She worked at the local hospital as a nurse, putting in overtime whenever possible to keep herself busy now that she was a widow. She tactfully left them alone in the lounge with their music but as the evening wore on so Amy began to feel ill again. At 9 o'clock she asked Mick to take her home.

"Maybe it's those dubes disagreeing with you," he suggested as he drove her home.

Amy shook her head. "I don't think so - it's that rotten dose of gastric flu. I'll be OK once I've taken some more grotty medicine."

Mick dropped Amy off at her home and said he'd see her Tuesday down the Scene. Indoors she went straight to bed with a hot water bottle to cuddle.

She still felt rough all day at work on Monday as she battled through the piles of agents' accounts and at lunchtime couldn't face eating a thing. She came home that evening and went straight to bed.

Next day she felt a lot better so she and Pam headed for the Scene that evening. "By the way, Bat, dad told me that your dad called in at Macfisheries to check up with him on your story about staying at my house last weekend," Pam said as the two friends strolled along with arms linked.

"What a snide!" Amy exclaimed.

"Dad didn't seem too bothered about me not staying at your house. It's mum who would hit the roof so I just hope he's not going to tell her."

"Well so far dad hasn't said a word to me about it and I'm sure if mum knew I'd been lying, she wouldn't be able to keep quiet."

Down in the dimly lit Scene Amy spotted Eric and a few other mates hovering near the record booth. There was no sign of Mick or Dick, which relieved Pam.

"All day I've been trying to decide exactly what I'm going to say to him tonight if he has the nerve to show his face," she said as she followed Amy, "but he is definitely going to get a right rollicking."

Eric saw Amy and grinned at her. "I've got a message for you from Mick," he said.

"Don't tell me he's packing me up!" Amy exclaimed in mock horror holding up her hands.

"Mick's been off work ill since yesterday. He's got a tummy bug of some sort. He wants you to give him a ring on Thursday - he's hoping he'll be back at work by then."

"If he's caught my gastric flu he'll probably be holed up for a week."

"And where's Dick tonight?" Pam demanded.

"I think he's keeping a low profile. He knows he's blown it with you."

"Huh, he can't keep avoiding me," Pam said crossly.

"Do you girls need any blues?" Eric asked wanting to change the subject. "I've got one packet of ten doubles if you're interested."

"We could do with some for Easter," Amy remarked glancing at Pam who just nodded. They paid Eric for the pills and then went for a dance.

Half an hour later as the girls emerged from the ladies they found Len with a mate waiting for them. Len grinned sheepishly.

"It's been a while since I last saw you," he said.

"I've been ill," Amy retorted coldly adding, "which you would have known if you had taken the trouble to ring me."

"I heard that you were going back out with your old boyfriend so I kept away," he explained, then asked, "is it true?"

Amy just shrugged. "It might be," she said offhandedly, "oh, and by the way, you still owe me ten shillings for those pills you had off me."

Len fumbled in his pocket and produced a ten shilling note. "Sorry, I forgot," he said handing her the money. He hesitated and then asked, "er - any chance of a dance?"

"No, I don't think so," Amy said and hurried off to catch up with Pam who was heading for the exit. They walked round to the Pic for a coffee and when they returned to the Scene there was no sign of Len and his mate - much to Amy's relief.

"At least you're no longer two-timing which makes for an easier life," Pam declared as they walked out into the middle of the floor to dance their Mod jive.

"It was probably best not to dance with him in case Eric saw us and told Mick," Amy replied.

During her lunch hour on Thursday, Amy rang Mick from a phone booth in the basement. He was back at work and feeling better though he was convinced Amy had given him her gastric flu, which she stoutly denied. They arranged to go to the flicks Friday evening.

Mick collected Amy from her house in his car and drove to Welling. 'The Ipcress File' was showing and they both enjoyed the film. Afterwards he brought her home but Amy didn't invite him in for coffee knowing that her parents would be lurking around. They sat in the car chatting between bouts of kissing and cuddling.

"It seems odd just the two of us going to the flicks," Mick commented.

"Is Dick still seeing that blonde?"

"I don't think so but I haven't seen him since Saturday. I'm pretty sure he still wants to go out with Pam."

"Well she's very unforgiving where unfaithfulness is concerned. He's only got himself to blame."

"Oh come on! He was only dancing with that girl, and you must admit, it was pretty sneaky of you two to creep back down the Scene last Saturday to check up on us after you said you were going home."

"Relationships are all about trust," Amy said getting a little annoyed with Mick's attitude, "Dick proved that he can't be trusted, and I'm not totally convinced that you were all that innocent. Maybe if we'd arrived a little later we'd have caught you smooching with someone too!"

Mick shook his head despairingly. "I can't win with you can I?"

Amy relented with a smile. "OK - innocent until proven guilty," she said snuggling up to him. She realised she was being a right hypocrite after two-timing him with Len. She just hoped he wouldn't find out because she would never hear the end of it.

Saturday night Pam and Amy met up with Mick down the Scene. There was no Dick or Len to make the situation awkward. Pat and Mary were there but Mary didn't stay for long as she was meeting Trevor over the road at the Red Lion. "He would rather have a quiet drink in the pub than bop to loud music down here," Mary said with a grin adding, "what an old frump I'm lumbered with!"

Pam and Pat went off for a dance. Amy spotted Graham and his mates so she went over to chat with him briefly while Mick was visiting the gents. She asked if he was intending to go to Brighton at Easter.

"You bet!" he said, "there's a crowd of us will be going down there."

Amy felt a tug on her arm. It was Mick keen to go round to the Piccadilly for a coffee. She suspected he was jealous of her chatting to other blokes. Out in the yard they paused to examine the repair on Pat's Mini and agreed it looked as good as new again.

"I expect daddy footed the bill for that," Amy said feeling a pang of envy. "I was thinking of sending off for a provisional licence so I can learn to drive."

"That's a good idea," Mick said enthusiastically, "if you like I'll give you some driving lessons in my car," he offered.

Amy sighed. "But I don't think there's any point as I'll never be able to afford a car for years."

"You could still learn ready for when you do get a car."

"I'll probably have forgotten all I've learnt by the time I get a car," Amy said with a laugh, "meanwhile it's buses and trains."

Mick accompanied Amy and Pam part way home on the train, alighting at his station, and arranged to collect Amy in his car Sunday afternoon.

At 3 o'clock next day Amy stood in the bay window of her lounge watching for Mick. As his car pulled up by the kerb she hurried outside and crossed the green. He took her back to his house as his mother was out at work. They played records and Mick persuaded Amy to cook some tea. After rifling through the contents of the fridge they opted for sausages and fried eggs.

"I think this is the only reason you bring me home," Amy said poking at the sizzling sausages in the pan while Mick, with his arms around her waist, was nuzzling her neck. "You'd go hungry if there was no-one to cook you a meal."

"I'd soon rustle up a sandwich," Mick mumbled through Amy's hair, "I'm a pretty mean sandwich maker."

"Well make yourself useful and butter some bread to go with this," Amy said transferring the food onto two plates.

They sat on the settee watching telly with trays on their laps.

"Are you planning on going down to Brighton?" Amy asked. Everyone seemed to be talking about the coming Bank Holiday and yet Mick hadn't mentioned it once.

"No way!" he said emphatically, "and if you've got any sense you'll keep well away from there too." It struck Amy that Mick was being unusually sensible.

"But it'll be a laugh," Amy protested, "there'll be hundreds and probably thousands going."

"Yes, and there will be nearly as many cops too who will arrest you as soon as look at you. I almost found myself arrested when I went to Clacton and I wasn't even doing anything. I was just standing around but the cops thought I looked suspicious. Property was getting trashed and they needed to make some arrests and weren't fussy who they nabbed. Eventually they released me with just a warning but it was no joke and I don't fancy a repeat of that fiasco."

Amy let the subject drop, realising she wouldn't be able to change Mick's mind but she remained convinced that Brighton was going to be exciting and she was determined to go.

At work on Tuesday Amy received a surprise phone call from Len. He wanted to take her to Brighton.

"Me and Trevor are going down there on the Sunday morning and wondered if you and Pam wanted to come with us?"

"Trevor?" Amy asked in surprise, "why isn't he taking Mary?"

"They've fallen out - had a bit of an argument."

"Mary hasn't mentioned it to me," Amy said suspiciously, "he's not wasting any time trying to home in on Pam."

"Well he does fancy her, and since Mary has given him the elbow, he's now a free agent."

"I shall check with Mary and if she doesn't mind then me and Pam will meet up with you down the Scene on Sunday morning," Amy said feeling fairly sure that Pam wouldn't object to the arrangement.

At lunchtime in the canteen Amy told Pam about Len's phone call. She quite liked the idea of going to Brighton with Trevor. "I don't want to upset Mary though," she said after giving it some thought.

"She'll be coming down here any minute so I'll ask her," Amy said.

"Just make sure she has definitely finished with Trevor, but maybe it would be best not to mention about the weekend in Brighton."

When Mary and Jeanette joined them Amy casually asked after Trevor.

Mary gave a contemptuous snort. "Don't talk to me about him - he has really pissed me off - the bugger!"

"Why? What has happened?" Amy asked.

"My brothers saw him out on Sunday with some girl on his arm. When I rang him up and asked him who she was, he denied it. Said he was indoors all day. I didn't believe him so I told him to get lost."

"Maybe your brothers were mistaken," Pam suggested.

"Nah, they know what Trevor looks like and were positive it was him."

"So you've really finished with him?" Pam asked, wanting to clarify the situation.

"You bet I have! And good riddance!" Mary's dark eyes flashed as she took a long drag on her cigarette and blew the smoke out forcefully through her nostrils reminding Amy of an angry dragon.

Now they had heard Len's news confirmed by Mary, Amy and Pam could make their plans for the coming weekend. They left Mary and Jeanette to head for the toilets.

"If we're going to Brighton with Trevor and Len, what will you tell Mick?" Pam asked as they stood in front of the washbasins brushing their hair in the mirror.

"Mick is a problem. He doesn't want me to go - I'm sure he'll try and talk me out of it so I think my best option is to simply finish with him. I'm meeting him tonight."

"I don't fancy going to the Scene tonight," Pam said as they emerged from the toilets and waited by the lifts, "I think I'll go home and wash my hair instead."

"I shan't be hanging around once I've packed him up. I'll probably get an early train home," Amy said as they entered the lift and pressed the buttons for their respective floors.

As Amy turned into Great Windmill Street that evening on her way to the Scene in Ham yard, she saw a familiar figure ahead of her. It was Mick so she hurried to catch him up.

"No mates tonight?" she asked grabbing his arm.

He grinned at her. "Most of them are broke so I came by train but Eric might come down later."

"Let's go for a coffee," Amy suggested.

In the Pic Amy sat staring into her coffee cup wondering how to say what needed to be said.

"Is something bothering you?" Mick asked noticing her subdued manner.

"I've decided I can't see you any more," Amy blurted out. She wanted to get it over with.

Mick looked at her momentarily lost for words. "Why?" he finally asked.

"Because I'm seeing someone else and don't want to two-time you." Amy had decided that a half-truth was the best policy. Mick looked crestfallen but quickly put on a brave face.

"Oh well, it was good while it lasted," he said. Then as an afterthought asked, "are you sure Pam didn't put you up to this because she's not seeing Dick any more?"

"Of course not!" Amy said indignantly, "I've told you the reason and it's got nothing to do with Pam. Anyway I'd better go." She wanted to get away before Mick thought of awkward questions to ask her about this new boyfriend. She finished her coffee and stood up. Mick walked back with her to the Scene where they parted company. He went down the stone stairs to the club while Amy headed for the station feeling waves of relief washing over her now that she was finally free for the weekend ahead. She felt no regrets so concluded that she couldn't have had any emotional ties to him.

With Easter imminent, Amy went to the market in Leather Lane next day in her lunch hour to buy some material to make a bag to take with her to Brighton. She found some suitable blue hessian and bought a length of it.

Next day, being Good Friday there was no work so she sat in the lounge sewing up the shoulder bag and listening to her records. Pam and Amy had decided to tell their parents they were going to Great Yarmouth as this was well away from Brighton. Amy was surprised when her parents accepted her story without a third degree.

"We don't mind so long as you aren't going anywhere near Brighton," her mother told her adding, "there will be a load of trouble there this weekend and I don't want you getting mixed up in it." Amy eventually managed to reassure her mother.

The next afternoon she met Pam on the train to London. They were both wearing their suedes and Levis.

"I like the bag, Bat," Pam said sitting down on the seat next to Amy and examining the hessian shoulder bag.

"Thanks - it was quite easy to make. Did you convince your parents that we're going to Great Yarmouth, Tibs?"

"I think so," Pam said sounding a little unsure, "mum never believes what I tell her as a matter of course. She just looked at me suspiciously and then left to go to work."

"Well, we're free of parents now for a few days which is great," Amy declared handing Pam a fag.

"It should be a good night with Zoot Money playing at the all-night session down the Flamingo," Pam said, adding, "when are we seeing Trevor and Len?"

"I arranged to meet Len down the Scene at around five o'clock tomorrow morning - I didn't want him hanging around me all night."

The girls wandered along Oxford Street and then headed for the Macabre coffee house to while away the time until the Scene opened.

They found it less crowded than normal for a Saturday night. "I expect a lot of people have left for the coast already," Pam remarked peering around the dimly lit club, "can't see anyone I know."

"That's probably a good thing," Amy said, "I don't fancy bumping into Mick and I don't suppose you want to see Dick either. C'mon, let's go and dance. We'll save the pills for later."

By ten o'clock they were beginning to flag from non-stop jiving and bopping so they went into the toilets to take the doubles they had bought from Eric.

The toilet was deserted. "I doubt if these will last us all night," Pam said studying the five tablets that Amy had handed her.

"Maybe we can score down the 'Mingo," Amy said producing a small bottle of water from her bag, "I brought this as I thought it would make taking the pills easier than trying to scoop water from the tap."

They each swallowed the pills with a swig of water from the bottle though in Amy's case it took five swigs, as she couldn't get the hang of swallowing whole tablets. She refilled the bottle at the sink, screwed the lid on and replaced it in her bag. "That's in case we score later on," she told Pam.

At one o'clock they went round to the Flamingo in Wardour Street and were pleased to find only a short queue. "See, Tibs, it pays to wait an hour then we don't have to queue for so long."

Inside they ran into Marilyn Cooper, an old school friend and her sister. They stood chatting to them near the cloakroom for a while and then pushed their way through the crowd to get near the stage.

As they had anticipated, it was a terrific atmosphere once Zoot Money and his band started thumping out their raunchy R&B numbers. The loud music pulsated around the confined space of the underground club enticing Pam and Amy to dance.

By 3 o'clock the effect of the pills was starting to wear off. They were squeezing through the crowd en route to the ladies when Amy felt a tap on her arm. A black boy grinned and leaned towards her.

"D'you want any gear?" he asked, "I've got some here if you and your mate are interested." Amy glanced down at the small packet he was holding.

"What are they?" she asked suspiciously.

"Specklers - ten will cost you a pound."

"I'll give you ten shillings for them," Amy said feeling a little irritated by his blatant profiteering.

"Make it fifteen bob and they're yours."

"Oh, OK," Amy said reluctantly and moved across to the side of the room where their transaction could be conducted more discreetly. She fished in her bag for the money and quickly exchanged it for the packet. As soon as he had the money he melted away into the crowd before Amy had a chance to check the contents of the packet. She looked around; there was no sign of Pam. She had continued to the ladies unaware that Amy was no longer following behind her. Amy pushed her way through the throng and caught up with her inside the toilet. The place was packed. Pam looked relieved to see Amy coming through the door.

"Thought I'd lost you," she said," where did you get to?"

Amy pulled Pam into a corner and quietly explained what had happened.

"You'd better take a look at what you've bought," Pam whispered. Amy nodded and went into an empty cubicle and locked the door. She carefully opened the packet and counted ten pills. They were blue and speckled so she assumed they were OK. She took out the bottle of water and swallowed half of the pills but it took the entire contents of the bottle to wash them down this time. Outside Amy could hear the chatter of numerous voices. She couldn't refill the bottle at a sink, as it would look odd. Pam would need water to take her half of the pills so there was only one option left. Amy flushed the toilet and held the bottle down the pan to half fill it, hoping the water was drinkable. She decided not to tell Pam what she had done. 'What she doesn't know, won't hurt her,' Amy thought, trying to convince herself.

She emerged from the cubicle and discreetly passed the pills and water to Pam.

"I think they're OK," she whispered as Pam went inside and locked the door. A couple of minutes later Pam came out and handed Amy the empty bottle.

"I was thirsty so I finished it off," she said.

"Let's get back out there," Amy said and pulled the door open.

Half an hour later she was trying to ignore the waves of nausea that kept sweeping over her. "Can we sit down for a while, Tibs," Amy said and made her way to where there were two empty seats down the front by the stage.

Pam sat down beside her. "What's up?" she asked.

"Are you feeling OK?" Amy asked, "only I don't think those pills were much good."

"I still feel about the same really; they haven't made any difference."

"I think he must have sold us some duff gear 'cos I'm feeling a bit sick," Amy said grimly.

They sat listening to the music and enjoyed watching Zoot Money performing the second part of his session. Sitting there reminded Amy of the last time she had sat in these red upholstered seats watching Zoot Money in the early hours of the morning only then she had been with her beloved Rob. She found the thought depressing so pushed it out of her mind.

Once Zoot Money had left the stage for the last time to deafening applause and whistles it was time for the girls to make their way back to the Scene and wait for Len. Amy felt a little better once she was out in the cool fresh air. It helped to clear her head and calm the nausea. She was puzzled why Pam hadn't been affected in the same way especially as she had drunk the water from the toilet but Amy thought it best to say nothing.

Just as the Scene was closing Len finally appeared wearing his long orange leather coat.

"Where's Trevor?" Pam asked expecting to see him come in behind Len.

"He wants us to call for him at his house," Len explained, adding, "Trevor doesn't like to miss out on his beauty sleep."

They caught a bus to Chelsea and Len took them along a couple of streets until they arrived outside what looked like a large block of flats set back from the road with an expanse of grass in front.

"This is where Trevor lives," Len said leading the way along a path at the side that led through a door into a foyer. Inside there were a couple of lifts. Len pressed the button and a lift door opened.

"We want the first floor," he told the girls following them into the lift. Amy pressed the button numbered one and the doors slid shut.

"These are all two storey maisonettes and are owned by Scotland Yard," Len said, "only policemen's families are allowed to live here."

"We'd better be careful then, Bat," Pam said with a grin, "don't want to find ourselves arrested for being in possession of drugs."

"You needn't worry - there are some right thieving buggers living here according to Trevor!" Len said with a chuckle.

The lift came to a halt and the door slid open. Len stepped out onto a wide balcony that overlooked the grass at the front. He walked along past a couple of front doors and then rang a doorbell.

After a few minutes the door was unlocked; it opened an inch and an eye peered out. When Trevor recognised Len he pulled the door open and invited everyone in. He was wearing pyjamas and a dressing gown and his hair stuck out in all directions. He had obviously just woken up.

"It's far too early," he complained in a hushed voice, "and don't make any more noise - I don't want to wake the olds." He took them into the lounge and told them to wait quietly while he dressed. "You can make yourselves some coffee in the kitchen if you like," he said before creeping back upstairs.

"I'll go and put the kettle on," Amy volunteered. She wasn't really thirsty but wanted to be doing something to pass the time. Pam came into the kitchen too and sat at the small kitchen table while Amy filled the kettle and hunted in the cupboards for mugs.

She was just pouring the water into the mugs when Trevor reappeared dressed in jeans and a polo shirt, his hair now tamed and combed neatly. He helped Amy carry the mugs through to the lounge and Pam brought the sugar bowl.

They sat sipping coffee and discussing their plans for the day ahead. After twenty minutes Trevor stood up and went out to the hallway and returned carrying a black leather coat.

"It's time we made a move," he said, "I think I can hear my mother getting up."

They quickly finished their coffee and left the maisonette. Victoria station was only a short bus ride away and they were soon on the platform having purchased their tickets. There was quite a crowd of Mods waiting to board the Brighton train.

"I need the ladies - come with me Bat," Pam said tugging Amy by the arm. They hurried off and found the toilets empty. Amy brushed her hair in front of the mirror while Pam went into a cubicle. Just then a tall lady came in wearing a skirt and blouse. The blouse had some of the buttons undone down the back. As she attempted to apply lipstick somewhat haphazardly, she spoke to Amy in a dark brown voice. "Oh dear, I'm late and had to dress in a hurry. Would you be a love and do up my buttons - I couldn't reach them all." Amy obliged but she was now scrutinising the woman more closely and noticed how she wobbled on her high heels, had a large muscular build and very hairy legs. There was also a hint of five o'clock shadow and a pronounced Adam's apple. Amy realised this was obviously no woman, but a transvestite. As soon as Pam emerged from the cubicle Amy grabbed her and dragged her outside before she had a chance to wash her hands. Amy explained why she didn't want to be in the ladies a moment longer and the two of them giggled all the way back to the platform and told the boys of their encounter.

"Do you realise, Bat, we could have been assaulted," Pam said.

"I expect he was pretty harmless," Trevor said trying to reassure her.

"Well he didn't have a clue about how to put on make-up," Amy said as they climbed into a compartment. They didn't have it to themselves for very long because it soon filled up. The other passengers were a boisterous, rowdy bunch of Mods who started singing "I'm in with the In Crowd' and kept up the noisy unmelodic songs for most of the journey.

"My younger brother, Kevin, said he might come down to Brighton later on today and try to find us," Trevor said having difficulty to make himself heard above the singing and yelling.

"I didn't know you had a younger brother," Amy said.

"He's got two," Len informed her.

"Kevin didn't fancy getting up so early on a Sunday to come with us," Trevor explained, adding, "the lazy git."

The train arrived at Brighton and crowds of Mods poured from the carriages to join others milling around the main entrance. Out in the street hordes of smart scooters festooned with mirrors and fox-tails meandered up and down along the seafront. Mods on the pavement were calling out to their mates on scooters who were yelling back at them. Scooters that weren't being driven were parked three or four abreast in the parking bays in front of the large hotels that took prime position overlooking the sea.

Pam and Amy hung on to Trevor and Len so as not to get split up in the crush. The promenade on the other side of the road was one mass of Mods.

"Let's go over there," Len said and crossed the road dodging the traffic with the others following.

Amy noticed the police were everywhere lining the seafront on both sides of the road. The local police wore white helmets, which Amy thought looked very cool for summer. Alongside them were other forces drafted in to help out. They found themselves with no choice but to move along with the crowd. After a while Amy spotted an empty bench on the promenade.

"Let's have a rest for a while," she said to Pam and tugged Len's arm.

No sooner had they sat down than a policeman appeared and ordered them to keep moving along.

"What a cheek!" Amy exclaimed indignantly, "we've got every right to sit on the promenade if we want to."

"Every other day except today," Trevor said as they walked on. "Their policy seems to be: Keep everyone on the move."

"I think we should go and find a cafe," Len suggested, "I'm starving - it must be the ozone. The others agreed so they crossed back over the road and found a side street that led away from the seafront. Before long they were sitting round a table and tucking into fish and chips in a bright, clean cafe where the food was well cooked although Amy and Pam didn't have much of an appetite so Len and Trevor finished their meals for them.

"We can't wander up and down the promenade all afternoon," Pam reasoned as they emerged back onto the street after their meal.

"Let's go and find a space on the beach to sit down," Amy said, "though I doubt your brother will ever find us amongst the crowds 'cos we've not seen anyone yet who we recognise."

"That's his problem. He should have got up in time this morning," Trevor said with a shrug.

They crossed the main road on the seafront and re-joined the throng of Mods being relentlessly made to move along the promenade by the hundreds of policemen. They pushed through the crowd and went down some steps to the pebbly beach. It was packed with people - mostly Mods - but there was the occasional family group bravely trying to enjoy a day at the seaside.

"At least I haven't seen any sign of Rockers on their motorbikes," Len commented as they found a space beside a groyne and sat down.

"Just as well," Trevor said, "Maybe the Greasers have some common sense after all."

"I hope there's not going to be any violence or fighting," Pam said looking uneasy.

"If there is, then we'll have to make sure we keep well away from it," Amy said firmly remembering what Mick had told her.

Up on the promenade the Mods were shouting and chanting. They seemed to be in high spirits despite being persecuted by the police.

"Does your dad know you are down here?" Pam asked Trevor.

"'Course not. I'm not that daft 'cos if I'd told him he would have tried to ban me from coming."

"Our parents think we are having a quiet weekend at Great Yarmouth," Pam said with a giggle.

"Mine don't care where I go so long as I keep out of their way," Len said gloomily.

"Well at least you don't have to worry about making up lies to tell them," Amy said trying to look on the bright side.

The sun shone weakly and a bitter cold wind blew in off the sea making the four of them huddle together for warmth. They had been on the beach for about an hour when a voice behind them said, "Watcha, I've found you at last!"

Amy turned her head and found a gorgeous boy standing behind her. Kevin gave her a dazzling smile of even white teeth as he gazed down at her with enormous soft brown eyes that made her heart give a skip. He was tall, though not as tall as his brother, with broad shoulders. Amy thought his physique was perfection. His brown, slightly wavy hair was neat and immaculately styled as were his clothes. He wore a dark tan jacket, brown trousers and matching shoes. Amy was so overwhelmed by his presence that she didn't immediately notice he wasn't alone. Her heart sank as she now registered that he was with a girl wearing a long black leather coat.

"About time too," Trevor said, "sit down here with us."

They walked round and sat next to Trevor who introduced them. The girl's name turned out to be Pauline.

"We're not staying long," Kevin said glancing back apprehensively at the chanting crowd on the promenade, "we're catching the train back to London in about an hour's time."

"We're going to check out the Brighton nightlife tonight," Len told Kevin, "I don't suppose the nightclubs here will be anything like as good as the Scene though."

Kevin suddenly turned to Trevor. "By the way, bruv, dad seems to know that you're down here. He's been doing his nut!"

"Who told him?" Trevor demanded crossly.

"He must have guessed 'cos I certainly didn't tell him."

"That's all I need," Trevor groaned, "more trouble."

After nearly an hour of lounging on the beach Kevin stood up and announced that it was time to leave. He helped Pauline to her feet. She seemed a rather shy girl who had said hardly a word apart from 'hello' when they arrived. With her mousy shoulder length hair and average looks, Amy couldn't help envying her ability to hook a dishy bloke like Kevin.

After they had left to catch their train, Len got to his feet and stretched. "Let's go and get a coffee," he said, "I need warming up."

They found the Zodiac coffee bar tucked away in a back street. It was packed with noisy Mods but they managed to grab an empty table. The place had a good atmosphere. Music was thumping out of a jukebox so Pam and Amy went over and selected some more tracks and then returned to the boys who had ordered the coffees. They relaxed, the boys telling jokes as they sipped hot cappuccinos from toughened glass cups and enjoyed the music. After whiling away an hour or more, Trevor suggested they check out the club scene.

Leaving the coffee bar, they wandered around the back lanes, which were crowded with Mods doing the same.

"Isn't this Blocker Tony from the Scene heading our way," Amy said pointing to a couple of blokes coming towards them.

"Yeah, you're right," Len said and shouted a 'hi' to Tony as he approached looking stoned out of his head as usual. "Hey, Tony, d'you know where the action is around here tonight?"

Tony smiled and cadged a fag from Trevor. "Two streets over there," he said waving his hand vaguely, "you'll hear the noise coming from the club - it's not bad considering it's not London."

They crossed the road and walked down a turning until they came to a junction. Opposite was the entrance to a nightclub with music throbbing away inside. Groups of Mods hung around outside.

"This must be it," Trevor said glancing up at the neon lights flashing above the open door.

Inside it opened out into a large dimly lit room with lights strobing around the packed dance floor. The music was thumping out of huge speakers. Pam and Amy went off to the ladies to freshen up.

"At least it's warm in here," Amy said tugging a comb through her wind-lashed hair. "Pity we can't afford a B & B for the night."

"We'd better make the most of it and stay here until the club closes," Pam said as she dabbed powder on her nose.

They re-joined the boys and spent the evening dancing with a break for soft drinks at the bar in an adjoining room where they discussed what they were going to do once the club closed.

"I guarantee we're going to be in for a cold night," Trevor surmised. "We'll need to find shelter from that icy cold wind."

Amy gave an involuntary shiver at the thought of the chilly uncomfortable night ahead.

"I remember seeing some upturned boats on the beach," Pam said, "if we got underneath one it would probably be quite cosy."

"That's a brilliant idea!" Trevor exclaimed and gave her a hug.

They returned to the dance floor for the last hour until the club closed at midnight and then reluctantly stepped out into the freezing night air, which hit them with an icy blast after the warmth inside. They made their way back to the moonlit beach and walked along the shingle. The crowds had now dispersed to the trains or to guest-houses. They came to an upturned boat and Trevor gave a knock on the side. A yell of 'piss off' came from inside.

"That one's obviously occupied," Trevor said. They walked on and tapped on two more boats getting a similar response from both.

"Unfortunately we're not the only ones with a good idea," Amy said.

But the next boat that Trevor tapped was silent. He heaved up one side and peered underneath. "It's empty!" he exclaimed with relief, "come on, get under quickly."

They crawled under the boat and found themselves squashed in a fairly confined space but there was enough room to huddle together. They scooped the shingle into a dip in the middle and piled it against the edges to seal up any cracks where a draught might get in.

"It's not too bad in here at all," Len said peering round and trying to adjust his eyes to the darkness.

"This shingle isn't exactly as comfortable as a mattress," Amy moaned, "I'll be black and blue with bruises by the morning."

"It's as good as it gets, so we'll just have to make the most of it," Pam said and turned to snuggle into Trevor's arms. Amy cuddled up to Len but only to keep warm, as she didn't feel like getting into a snogging session with him. She found herself thinking about Kevin. If only it was him she was cuddled up to right now - that would be fantastic.

They had been under the boat for about half an hour when they heard the shingle crunching outside and then one side of the boat was suddenly yanked up.

"Come out of there," commanded a stern voice. There stood two burly policemen silhouetted in the moonlight who weren't going to brook any arguments. Trevor started to protest but then thought better of it. They crawled out into the biting cold wind, which was spotting with rain.

"Move along now, and don't come back," the policeman warned them, "these boats are private property and out of bounds."

They stumbled along on the shingle not sure where to go and eventually came to an area where public gardens rose up against a sheer cliff face across the road from the beach. They crossed the road and followed the narrow meandering path up the cliff. At intervals there were shelters with a bench where tourists could sit and gaze out to sea. They decided to make the most of a bad situation by huddling on one of these benches. But there was no protection from the elements. The wind and rain blew straight in off the sea. They tried turning the bench over and got behind it in a vain attempt to find some shelter but the slatted seat and back did nothing to stop the icy wind from blasting through.

They lay on the ground and the boys gallantly undid their coats so the girls could snuggle up inside. Amy felt almost suffocated by the overwhelming stench of body odour coming from the underarm area of Len's lining inside his coat.

The relentless cold deteriorated into freezing sub-zero temperatures as the night progressed. Amy was sure she had never felt so cold before in her whole life as she did right now on that cliff face overlooking the open sea.

"Bloody hell!" she yelled peering out over the bench, "it's only snowing!" Sure enough mixed in with the rain, snowflakes were being driven in by the wind.

"This is hopeless," Pam said standing up, "my hands and feet are completely numb with the cold. I've got to move around else I shall end up with frost bite."

"Good idea, Tibs," Amy agreed and stood up too, relieved to be breathing fresh air again. "Let's run up and down to get the blood circulating and maybe it'll warm us up."

They left the boys still huddled on the ground and ran along the pathway, stamping their feet and banging their arms and hands on their sides. After ten minutes of this exercise they were breathless but felt a little warmer.

"Who's stupid idea was it to come to Brighton?" Pam demanded breathing heavily as they rested against the upturned bench.

"Well we weren't to know it was going to flippin' well snow at Easter!" Amy said indignantly. Just then a couple of Mods came jogging past wearing parkas. It seemed they had the same idea as Pam for keeping warm. Amy asked if they had the time.

One paused and glanced at his wrist. "It's just after four o'clock," he said adding, "we're in the next shelter further up."

"They are hardly shelters," Amy said scornfully.

"Roll on seven o'clock when Lyons opens up," he said and continued jogging up the path.

"C'mon Bat, let's do a bit more running - I'm still freezing cold," Pam said and started running up the path again. Amy groaned and followed her half-heartedly.

"I don't think I've got the energy, Tibs. What I really need is some sleep but it's just too cold."

"I think Trevor and Len have managed to doze off 'cos they're pretty quiet and I think I heard a snore just now," Pam said.

"Lucky buggers!" Amy said between puffs as she tried to keep up with Pam. "If this sleet gets any heavier it'll ruin our suedes."

After running up and down for ten minutes they returned to the comparative warmth inside Len and Trevor's coats where they were more protected from the weather.

A grey dawn broke in the eastern sky; the rain and snow had stopped now. Amy heard voices and peered over the bench as the same two Mods came walking down the path. They spotted Amy and called out a cheery "hello." "We're gonna wait for Lyons to open," one of them said, "it shouldn't be too long now."

Amy gave Len a shake.

"C'mon Len, I don't know how you manage to sleep on such hard cold ground. Let's get moving."

Pam got up and prodded Trevor who sat up and yawned.

"I haven't slept a wink," Pam said to Amy, "unlike these two. How on earth did they manage it?"

Amy was glad to be on the move again. The icy wind still blasted in off the sea and she desperately wanted to get inside somewhere warm. They followed the two Mods in parkas until they reached the cafe. Although it was Bank Holiday Monday the sign on the door said it would be open at 7a.m. Already there was a queue forming along the pavement. Everyone looked washed out and frozen with the cold. Then a cheer went up as the door was unlocked and they started to move inside.

"You two girls go and grab a table while me and Len fetch the drinks," Trevor said as the cafe quickly started to fill.

The warmth inside the cafe soon restored flagging spirits and the queue at the counter was quick to take advantage of a large tray of hot cross buns. Every time the waitress turned her back to fill the teapot, buns were grabbed and thrust into pockets or thrown across the room. Pam and Amy managed to catch three. Trevor and Len arrived at the table with mugs of tea and pockets bulging with buns. The hot tea and buns were just what they needed after their prolonged exposure to the freezing weather.

Len pulled out a handful of change from his pocket and sighed. "I don't think I've got enough money left for the train fare home. Can you lend me some Trevor?"

Trevor dug down into his pocket, pulled out a few coins and counted them. "You must be joking," he said, "I've got less than you."

Amy and Pam quickly checked their finances and found them to be sorely lacking too.

"It's no big deal," Trevor said giving Pam a reassuring hug as she was looking quite concerned, "I'll give Mary a ring and explain the problem to her. I'm sure she and Pat will come down and collect us in Pat's Mini."

Pam brightened up. "Yeah, that's a good idea, Trevor."

Having finished their tea and buns, they left to search for a telephone box. Arriving at the far end of the promenade, they found an empty kiosk and everyone crammed inside.

"Maybe it would be better if you asked Mary," Trevor said to Amy, "since we aren't on very good terms at the moment." He produced some coins and pulled a small notebook out of his inside pocket. After thumbing through it he found Mary's number. Amy dialled it and waited apprehensively; then she heard Mary's cheerful voice at the other end. She explained their predicament and asked the big favour of Pat and Mary. The tone of Mary's voice changed from friendly to cold in an instant when she realised that Pam and Amy were accompanied by Trevor.

"I don't want to speak to that git," Mary snapped when Amy offered to pass the phone to him. "If it was just you and Pam, then we'd come down and get you but there's no way me and Pat are going to go all that way just to rescue him!" She was adamant and Amy knew she wasn't going to change her mind so she hung up.

"Well, that's that!" she said. "We're stuck here with little money and no way of getting home."

"That Mary can be a hard-nosed cow," Trevor said bitterly as they emerged from the booth, "I bet she's having a right laugh now at my expense. She leaves us with no other option but to hitch-hike back to London."

"There won't be many cars with room for four hitch-hikers," Amy pointed out gloomily.

"Oh I'm sure we'll find some," Trevor said optimistically.

"I just hope we get a lift fairly quickly," Amy said, "I'm dreading the thought of walking for miles after nearly three days without sleep."

"I'm sure we will," Len said, "once we locate the main road to London."

"Oh, it's bound to be signposted," Trevor said. "All we've got to do is head for the outskirts of town and look for a sign that says A23 to London."

This proved to be easier said than done. They wandered around the streets and had to ask several people before they found themselves in the sprawling suburbs heading in the right direction.

A few miles out of town, Amy stopped and sat down on the grass verge and Pam joined her.

"I can't walk another step," she moaned, "I'm completely knackered."

"Me too," Pam agreed rubbing her legs.

Then a miracle happened: A car drew up and a voice called out. "Want a lift?"

With a chorus of "Yes please!" Pam and Amy leapt to their feet and hurried over to a large black car. Amy, Pam and Len piled into the back seat while Trevor got in the front seat next to the driver. He was on his way to London and obviously fancied some company for the journey.

Trevor was left with the task of keeping awake and chatting to the driver as all three in the back seat were quickly lulled into a deep sleep by the warmth inside the car.

Amy roused as the car came to a stop in Chelsea. She nudged Pam and Len awake. They thanked the man for his kindness and climbed out feeling stiff and tired.

As they stood in a group trying to decide what to do, Trevor suddenly pointed across the road. "Look, there's Donovan."

A scruffy youth with a guitar slung across his back was walking along the pavement. He stopped and pushed open the door of a cafe and vanished inside.

"How about we go and get his autograph?" Len suggested.

"No thanks," Amy said, "I'm too tired and besides I'm not that keen on his music."

Suddenly a familiar voice behind them made them turn round.

"So you managed to get back OK." There was Kevin standing in the same clothes as the day before. He grinned broadly at them and Amy felt a tingle of excitement. "Dad's in a right mood. He's been on to Brighton police to be on the lookout for you."

"Oh bugger!" Trevor gasped in horror.

"So if we'd gone to the police station and told them who we were, we could have been chauffeur-driven home in a police car," Len said with a chuckle.

"Or maybe just arrested," Trevor retorted and then groaned. "S'pose I'd better go home and face the music."

He walked off with Kevin while the others headed for Sloane Square tube to catch their trains home. Amy said goodbye to Len as they split up to catch their different trains but didn't bother to make any arrangements to see him again.

She finally arrived back home at around 5
p.m. and walked in the back door to be greeted by
a barrage of questions from her very suspicious
mother who firmly believed that her daughter had
been hanging out with all the other Mods at Brighton
despite Amy's protestations and claims to being at
Great Yarmouth all weekend.

At the first opportunity Amy escaped to her
bedroom and collapsed into bed exhausted. She
definitely wasn't looking forward to getting up for
work next morning.

Tuesday morning Mary apologised to Amy for
letting her and Pam down by refusing to collect them
from Brighton. Amy assured her that it didn't matter
and told her about the great lift they had all the way
back to London. She didn't want to fall out with Mary
so was glad to put the incident behind her.

For a week Amy kept a low profile and came
home after work to get back into her parents' good
books. Then she arranged to go down the Scene with
Pam, as it was her turn to celebrate her eighteenth
birthday.

This was only the second time they had been
down the Scene on a Thursday. It wasn't as packed
as Tuesday evenings but they enjoyed themselves
dancing to the music and when their dancing took
them near the booth in the corner where Blocker
Tony sat playing the records, he gave them a wave.

Halfway through the evening who should come
strolling in - none other than Kevin. Amy's heart
skipped a beat. He spotted Amy and Pam and walked
across the floor between the dancers to reach them.
Another boy trailed along behind him, not as tall as
Kevin and smaller built but not bad looking. Kevin
introduced him as his cousin Ken. Amy was pleased
to see that there was no sign of Pauline and Kevin
didn't mention her.

They stood around chatting for a while and Ken
cracked a few jokes. Amy hoped that Kevin might

ask her for a dance but he seemed to be a little shy and she lacked the nerve to ask him. Eventually he said he would have to get back to the Red Lion where he was meeting Trevor. Before leaving he mentioned that they would probably come down the Scene the following Thursday.

"Things are looking up, Tibs," Amy said excitedly after Kevin and Ken had left.

"Don't forget Kevin's already got a girlfriend."

"So why wasn't she with him tonight?" Amy demanded.

Pam shrugged. "Could be any number of reasons, so don't go getting your hopes up."

Chapter Ten

May - Kevin Appears on the Scene

Saturday evening Amy met up with Pam on the train to London. They had decided to stay down the Scene all night.

"Did your mum buy the story that we're going to a party at Pat's house?" Amy asked as Pam dropped onto the seat next to her.

"Sort of, but she wasn't happy about me being out all night. Once she'd agreed that I could go to the party, I quickly dashed out of the door before she could change her mind."

"Mine was just as suspicious," Amy said and gave a sigh, "parents can be such bores when all we want to do is enjoy ourselves."

"For some reason they think we're safer at an all-night party but I know I feel far safer in a nightclub than at a drunken party," Pam declared with a toss of her head. She took out her cigarettes and gave one to Amy.

"Ta," Amy said distractedly, "I hope we can get hold of some gear else it'll be hard to keep going all night." She patted her bag. "I've brought a bottle of water just in case."

Down the Scene they discovered that a live group would be appearing on stage later on though it wasn't one that either of them had heard of before.

They had just finished dancing to 'Shotgun' by Junior Walker and the All Stars when someone tapped Amy on her shoulder. She turned to find Eric standing there and behind him lurked Mick with his hair cropped really short. Amy thought it looked terrible.

"I've got some dubes if you're staying here all night and need something," Eric offered.

"Yeah, that would be great," Amy said and grinned at Pam.

"My car's in the yard - let's go and sort out up there," Eric suggested and headed for the exit.

Mick sat in the front with Eric while Amy and Pam got in the back seat. They sorted out their money and paid Eric for ten dubes each.

"D'you need a drink like last time?" Mick asked Amy.

"No thanks - I've got some water here," she said and produced the small bottle from her bag, "by the way, who scalped you?"

Mick gave a sheepish grin. "Just fancied a change - takes a bit of getting used to."

"Preferred it how it was - don't you Tibs?"

Pam nodded. "Definitely. Er - where's Dick got to tonight? I hope he hasn't had his locks shorn off too."

"Dick likes his hair hanging round his face," Mick said, adding, "he's gone to some do. Wanted me to go too but I didn't fancy it."

The girls shared the water between them to take the pills, thanked Eric and then returned back down the Scene.

The group started up a little later and thumped out some good numbers so Pam and Amy danced their Mod jive energetically as the effect of the pills kicked in.

When a slow number was played two boys came over and asked the girls for a dance. The tall blonde boy who danced with Amy said his name was Tony, "but everyone calls me Nobby," he told her. His shorter dark-haired mate was called Bob. At the end of the dance Nobby suggested they all go for a coffee. Once outside, instead of heading through the garage to the Piccadilly, he took them on a longer walk to the Coffee An.

The four of them chatted over coffee and Amy was surprised to discover that Nobby only lived a couple of streets away from her and yet she hadn't seen him around town or hanging out in the local Wimpy Bar.

Back at the Scene Nobby and Bob danced with the girls for the rest of the night and when it closed at six in the morning they suggested moving on to the Last Chance in the Strand. The girls were impressed by the boys generosity as they insisted on paying for them to get in. The club was packed as usual and Amy hung on tightly to her bag remembering what had happened previously. They had no problem dancing non-stop 'til 9 a.m. when the club closed.

As they emerged onto the Strand, Amy said she wanted to go to Petticoat Lane and get a new leather handbag so they said goodbye to the boys.

"Will you be going to the afternoon session at the 'Mingo?" Nobby asked.

"Probably, but if not then we'll be at the Scene again tonight," Amy told him.

"See you there," he said with a wave as he and Bob walked off in the direction of Charing Cross station.

"They were quite nice, don't you think, Tibs?" Amy said as they went in search of a bus that would take them to Petticoat Lane.

"Mm, Bob was OK I suppose," Pam said casually, "anyway, you've finally decided to get a handbag the same as mine have you? I think I'll see if I can get a pair of black leather gloves."

Amy arrived at Pam's house later that day carrying her new handbag.

"I thought we were going to the Flamingo this afternoon," Pam said as Amy flopped down in an armchair exhausted from the long walk.

"When I got home this morning I lay on my bed for a rest and dozed off. I woke up this afternoon and dashed to the station but missed the train so decided to walk all the way here instead since the buses only run once an hour on a Sunday," Amy explained.

"Never mind, we'll have some tea and then get the train up to town."

The girls arrived at the Scene and found Nobby and Bob sitting on a bench in one of the alcoves. Amy sat down next to Nobby while Pam went off to the ladies. Amy thought Nobby was looking a bit vague and wondered whether her presence had actually registered with him. The next moment he flung an arm around her shoulders and produced a small bottle from inside his jacket.

"Take a good sniff of this," he said thrusting the bottle towards her. His words sounded slurred.

"What is it?" Amy asked suspiciously pushing the bottle away from her face. 'He's blocked out of his head,' she thought starting to get irritated.

"Chloroform," he announced, adding, "it's really great." He thrust the bottle back under her nose.

"Leave it out!" Amy said crossly. She pushed him away, stood up and went off to the ladies in search of Pam.

"You'd better avoid him tonight, Bat," Pam advised after Amy had told her what had happened, "chloroform's a new one on me. I didn't know you can get high on it - I thought it just put you to sleep."

"Well Nobby seems pretty stoned on it," Amy said as they came out onto the dance floor again.

They danced all evening and didn't see Nobby until they were about to leave for the station when he came over, apologised for earlier and asked if he could take her home. His speech had improved and he seemed to be more in control. There was no sign of Bob so Amy said he could catch the train home with them if he liked.

He walked Amy home from the station and asked to see her at the Railway Tavern the following evening so she arranged to meet him outside at eight o'clock.

After a grotty Monday at work Amy managed to grab a seat on the crowded fast train home. Jennifer had left the Pru at Christmas so Amy's journeys home were now alone as Pam needed to catch the slow train which stopped at her station. On the journey she mulled over the previous evening with Nobby and the incident down the Scene with the chloroform. She concluded that she really wasn't interested in seeing him any more so decided to stand him up and not bother meeting him at the Railway.

The following evening she and Pam met up with Mary and Pat down the Scene. They were relieved to find no ex-boyfriends lurking down there so the four of them could relax and enjoy themselves. Later in the evening Ken arrived with a couple of mates who he introduced as Tom and Bill, but there was no sign of Kevin, which disappointed Amy. Ken asked Amy to dance a couple of times when slow numbers came on. She liked Ken but couldn't help wishing it was Kevin she was smooching with.

She tried to sound casual when she asked Ken where Kevin was.

"I dunno what he's doing tonight," Ken replied, "but I think he wants to come down here on Thursday."

Amy was pleased to hear this and quickly changed the subject so that Ken wouldn't twig just how much this news meant to her.

Tom and Bill were friendly and cracked a lot of jokes which made the girls giggle. They all danced together in a group until it was time to leave and wend their various ways home.

Amy was impatient waiting for Thursday evening to arrive. During her break Thursday afternoon, Mary came over while Vera was out of the room.

"I've been hearing on the grapevine that both Ken and Kevin like you."

"Who's been telling you that?" Amy asked trying to sound offhand while inside her stomach was doing cartwheels with joy. Just then Vera returned, marching up the aisle between the desks and gave Mary a black look.

"Here comes trouble - I'd better go," Mary said hastily and beat a retreat back to her desk.

Mary's news made Amy even more eager to get to the Scene that evening. As she and Pam walked into the club through the swing doors Amy scanned the crowd dancing and the groups standing around at the side or sitting on the benches. There was no sign of Kevin or Ken. All through the evening as Amy danced she kept one eye on the door checking on every person that came in. Towards the end of the evening she had all but given up when in came Ken with Kevin following behind. They stood over by the stage so Amy quickly tugged at Pam's arm and pushed her way through the crowd towards them. She was relieved to see no Pauline accompanying Kevin. He smiled his slightly shy smile when he spotted Amy and Pam approaching.

They chatted intermittently trying to make themselves heard over the loud music. Amy was worried in case Ken asked her to dance again so she kept Pam between herself and Ken.

"Me and Pam are going to try and get to the all-night session at the Flamingo tomorrow night," she told Kevin, "Georgie Fame is billed to appear so it should be fantastic."

"I love Georgie Fame, but I've never managed to see him perform live," Kevin said somewhat wistfully.

"Well, why not go tomorrow," Amy coaxed, "I know you'd enjoy it there."

"Are you definitely going?" Kevin asked eagerly.

"It all depends on whether we can escape out of the bedroom window again like we did once before," Amy said.

Kevin laughed. "Sounds like you have as much trouble as I do staying out all night, but I shall try my best to come if I can."

This was music to Amy's ears: Georgie Fame at the Flamingo all night with Kevin for company. What more could she want. She was a little disappointed that Kevin didn't seem interested in dancing but she was content just standing around chatting to him. They hadn't been there very long before Ken announced that he had to leave which meant Kevin would also be leaving.

"See you tomorrow down the Flamingo," Kevin said as he turned to go.

"Do you really think we can pull off another escape out of your bedroom window, Bat?" Pam asked as they relaxed on the train home.

"Well it was a bit dodgy last time with my parents sleeping in the next room. I'm still surprised we didn't wake them up with all the noise we were making. How about a slight change of plans?" Amy suggested with a grin.

"What do you mean?" Pam demanded looking a little puzzled.

"Well, instead of sleeping in my bedroom, I'll ask if we can sleep on the divan in the lounge as it opens out into a double bed so it will be more comfortable for us. I'm sure my parents won't object to that and it means that we can climb out of the window far more easily being downstairs, and they are less likely to hear us if we make a noise."

"I like the sound of that, Bat," Pam declared firmly adding, "I didn't much care for climbing down from your porch roof before - I don't have much of a head for heights."

"Tell your parents that you're staying at my house and it won't matter if your dad checks up with my dad because he'll just confirm that's where you were all night."

Friday evening Amy and Pam's plans were put in jeopardy by an unexpected visit from Mrs Bullen and Katy. Pam arrived looking very pleased with herself having convinced her parents that she would be sleeping over at Amy's.

Amy had got her mother to agree to the girls sleeping downstairs on the divan so everything was set up ready and then in walked Mrs Bullen and Katy unaware that they had thrown a spanner in the works. They stayed for tea and were in no hurry to leave as the evening wore on. Pam kept glancing at Amy wondering what she was going to do while Amy got more and more agitated with the situation. Everyone was sitting around chatting nineteen to the dozen catching up with over six months' worth of news.

"Me and Pam are going up to my bedroom for a while," Amy said jumping up and beckoning to her friend.

"Can I come too?" Katy asked, standing up.

"Er, yes of course you can," Amy said wondering whether it would be safe to confide in Katy what they had planned for the evening and night ahead.

Amy decided to let Katy in on their plans and she was as excited as they were at the prospect of them escaping out of the window.

"We must leave in time to catch the last train to London though," Amy told her, "which means getting everyone out of the lounge."

"I'll help if I can," Katy offered, "but you know what mum is like when she gets nattering - there's no stopping her!"

Pam and Amy laid out their make-up, brushes, combs and hairpins, and started to get themselves ready.

"We've decided to wear our hair up tonight for a change," Pam said as she scooped her hair into an elastic band on top of her head.

"It gets really hot down the Flamingo so it might feel a bit cooler with our hair out of the way," Amy explained.

"Let me give you a hand with your hair," Katy offered coming over and grabbing a handful of pins. She deftly tucked in the ends and pinned Amy's hair neatly and then did the same for Pam. "How will you explain to your mum and dad going to bed with your hair piled up on top of your head and wearing make-up, when you go back downstairs?" Katy asked, "they're bound to comment on it."

Amy and Pam looked at each other and groaned.

"Hadn't thought about that," Amy confessed, "maybe if they're too engrossed in chatting, they won't notice. Anyway somehow we've got to shift them all out of the lounge."

The girls returned downstairs and were immediately confronted by Mrs Bullen exclaiming: "I see you've been busy trying out fancy new hairstyles."

"Er, yeah." Amy hesitated aware of quizzical eyes staring at her and Pam. "We were just experimenting to pass the time." She gave a yawn. "Me and Pam are getting pretty tired. Do you mind if we make up the divan into a bed now?"

"Why don't we all go and sit in the dining room and leave these two to get ready for bed?" Katy suggested rounding up her mother and ushering her out of the room.

Amy heaved a sigh of relief once they were alone in the lounge. She and Pam quickly opened out the divan and made up the bed. She poked her head out of the door leading to the dining room and wished everyone goodnight, apologising for kicking them out of the lounge and then quietly locked both the doors so no-one could get in.

They donned their suedes and carefully climbed out of the bay window closing it behind them and then hurried round the Crescent hoping no neighbour had spotted them making their escape.

They caught the last fast train up to town and were soon revelling in the hot, humid atmosphere of the Flamingo and applauding as the M.C. introduced Georgie Fame who launched into 'Can't Sit Down' on his Hammond organ. The girls found a small space to dance and kept going all night with only a brief rest at three in the morning when they sat in the plush red seats down the front.

"See, Bat, we can get by OK without taking anything," Pam said as they lit their cigarettes and relaxed.

"Yeah, but it's always around this time of the morning that we start to flag a bit."

"We'll be fine after a half-hour break," Pam said firmly.

"It doesn't look like Kevin's going to turn up," Amy said despondently.

"I expect he couldn't get out. Having a copper for a dad must be pretty restrictive," Pam declared.

Leaning back in the seats, they allowed the music to wash over them as Georgie Fame started into 'Work Song.'

They eventually staggered up the steps of the club and out into the grey dawn at five in the morning feeling tired and bedraggled but exhilarated by the fantastic music. They waited at Charing Cross station until they could catch the first train home and crept back in through the lounge window.

"I hope Katy covered for us last night," Amy whispered as they undressed and collapsed into bed.

It felt like the very next minute they were rudely awakened by a knocking on the door.

"Are you girls awake yet?" It was Amy's mum calling through the locked door. Amy tumbled out of bed and unlocked the door. Her mother came in with two mugs of coffee. "Did you sleep more comfortably in this bed?" she asked setting the mugs down on the coffee table.

"We had a really great night, thank you Mrs Brown," Pam mumbled from under the sheets. Amy giggled causing her mum to look at her sharply.

"Your hair has stayed in place remarkably well," she observed. Amy discreetly tugged a strand loose in a belated attempt to make her hair appear more dishevelled.

"I expect I put too much lacquer on it last night," she said lamely and quickly changed the subject. "Thanks for the coffee - we'll get up in a little while and put the bed back to a divan."

"We've had breakfast so you two will have to get yourselves something when you're dressed," Mrs Brown said as she walked out.

"Looks like we've done it!" Amy exclaimed gleefully passing Pam a mug of coffee, "they don't suspect a thing."

"Another successful escapade accomplished, eh Bat?" Pam said sounding relieved.

Although they still felt really tired after very little sleep, they got up, dressed and made themselves some toast and more coffee. Then Pam headed for the bus and home while Amy soaked in the bath and washed her hair in readiness for another Saturday night down the Scene.

That evening she met Pam as arranged on the London-bound train and before long they were dancing to the music in the gloom of the Scene. There was no live group playing tonight but the club was still pretty crowded. Amy spotted Nobby sitting in an alcove but decided to ignore him. Later on Ken came in followed by Trevor. Amy looked in vain for Kevin. They came over and chatted to the girls and danced with them when a slow number was played - Trevor smooching with Pam and Ken with Amy. Then they took the girls round to the Piccadilly for coffee.

"We've been invited to a party tonight," Trevor informed them as they sat down by the window, "why don't you two come with us?"

"We were out all last night," Pam said, "so I don't think we can get away with an all-night party. I know my mum would hit the roof. She's getting very fed up with me staying out."

"I wouldn't mind going," Amy said, "but our parents are expecting us home tonight - what a bore!"

"That's a pity," Ken said, "it should be a really good party - there's a load of people going to it."

"What happened to Kevin last night?" Amy asked Trevor, "he said he'd try and get to the Flamingo."

"Oh, is that where he wanted to go. I heard him having an argument with dad about going out and it sounded like dad won."

"Just as I said," Pam whispered giving Amy a nudge.

"How come you're allowed out all night and Kevin isn't?" Amy demanded.

"I'm older than him, after all he's barely out of school," Trevor said matter-of-factly.

"What!" Amy gasped in surprise. "How old is Kevin then?"

"How old do you think he is?" Trevor countered with a grin.

"Well I assumed he's about my age - seventeen or eighteen."

"He's fifteen," Trevor announced flatly, enjoying seeing the look of amazement spread over Amy's face.

"He doesn't look it," she said finally after the shock news had sunk in, "no wonder your dad doesn't like him staying out. How come he's not still at school?"

"Got himself expelled - can't remember why - you'll have to ask him for the reason."

Back down the Scene they had another slow dance and then Trevor and Ken left to go to the party. The girls were squeezing between the gyrating bodies on their way to the ladies when Amy felt a tug on her arm. She turned round to find Bob behind her.

"Nobby wants to know if you're staying down here all night," he said.

"Why doesn't he come and ask me himself?" Amy asked peevishly.

"I think he's a bit unsure of the reception he'd get after you stood him up the other night," Bob said with a grin.

"Well, as it happens, we're leaving very soon so we won't be staying all night," Amy informed him and then continued into the ladies where Pam was brushing her hair.

"Nobby didn't have the courage to come and speak to me himself so he sent Bob," Amy said scornfully rummaging in her make-up bag.

"You'd think he'd take the hint when you don't bother to meet him," Pam commented. She glanced at her watch and gasped. "Oh, Bat we'd better hurry if we're going to catch the last train."

They arrived at Charing Cross just in time to leap onto their train, as it was about to leave. They slumped onto a seat in an empty compartment and Pam handed Amy a fag.

"I've got a rash come up on my back and front," Amy said, adding, "mum suspects it's caused by pills - I hope it's not."

"Does your mum know you take pills?" Pam gasped in surprise.

"No, of course she doesn't. She just comes out with these things to make me think that she knows. In her mind nightclubs are synonymous with drug taking."

"Still, I shouldn't think it's pills, Bat, 'cos I've taken the same as you and I don't have a rash."

"Anyway she's made an appointment for me to see the doctor on Monday so I shan't be in work until the afternoon."

After work on Tuesday evening, Pam and Amy walked across town to the West End after a snack of poached egg on toast in the Lyons cafe.

Down the Scene they met Carol and Margaret so they danced together in a group for over an hour and then Amy spotted Trevor strolling in followed by Kevin. There was still no sign of Pauline and Amy's heart skipped a beat. The brothers stood near the record booth in the corner so Amy beckoned to Pam before pushing her way through the crowd with the other three trailing behind her. She got the impression that Kevin was pleased to see her. A slow number came on and Trevor asked Pam for a dance.

Kevin shuffled nervously and then held his arms outstretched. "Anyone care to dance?" he asked shyly. Amy saw Carol make a move towards him so she quickly threw herself into his arms, surprising herself at her forwardness, but the prospect of competition for Kevin made her throw caution to the wind. He folded his arms around her and Amy felt her knees go weak. She wanted that number to last forever but all too soon it came to an end and she reluctantly stepped back. He apologised for not making it to the Flamingo on Friday. As Trevor had already explained, his father had put his foot down.

"You missed a terrific night," Amy told him and then she hesitated as she tried to pluck up the courage to ask Kevin the question that had been bothering her. Hoping she sounded casual, finally she asked, "where's your girlfriend tonight?"

"My girlfriend?" Kevin looked puzzled.

"Pauline."

"Oh!" He grinned. "You thought Pauline was my girlfriend?"

"Well isn't she?" Amy demanded. It was her turn to look puzzled.

"Pauline is my cousin," he explained, "she often comes out with me or Trevor." Waves of relief mingled with elation swept through Amy as her imagined rival for Kevin's affections melted away.

Another slow number started up and Amy found herself once again wrapped in Kevin's arms. She was still adjusting to the fact that a gorgeous looking boy like Kevin was available and not involved with anyone else. After the slow number ended they all stood in a group chatting and joking until Trevor announced they had to leave.

"Maybe I'll see you down here on Thursday," Kevin said to Amy flashing her a smile as he turned to follow Trevor. Amy nodded and returned his smile. She was on cloud nine for the rest of the evening.

On the train home the girls sat puffing on cigarettes.

"What did the doctor make of your rash yesterday?" Pam asked.

"I don't think he knew what it was. Muttered something about athlete's foot on the body, which sounds disgusting and ridiculous. He gave me some cream - I just hope it works." She gave a sigh. "At least it's not contagious."

Amy could barely contain her impatience for Thursday evening to arrive. Wednesday she stayed at home after work and washed her hair in readiness.

At the office on Thursday she buried herself in her work in an attempt to make the time pass more quickly.

Finally she and Pam were once again back down the Scene. Amy danced keeping one eye on the double doors at the entrance. She was beginning to give up hope when finally the familiar leather coat belonging to Trevor appeared with him inside it. A brief pause and then Kevin came in wearing his usual jacket. They came over and chatted for a while. When a slow record began to play, Amy found herself once more in Kevin's arms while Pam danced with Trevor. They stayed together for the rest of the evening until it was time for the girls to leave.

"Do you mind if we walk you to the station?" Kevin asked.

"Of course we don't mind," Amy said emphatically without considering whether Pam would mind. Amy glanced across at her friend; she seemed content enough in Trevor's company.

They strolled down to the Strand arm in arm. Amy hadn't felt so deliriously happy for a long time, not since Rob in fact. At the station they just had time to agree to meet at the Scene on Saturday evening before the train whisked the girls away into the night.

"You really like Kevin don't you?" Pam said seeing the ecstatic look on her friend's face as they stretched out on the seats in their empty carriage.

"He's such a dish," Amy said dreamily.

"But he's quite a bit younger than you," Pam pointed out.

"I don't care - he looks older and that's what counts. How are you and Trevor getting on?"

"He's OK," Pam said offhandedly, "he makes me laugh with his jokes."

"I fancy staying down the Scene all night on Saturday. It'll probably be best to tell our parents we're going to a party."

"Mm, I think you're right, Bat. It'll cause the least strife."

Saturday afternoon Amy met Pam in her town and they wandered around the shops until closing time and then went in the Wimpy Bar for egg and chips to kill time before taking the train up to London.

The waitress arrived with two plates piled up with chips and a fried egg. Amy gazed at the food being put in front of her and sighed.

"I do wish they wouldn't serve their eggs sunny side up."

"I think it's the way Americans cook their fried eggs," Pam mumbled through a mouthful of chips. She was hungry and had already started on her meal.

"Were your parents OK about you going to an all-night party tonight?" Amy asked.

"They weren't exactly over the moon but said I could go as I would be with you. For some strange reason they seem to trust you."

Amy grinned. "I always knew your mum and dad had good taste. Mine didn't mind but asked a lot of awkward questions about where the party was being held and if there would be any adults around. I had to do a lot of quick thinking, but I'm sure they believed me."

"I would really love to get away from home and be independent," Pam declared wistfully.

"Your mum would go potty if you left home," Amy said, and took a sip of coffee.

"Yeah, you're right, Bat. She's always moaning about girls who have flats. She's convinced they have non-stop orgies in them."

"I don't think our flat would be like that," Amy said giggling.

"It certainly wouldn't!" Pam said emphatically with a toss of her head.

"Sometimes I wonder whether your mum really knows you at all," Amy mused.

"Anyway, drink up and let's get going. We've got to stay awake all night without any help," Pam said, picking up her handbag.

Amy groaned. "Maybe we'll be able to get hold of some pills - it makes staying awake so much easier."

They arrived at the Scene to be greeted by Mary and Pat as they walked in.

"You've just missed Trevor and Kevin," Mary yelled in Amy's ear over the music, "they popped in and then left a little while ago to go to a party."

Amy tried to hide her disappointment at this news. She felt a bit vexed that Kevin had opted to go to a party instead of waiting for her.

"Kevin said he'd try and get back here later," Mary added, as Amy turned to follow Pam to the ladies. This cheered Amy up somewhat. The four friends spent the next few hours dancing with a break for coffee round at the Piccadilly. Then Pat announced she was feeling tired and wanted to go home so she and Mary left.

Pam and Amy launched into their Mod jive as Hank Jacob's 'So Far Away' started to blast out and when it finished Trevor appeared through the doors with Kevin trailing behind. As they approached Amy tried to look annoyed with Kevin but it didn't work because her irritation melted away under the gaze of his large soft brown eyes.

He immediately apologised for leaving earlier. "Trevor refused to leave me down here, and as he wanted to go to this party, I didn't get any choice."

"The joy of having a bossy older brother," Amy commented with a grin. Trevor overheard what Amy said. He had been busy making his peace with Pam though she hadn't seemed particularly bothered that he had been missing for most of the evening.

"I've got strict instructions from my father to keep an eye on Kevin," he explained defensively, "else he probably wouldn't be allowed out. Our parents think we're at a party so we had to go and put in an appearance in case word gets back that we weren't there. They're not keen on us frequenting clubs."

"Oh you too!" Pam exclaimed. "What is it with parents and nightclubs?"

Kevin pulled Amy into his arms as a slow number started. "It was a lousy party anyway," he whispered, "I couldn't wait to leave and get back here."

Amy was happy again and Kevin was back in her good books. They danced and chatted until nearly midnight when Trevor decided it was time for them to go home. Kevin looked unhappy with the news that Amy and Pam planned to stay there all night.

"I wish I could stay with you," he told Amy as they stood outside in Ham Yard saying their goodbyes. He took out a pen and piece of paper. "Give me a ring in the morning," he said, writing down his phone number.

Amy promised she would and then she and Pam returned back down the steps to the noise and heat of the club. There was no sign of Eric, Mick or Dick down there but Amy noticed Graham dancing with a group of Mods so she went over and asked if he had any spare pills.

He shook his head. "Sorry Amy, couldn't get hold of hardly any tonight," he said, "but if another mate of mine turns up he might have some. If so I'll come and find you." She thanked him and returned to Pam who was busy miming to Blocker Tony through the glass window of the record booth to play the Blendells. Tony finally got the message and gave her the thumbs up.

After an hour of dancing they headed for the Coffee An near Leicester Square for a rest and a cup of indifferent instant coffee. They returned to the Scene feeling refreshed and able to continue dancing until the club closed.

After a few more hours of dancing in the Last Chance, they headed for the nearby coffee bar in the Strand where they sat drinking coffee and smoking.

"We managed OK without any pills didn't we?" Pam said sounding quite proud of her achievement.

"Pity Graham's mate never turned up though," Amy said with a sigh, "it's not easy dancing all night."

"I feel I need to freshen up," Pam said, pushing her hair back from her face, "let's go over to the station wash-room."

The girls walked across the road to Charing Cross station and spent half an hour washing and reapplying their make-up. Then, feeling tired, they went into the waiting room and tried to get comfortable on the bench to have a brief kip. No sooner had they settled down than in walked a big policeman and frowned at them.

"This is a waiting room not a doss house," he informed them curtly, "so you had better leave now." Amy groaned and picked up her bag. She just scowled at the policeman as she left with Pam following her. There was obviously no point in trying to argue with him. They stood under the clock undecided on what to do or where to go.

"It's probably too early to phone Kevin," Amy said, "he'll still be in bed asleep."

"Let's ride up and down on the trains for a while," Pam suggested.

"Good idea, Tibs," Amy agreed, "at least it's warm and comfortable in a carriage and it won't cost us anything."

After an hour of dozing in a warm carriage, lulled by the rhythmic motion of the train, they arrived back at Charing Cross and headed for the phone booths. Amy dialled the number Kevin had given her and was relieved to hear his voice answering the phone. He answered so quickly that she felt sure he must have been hovering next to it. He wanted to know everything she had done since he left and whether she had danced with anyone else. Amy felt flattered to hear a touch of jealousy in his questions. It meant that he cared which pleased her immensely. He suggested they meet at two o'clock to go to Battersea funfair. Amy readily agreed and then said goodbye. Pam was dubious about playing gooseberry to the two of them and proposed that she go home. Amy convinced her that she needed her there for moral support.

"It'll be the first time I've met Kevin on his own - I promise you won't feel out of place," she pleaded. Pam finally agreed to accompany her friend so they went in search of a Wimpy Bar to kill time until the afternoon.

As they sat eating rum babas and drinking coffee, the heavens opened and rain poured down in torrents. It beat on the plate glass windows and the gutters were soon awash with brown gushing water gurgling down the drains.

"I don't much fancy a fairground in the pouring rain," Pam said hunching her shoulders.

"What a bummer!" Amy exclaimed crossly, "that rain will ruin our suedes and we don't have a brolly between us."

"Maybe you should give Kevin a ring and cancel your date," Pam suggested, "you need good weather to enjoy fairground rides."

"Yeah, you're right," Amy agreed glumly, "as soon as the rain eases up we'll make a dash back to the station and I'll ring him from there."

Monday evening Amy and Pam didn't bother going to their typing class as they hadn't done much practising so decided to give it a miss.

Amy waited impatiently for ten thirty to arrive when she hurried round to the phone box on the corner to ring Kevin for a chat as she had promised she would when she spoke to him the previous day to cancel their date at the funfair. She found chatting to Kevin came easy and after half an hour had to tear herself away as there was an impatient man outside the box glaring at her. She arranged to meet Kevin the following evening down the Scene before hanging up. On her way home she felt as if she was floating six inches above the pavement, her thoughts filled with Kevin.

Pam and Amy walked into the Scene Tuesday evening and stopped dead in their tracks. Bright spotlights had transformed the familiar gloomy club.

"What on earth is going on here!" Amy gasped.

"There are cameras over there," Pam said pointing to where large tripods were set up by the side of the room with men operating the cameras fixed to the top, "looks like they're filming."

A man who appeared to be in charge was busy moving groups of Mods into the best positions for dancing in front of the cameras.

Amy caught sight of Graham over by the stage so she went to ask him what was happening.

"They're making a film about this club which is going to be shown in America," he explained, "trouble is the bright spotlights show up just how scruffy this place really is."

"Yeah, you can't see how rough it looks when it's dark, but I don't fancy dancing under those bright lights," Amy said, and then, with a change of heart, added, "still, if it means being in a film then maybe I will."

She and Pam went to the ladies to brush their hair and freshen up their make-up before going to the cloakroom to check in their coats and handbags. They quickly joined in the dancing in the centre of the floor where the filming was taking place.

"This feels weird when you can see everything and everyone around you," Pam said, and then grabbed hold of Amy, "let's show the yanks our Mod jive."

Twenty minutes later Kevin arrived with Ken. They stopped and stared in disbelief. Amy saw them and waved them over.

"Come and dance with us and you might end up as a Hollywood film star," she told them with a giggle. The filming lasted for just over an hour and then the men packed away their equipment and the spotlights were turned off.

Amy heaved a sigh of relief. "Thank goodness it's back to the gloom that we know and love."

Kevin and Ken took the girls round to the Piccadilly for coffee and their only topic of conversation was the filming session they had just been a part of.

"I hope we get to see that film one day," Pam said wistfully.

"Maybe it'll be shown on the telly," Ken said.

"Let's face it, with the Scene making such a tacky backdrop to the dancing, they'll probably ditch the whole film," Amy said pragmatically with a sigh.

"Well, let's look on the bright side," Kevin said putting his arm around her shoulders, "there's always the chance that it could be the start of something big,"

At the end of the evening, Kevin and Ken walked the girls to the station and Kevin promised to ring Amy next day at work.

Amy was taking her tea break the following afternoon when Kevin phoned. Fortunately Vera and her sidekick, Audrey, were out of the room so Amy could relax and chat to him. Mary realised Amy was talking to Kevin so she came over from D division and joined in the conversation which became very high-spirited with a lot of yelling and laughter down the phone. Kevin invited Amy to the Goldhawk Club Friday evening but she reluctantly decided it was too far to travel to the Goldhawk Road so Kevin suggested they meet up outside the Scene Saturday night instead.

Amy spent Saturday afternoon soaking in the bath and getting ready for her date with Kevin. She sat in front of her dressing table mirror and carefully put her hair up in a half bun, lacquering it in place.

The train arrived at Pam's station and she jumped into the carriage as they headed for another evening at the Scene. They found Kevin waiting outside accompanied by Mary and Pat.

"We've been invited to a party tonight," Mary announced, "why don't you come too? It's at a cousin of mine's."

Amy and Kevin decided to stay down the Scene but Pam agreed to go to the party. The girls piled into Pat's Mini Traveller and drove off with much horn beeping and then Kevin and Amy headed down the stairs to the gloom of the club. It was fairly crowded so they found a seat in an alcove where they could sit and chat and comment on the dancers. Amy spotted Eric but didn't see any sign of Mick or Dick. They had a few dances when slow numbers came on and Kevin bought Amy a cold drink at the snack bar in the corner. She found the time flying by in Kevin's company and suddenly it was time to leave and catch her train home.

As they headed for the exit Pam came in. Mary and Pat had dropped her off and then driven home.

"How was the party?" Amy enquired.

"It was at a large Victorian house in North London. Quite a crowd and loads of food and drink so we really enjoyed ourselves. I think someone was celebrating a birthday and Mary seemed to know everyone there."

The three of them walked to the station and Kevin suggested they meet up Sunday afternoon to go to Battersea funfair, as they hadn't made it there the previous Sunday.

"You must come too, Pam," he added not wanting her to feel left out, "it'll be good fun."

"Yeah, why not, it'll be better than staying at home," Pam said with a smile even though she was really only agreeing for Amy's sake.

The next day Pam and Amy caught the train and then the tube to Sloane Square where they had arranged to meet Kevin. He didn't have far to come as he only lived round the corner but he still managed to arrive late. They caught a bus to Battersea and strolled through the gardens to the funfair.

They were greeted by loud music and lots of flashing lights from the various rides and sideshows. They stopped at the dodgems and perched on the perimeter railing watching the cars whizzing around and crashing into one another. When the bumper cars stopped, Kevin was keen to have a go but Pam refused point blank to get into one. Kevin grabbed hold of Amy and dragged her to the nearest car. She squeezed in beside him and let him do the steering while Pam looked on from the safety of the railing.

"No head-on crashes, please," Amy begged as the cars began to move off.

Kevin grinned. "I'll try, but the others will probably hit us anyway." They careered around the floor with deafening music blaring and Amy hanging on for dear life. She caught occasional glimpses of Pam looking a bit fed up and guessed she wasn't really enjoying herself.

At the end of the ride they clambered out of the bumper car and re-joined Pam who announced that she had decided to go home. No amount of cajoling could persuade her to change her mind and stay. After Pam had left they spent the rest of the afternoon wandering around and enjoying the various rides. By early evening they had had enough so Kevin suggested they head for the Scene.

They arrived to find it closed. A notice pinned to the door gave no explanation but promised it would be open as usual on Tuesday.

"Let's go and get something to eat – I'm starving," Kevin said so they walked through the multi-storey garage to the Piccadilly cafe and ordered two plates of chips and two coffees. They took their time over the meal while trying to decide where to spend the rest of the evening. With nothing better to do, they headed for Trafalgar Square and sat on a bench watching the pigeons and fountains. Amy was surprised at how few people were in the square.

"Probably because it's a Sunday," Kevin surmised. Amy shivered as a cool breeze swept through her hair so Kevin put his arm around her and Amy snuggled up close to him. She realised she was falling in love and sensed that Kevin was keen on her too. They sat there oblivious to the chill night air until it was time for Amy to catch her train home. Kevin kissed her goodbye and promised to ring her at work the next day.

Tuesday evening, as Pam and Amy arrived at the Scene, Amy scanned the crowd inside hoping to catch sight of Kevin, but she was disappointed. The girls made their way to the ladies and stood in front of the mirror tidying their hair.

"I thought Kevin would have been here waiting for me," Amy said peevishly tugging a comb through her hair, "when he rang me yesterday he said he would meet me here at seven thirty and it's now eight o'clock."

"If he said he was coming then I'm sure he'll turn up," Pam declared trying to console her friend, adding, "he seems to really like you."

They went out into the gloomy, smoky atmosphere and danced to the loud music. After half an hour Mary and Pat came in.

"Where's the delectable Kevin?" Mary asked. She had overheard the arrangements being made at work the previous day when Kevin had phoned. She had joined in by yelling insults at him down the phone as she walked past ignoring the dagger looks from Vera.

"He hasn't shown up, the sod," Amy said with a toss of her head.

"Well go and ring him and tell him to shift his arse!" Mary shouted bursting into laughter.

"I'm not ringing him," Amy said indignantly, "it'll look like I'm crawling after him."

"I'll ring him if you like," Pam offered, "at least then you'll know what's happened to him."

Amy reluctantly agreed so the two of them left the club and walked round to Great Windmill Street where there was a phone box. Pam dialled the number and waited.

"Don't let on that I'm here with you," Amy hissed in Pam's ear.

Kevin answered the phone and Pam immediately demanded to know why he was messing Amy around and why he was still at home. Pam held the handset so that Amy could hear what was being said.

Kevin apologised and explained that he had no trousers to wear. His one and only pair of trousers were in the wash. He told Pam to give Amy his apologies and said he would ring her at work next day.

Pam hung up and the girls collapsed in giggles.

"Can you believe that!" Pam exclaimed, "it's such a ridiculous excuse that it must surely be true." Amy felt relieved now that she knew what had happened.

"Come to think of it, Kevin has only ever worn the same trousers and jacket ever since I first set eyes on him at Brighton."

"He obviously can't earn much money from his Saturday job at the hairdressers," Pam said as they arrived back at the Scene.

"He told me that he also helps his mum and aunts. They clean an office block each evening after work."

"But it's not like having a proper full time job so I'm not surprised he's broke and can't afford a second pair of trousers."

They re-entered the club and went across the floor to where Mary and Pat were sitting. They fell about laughing when Amy told them what Kevin had said.

"If he really loved you nothing would stop him from coming out tonight," Mary said emphatically.

"He couldn't borrow a pair of trousers from Trevor because he's taller and skinnier than Kevin, and I definitely don't want him arriving here in his Y fronts," Amy declared with a grin."

"It would cause a bit of a stir," Pam said, "but I think they would let him in."

"By the way, I've just seen Mick and Dick," Mary said, "they arrived about ten minutes ago and Mick has got some drippy looking girl in tow."

"I wish Kevin was here so I could parade him in front of Mick," Amy said wistfully.

The girls danced to a couple of records and then, as a slow record started up, a familiar figure appeared hovering nervously behind Pam. It was Dick. He hesitated and then tapped her on the shoulder and coyly asked her to dance. Amy thought Pam appeared quite keen to fall into Dick's arms and they smooched off into the crowd.

Pam didn't return until the end of the evening when it was time to leave. Mary and Pat stayed longer than intended; waiting to hear what Pam had to say. She received a chorus of "Well?" from the other three.

"It looks like me and Dick are going out again," she announced sounding quite surprised by the news.

Amy groaned. "How many times is it now?" she demanded.

Pam sighed. "I know, Bat, but at the moment even Dick is better than no boyfriend at all. You know how much I hate playing gooseberry to you and Kevin."

They said goodbye to Pat and Mary out in Ham Yard before heading for the station and home.

"So when are you seeing Dick next?" Amy asked as they walked along.

"Well, surprise, surprise, he wants to take me to the pictures on Friday," Pam replied.

"Just like the old times," Amy said scornfully.

"I don't know why, but there is something reassuring about Dick's predictability," Pam declared.

The next day at work was payday - Amy's favourite day of the month. It meant she could afford to upgrade her cigarettes from Piccadilly to Peter Stuyvesant or Benson and Hedges. As the month progressed and the money got tight, she usually ended up downgrading her cigarettes back to Piccadilly.

Kevin rang Amy full of apologies for the previous evening. She waited a full five minutes before forgiving him, as she didn't want him to think she was a complete pushover. He asked her to meet him the following evening in Shaftesbury Avenue where his bus stopped.

Thursday evening at eight o'clock Amy and Pam stood waiting at the bus stop in Shaftesbury Avenue but although several buses arrived there was no sign of Kevin.

"Let's go down the Scene, Bat," Pam coaxed, getting impatient with all the waiting around. She glanced at her watch. "It's gone eight thirty - he's over half an hour late."

"Let's wait a bit longer, Tibs - maybe he got held up," Amy said, trying to make excuses for his lateness.

The girls were about to give up and leave at ten to nine when Kevin came bounding off a bus full of apologies yet again.

"I'm so broke, I had to borrow the bus fare to get here," he explained, "so I can't afford to go to the Scene."

Pam gave an exasperated look behind Kevin's back, which Amy ignored.

"I got paid yesterday, so I'll pay for you to get in," she offered.

Kevin at first refused but then reluctantly agreed when she insisted because she didn't want him to get on the next bus home again.

Pam stayed for only half an hour and then decided to go home leaving Amy and Kevin to smooch to their hearts content without feeling guilty about Pam standing around on her own.

Amy enjoyed her evening with Kevin. He walked her to the station and saw her onto her train, promising to ring her at work the next day.

The carriage was fairly empty and at London
Bridge the door opened and a man jumped in and
sat down opposite Amy. She glanced across and then
stared hard scarcely able to believe her eyes. Sitting
opposite her was none other than Manfred Man with
his unmistakable neat beard edging his chin and
black-rimmed glasses. He held his ticket between his
teeth and carefully placed a bottle of milk in the far
corner of the seat next to him. Every time the train
lurched the bottle overbalanced and he dived across
to grab it before it fell and then carefully replaced it
in its original position.

Amy watched, bemused, as this fiasco continued
all the way to Blackheath where he alighted with his
bottle of milk intact. She couldn't help wondering
why on earth he hadn't just simply held on to the
bottle - it would have been far easier. She concluded
that he was probably high on drugs.

Friday afternoon Kevin phoned Amy at work. Vera
was in a rare good mood and didn't glare at Amy
while she chatted on the phone. Amy didn't want
to push her luck so she told Kevin she'd ring him
back at home that evening as Pam was going to the
pictures with Dick so she would be staying in.

That evening Amy walked round to the phone box
and spent nearly an hour chatting to Kevin. He asked
her to meet him next day in his lunch hour at the
hair salon where he worked in South Kensington.
Amy agreed as she had decided to go shopping up
Oxford Street Saturday morning and could easily
catch the tube to South Kensington.

After a fruitless shopping spree in Oxford Street
where she hadn't found anything she liked enough
to buy, Amy arrived at the hairdressers in South
Kensington having successfully followed Kevin's
directions to the salon. She peered in at the open
doorway to find Kevin busy washing an elderly
lady's blue rinsed hair at the sink while he chatted
politely to her as he worked. He glanced across and,

seeing Amy grinning at him, quickly rinsed and then wrapped the lady's head in a towel.

"I'm off to lunch now," he called out to his boss who was cutting hair and then joined Amy giving her a hug.

"Where shall we go?" Amy asked.

"How about the Science Museum as it's only around the corner," Kevin suggested.

They spent best part of an hour wandering around the museum pressing buttons and experimenting with gadgets until it was time for Kevin to return to work.

"Me and Pam have arranged to stay down the Scene all night tonight," Amy said as they stood outside the salon. "We've told our parents we're going to an all-night party. D'you think you can stay all night too?"

"I'll try the same story on my folks and see if it works," Kevin said with a grin adding, "if it doesn't work then I might just come anyway."

"I don't want your dad sending cops down the Scene to search for you," Amy declared.

"Oh he wouldn't do that - at least I don't think he would." Amy was a little uneasy at the uncertainty in Kevin's words but they agreed to meet up at the Scene later that evening regardless.

Amy went home to get ready and then met Pam as usual on the London-bound train. Pam had arranged to meet Dick down the Scene and when they arrived they found Dick already there with Eric and several other mates, but not Mick. The girls stood chatting to Dick and Eric for a while, though Amy couldn't help glancing impatiently at the entrance doors willing Kevin to walk in. Ten minutes later her prayers were answered when he appeared on his own wearing his one and only set of clothes. Amy went over and, grabbing his arm, drew him across to where the others were standing and introduced him, knowing that news of her new boyfriend would find its way back to Mick.

A little later Amy was smooching with Kevin when Pam tapped her arm.

"I'm going round to Eric's house for a while with Dick and the others," she informed her.

"Is there a party on?" Amy asked in surprise.

"Oh no, we're just going for a coffee - d'you two want to come? It'll be a bit of a squeeze in Eric's car though."

Amy shook her head. "No thanks, we're OK here." She snuggled up to Kevin again while Pam picked her way back through the dancers to where Dick was waiting.

At twelve thirty Amy and Kevin walked along to the Coffee An. Down in the dingy underground room they sat opposite each other at the only two empty seats available as the place was packed.

"So you persuaded your parents that you were going to an all-night party tonight then," Amy said.

"Well, no not really. I did try asking if I could stay out all night but dad insisted that I must go home."

"Isn't it a bit too late now? Your last bus will have gone."

"I know, and I don't care," Kevin said defiantly with a grin and reached across the table and took hold of her hand. "I want to stay down the Scene with you and I'll just have to face the music when I get home tomorrow."

"So long as your parents don't ban you from the Scene altogether," Amy said.

"Oh I'm sure they wouldn't try to do that - they're not *that* bad," Kevin declared.

"Well let's head back - maybe Pam and Dick will have returned by now. That coffee, although it's pretty awful, has woken me up so I don't feel at all tired - just as well since Eric didn't have any spare pills tonight."

"Do you take them very often?" Kevin asked sounding a little surprised.

"Only when I'm dancing all night – stops me from flagging."

They reached Ham Yard to find it swarming with police so they quickly made for the entrance to the Scene and went down the stairs.

"What's going on up there?" Amy enquired of Harry the bouncer.

"The fuzz are searching all the cars parked up there - looking for drugs," Harry replied as he checked their pass out marks under the fluorescent light.

"They won't be coming down here will they?" Amy asked anxiously.

"I doubt it. If they intended raiding the joint they would have done that first. If they do it now they'll have lost the element of surprise."

After half an hour Mary and Pat came in followed by Pam and Dick and his mates.

"Have the police gone from the yard?" Kevin asked Mary.

"What police? I didn't see any."

"A good job you didn't get here earlier else your car would have been searched for drugs," Amy told Pat.

Pat shrugged. "I've got nothing to hide," she said handing round her cigarettes.

"For once my car is clean of pills," Eric said looking relieved.

Mary and Pat only stayed for a short while and then left to go home. While Pam and Dick smooched around to the music, Amy and Kevin sat cuddled up together in an alcove.

At 6 a.m. they left the club and the four of them walked to Charing Cross Station in the grey of the morning dawn.

Dick was getting a lift home in Eric's car so the girls said goodbye to the boys on the platform.

"Hope you don't get into too much hot water," Amy whispered in Kevin's ear, adding, "I really thought for a while that those cops had been sent by your dad."

Kevin smiled, held her close and whispered, "I love you - phone me tomorrow."

The whistle blew and the girls had to quickly jump into the nearest carriage. They waved goodbye out of the window, and then Amy flopped down on the seat, bursting to tell Pam of Kevin's declaration of love for her.

"Huh, that's more than I've got out of Dick after all this time we've been going out together!" She exclaimed with a flick of her hair. She seemed a little peeved.

Amy arrived home just after seven thirty, crept in the back door and up the stairs to bed. She fell asleep dreaming of Kevin and didn't wake up until three in the afternoon. When she eventually put in an appearance in the lounge she was horrified to find an array of glassy Arthurs occupying all the seats. They were six of mum's relatives (mum, dad, three sons and a daughter) who occasionally descended unannounced and unwanted from Essex. They all wore glasses - hence the nickname that her father had bestowed on them, and they were all a little odd.

One of the sons, in his early twenties sat engrossed in a Beano comic while his teenage brother absently tugged out tufts of hair from his scalp. Their father was in the middle of a lengthy explanation of the procedures he underwent during his last operation, one of many, and insisted that his insides were now held together with rope and a broom handle!

After a hasty 'hello', Amy quickly retreated using the excuse that her hair was in need of an urgent wash.

Chapter Eleven

June - The Flat

Amy ploughed through her usual heavy Monday morning workload updating her ledgers with the agents remittance advice for insurance premiums collected the previous week. She was looking forward to ringing Kevin during her lunch hour when he pre-empted her by calling her instead. His voice on the phone lifted her spirits and sent them soaring. Suddenly her drab job no longer mattered, now that she had Kevin to talk to.

"Did you get into trouble with your dad on Sunday morning when you arrived home?" Amy asked as soon as she recognised his voice.

"Oh, he blew his top, as expected, but I cooked him a huge fried breakfast and that helped to mollify him. How about meeting me after work on Wednesday evening then you can come to work with me."

"That would be great - I'd like to see where you work," Amy said.

"The only trouble is, it'll mean you meeting my mum and my aunts." Kevin sounded dubious.

"I don't mind that," Amy insisted, "in fact I'm looking forward to meeting your mum."

"That's settled then," Kevin declared, "meet me at Victoria Station at five thirty."

Amy hung up feeling happy after her chat with Kevin but a little apprehensive at the prospect of meeting his mum and aunts. She decided to be on her best behaviour knowing that first impressions were vitally important and his mum and aunts would definitely be sizing her up.

After work on Wednesday Amy hurried to the tube where she caught a train across town to Victoria and found Kevin waiting for her outside the station.

"It's not far from here," Kevin said as Amy took his arm and they walked along the road, "I help with the cleaning at an office block two or three evenings a week. Don't like doing it but it puts a few much needed pennies in my pocket. I told mum I was bringing you this evening."

"You mean you warned her," Amy corrected him with a grin.

"I know mum will like you," Kevin declared confidently. Amy didn't feel so sure as she followed Kevin into the entrance foyer of a large building. They stepped out of the lift at the second floor into a corridor that had empty offices on either side. Voices could be heard chattering in one of the offices further along so Kevin took Amy in that direction. Outside the office a large trolley stood loaded with cleaning materials and equipment.

They walked in and Amy was surprised to find three diminutive women in overalls busy emptying waste paper bins and ashtrays into large rubbish bags.

"Hello mum, er - this is Amy," Kevin announced sounding a little nervous. The women stopped work and turned to stare. Amy smiled and said 'hello', hoping she passed their scrutiny.

One of the women put down her rubbish bag and walked over.

"Your late," she snapped at Kevin and then turned to give Amy a warm smile. "I've heard quite a bit about you from Kevin, dear. Nice to meet you at last."

Amy gazed at the petite attractive woman with dark brown curls reaching to her shoulders. Amy guessed she couldn't weigh above six stone.

"It's nice to meet you too, Mrs White," Amy replied politely. Kevin's mum then proceeded to introduce Amy to her two sisters and Amy was struck by the obvious family resemblance. Then she turned back to Kevin.

"Make a start on the two offices at the far end of the corridor and then you can clean the men's urinals next to them. I don't like going in those smelly places to clean."

"Oh thanks - give me the grotty jobs," Kevin moaned, then he glanced at Amy and winked. "Come and give me a hand," he said and they walked back along the corridor.

"I've finished work for today," Amy said firmly, "I shall enjoy sitting back and watching while you slave away."

Amy sat on a desk swinging her legs and chatting as Kevin walked up the aisle emptying the bins and cleaning the ashtrays.

"Your mum and aunts seem quite nice," she commented casually.

"She's OK - I can usually get round her if there's something I want," Kevin said, carrying a bag of rubbish out to the corridor, "it's dad that's the problem; he has rules and expects everyone to stick to them. He thinks he can order us around like he does his underlings in the force. He and Trevor have fallen out badly at times - I'm surprised Trevor hasn't left home before now. Right, I've finished in here, let's go to the bogs next door."

Amy followed Kevin somewhat reluctantly into the men's toilets feeling a bit uncomfortable at being where she ought not to be even though the offices were closed. She was surprised how different they were to ladies toilets with the urinals lined up along one wall. She had gone into men's toilets a few times in the past, but purely by accident, and because of her acute embarrassment, hadn't stopped to take in the surroundings, being intent on getting out as quickly as possible.

Kevin donned rubber gloves and set to work with disinfectant and brushes cleaning each urinal and cubicle.

"I'd want double time if I was doing this job," Amy declared.

"You get used to it," Kevin said giving each toilet a flush, "it doesn't take very long." After cleaning the hand basins Kevin was finished. "Mum and my aunts will do the floors," he said packing away the cleaning materials.

Amy was relieved to leave the men's toilet and return to the corridor. Kevin poked his head back round an office doorway to say goodbye to his mum and aunts and then walked along to the lifts with Amy.

Outside they hopped on a bus for the short journey to Sloane Square and walked round the corner to Kevin's house. Indoors Kevin's younger brother, Stuart, was slumped on the settee watching T.V. Kevin introduced him to Amy and she was struck by the likeness to his older brother, having the same dark hair and large brown eyes. He grunted a 'hello' and then returned to watching cartoons. Kevin took Amy into the kitchen and started making some beans on toast for their tea while Amy busied herself brewing a pot of tea.

"How come Trevor doesn't look anything like you or Stuart?" Amy asked.

Kevin shrugged. "Maybe he was adopted," he said with a grin, spooning the heated beans onto pieces of toast. They sat at the small kitchen table to eat their meal and had just finished when Trevor arrived home. He came into the kitchen and made himself a coffee.

"What are you two up to this evening?" he asked.

"We'll probably go round to Ken's," Kevin said and drained his mug of tea, "are you ready Amy?"

Amy nodded, stood up and put her coat on.

"Mum will be home anytime now," he told Trevor as he ushered Amy towards the front door.

"Good, I'm hungry and want my tea," Trevor said slumping into the chair that Amy had vacated.

"You could always try cooking it yourself," Kevin called out and then slammed the door shut behind him and Amy, not waiting to hear the sarcastic retort from his brother.

They caught a bus over to Ken's house and found him indoors on his own playing records. He made them a mug of coffee each and they sat in the lounge chatting and joking while listening to records until it was time for Amy to catch her train home. As she got up she dropped her handbag and the contents spilled out onto the carpet. Kevin pounced gleefully on the photo of Amy and Mick and held it out of her reach. As she leapt on him trying to get it back Ken gave a whoop. "Look what I've found," he said waving Amy's diary at Kevin.

"Don't you dare read that," Amy shouted and lunged across the room at him knocking him onto the sofa. She wrestled the diary from him and they ended up falling onto the floor giggling helplessly. Then she quickly thrust her things back into her bag.

"I'm not bothered about that photo - you're welcome to it - it's pretty awful," she said to Kevin.

"I'll cut him off and just keep you," Kevin said pocketing the photo.

The following evening Amy and Pam met Kevin at the bus stop in Shaftesbury Avenue and they headed for the Scene. Pam was meeting Dick there and being a Thursday, it wasn't quite so crowded. There was no sign of Dick and after half an hour Pam spied Eric and went over to find out what had happened to him.

Amy and Kevin were sitting in an alcove wrapped up in each other when Pam returned and flung herself down next to them, her face contorted with anger.

"That's it, Bat," she snapped, "Dick has blown it this time."

"What's he done now?" Amy asked pulling away from Kevin.

"Eric has just informed me that Dick has gone off to a party this evening. He didn't mention any party when I phoned him at lunchtime."

"Maybe it's something that came up at the last minute and he couldn't get out of it?" Amy suggested somewhat lamely. It was the best excuse she could think of on the spur of the moment to try and put Dick in a better light.

Pam gave a derogatory snort. "Eric was being a bit cagey so I wouldn't be surprised if Dick has taken some girl to the party. Well I'm definitely finished with him now so I'm not going to hang around here any longer - I'm going home." She stomped off towards the exit.

"Perhaps I should go with her," Amy said, glancing at Kevin.

"She'll be fine," Kevin said confidently, "there's no need to spoil our evening too"

"I suppose you're right." Amy didn't take much convincing because she was enjoying snuggling up to Kevin in the alcove. Percy Sledge started crooning 'When a Man Loves a Woman' so they got up for a smooch on the dance floor. Halfway through the dance Kevin murmured in Amy's ear: "I think we should get engaged next year."

Amy giggled. "You're nuts!" she exclaimed. "You're not serious?" Kevin was serious but Amy's reaction unnerved him so he laughed it off as a joke.

"It's bank holiday this weekend so why don't we go down to Brighton?" Amy suggested changing the subject.

"We could go on Sunday but I'm not sure about staying over to the Monday," Kevin said as they sat down again, "it could cause ructions."

"Perhaps if you got round your mum, she could convince your dad that it'll be OK?"

"Maybe," Kevin said doubtfully.

At the end of the evening Kevin walked Amy to the station and they arranged to meet on Saturday evening at Sloane Square.

Pam arrived at Amy's house Saturday afternoon. She seemed to be over Dick and back to her usual cheerful self.

"I've told my parents I'm staying here tonight so we can go down the Scene all night Bat - that's if you can stay out all night too."

"Mine don't put up much resistance these days and just accept it when I tell them I'm going to a party or staying over at yours."

"You're lucky then; my mum always has a good moan."

"I'm meeting Kevin at Sloane Square but you can come too and then we'll go down the Scene later on," Amy suggested.

"Won't Kevin mind me tagging along?"

"'Course he won't, Tibs," Amy assured her friend, "and he won't be staying out all night so we'll have a great time by ourselves."

After informing her mother of the all-night party they were going to, Amy got ready and then she and Pam caught the train to London and dived onto the tube to Sloane Square where they found Kevin already waiting. He didn't look surprised at seeing Pam arrive with Amy.

"Ken asked me to go over to his house so I told him we'd go for a while this evening," he said.

"That's a good idea," Pam said eagerly. At least now there would be four of them and she wouldn't feel *de trop*.

They caught a bus to Ken's house and spent the evening drinking coffee and chatting while listening to records until Ken's mum arrived home at eleven when they decided it was time to leave. Ken walked to the front gate with them.

"Are you ones going up West all night?" he asked.

"These two are but I've got to go home," Kevin said sounding a bit disgruntled.

"You boys need your beauty sleep," Amy teased, "so while you're getting your zeds in we'll be dancing the night away."

"I think I'll set my alarm for about four in the morning so that I can get down the Scene for the last hour before it closes," Ken said.

"Well don't bother calling for me at that unearthly time," Kevin said emphatically, "it won't be appreciated."

At the bus stop Kevin caught his bus home and Amy promised to ring him in the morning.

"Try not to make it too early," Kevin pleaded as he boarded the bus.

The girls hopped on a bus to the West End and alighted in Leicester Square. They headed for the Coffee An as it was just round the corner and got chatting to a boy who shared their table. He offered to sell them ten doubles each, which they quickly accepted and discreetly swallowed with their coffee.

Down the Scene as the pills took effect they really began to enjoy themselves dancing and chatting non-stop with all and sundry. A girl called Toni who they hadn't seen down there before attached herself to them. Pam and Amy didn't mind, as she seemed to be on her own.

At around four in the morning Toni wanted to go round to the twenty-four hour chemists in Piccadilly so Pam and Amy offered to accompany her.

"Are you ones going to the coast tomorrow?" Toni asked as they emerged from the chemist's.

"I'm not," Pam said, "but you're going with Kevin aren't you, Bat?"

"If I can get him out of bed," Amy said.

"Do you think I could come with you?" Toni asked. Amy wondered why she would want to play gooseberry to two comparative strangers but she merely nodded.

"'Course you can, I'm sure Kevin won't mind."

As they turned into Great Windmill Street they bumped into Graham and his mates.

"Don't go back to the Scene just yet girls," Graham said, "it's being raided - police are swarming all over the place."

"It was lucky we left when we did then," Pam said peering along the street to the turning into Ham Yard. "I can see the meat wagons parked up ready to load up the unlucky ones that get arrested,"

Graham and his mates walked off and the girls stood huddled together uncertain where to go.

"Let's go and get a coffee at the self-service machines in Piccadilly," Toni suggested. They retraced their steps and managed to find the change needed for three coffees at the newly installed machines in a recessed area where hot and cold snacks and drinks were dished out at the press of a button. The girls stood drinking coffee out of plastic cups.

Amy gave a shiver in the chilly morning air. "If I'd known we were going to be out for so long I'd have brought my suede," she complained. After finishing their coffee they returned to Great Windmill Street and found the meat wagons had gone. They cautiously made their way back to the Scene but there were only two coppers hovering in Ham Yard and they took no notice of the girls as they tiptoed back down the stairs.

"How did it go?" Pam asked George as he checked their pass out marks under the fluorescent light.

"There were a few arrests for possession," George said with a shrug," "but I think most of the kids managed to flush their pills down the loo before they could be searched. The fuzz must be hard up for something to do to come down here and cause trouble for no good reason."

"So now the loos are blocked too!" Pam said with a laugh as they went inside. Most of the people were standing around talking, evidently still unsettled by the raid and no longer inclined to dance. But the music soon had the girls dancing again and at the end of the second number in walked Ken accompanied by Len wearing his long orange leather coat.

Ken grinned at Pam and Amy. "I told you I'd get here around five," he said.

"Didn't really think you'd make it," Pam said.

"I even managed to get Len up to come with me," he added.

"I'd been to a party and only just got to bed when he comes banging on my door," Len said, "I don't think my mum was too pleased at being woken up at that hour."

"It's just as well you didn't get here any earlier," Pam said, "else you might have ended up in a police wagon." She told them about the raid and introduced them to Toni. Len looked quite taken with her and as soon as a slow number came on he asked her to dance. That was the last they saw of them. When the Scene closed Amy and Pam decided to go to the Last Chance and Ken caught a bus home again.

The girls still had plenty of energy and danced non-stop 'til eight o'clock when Amy thought it wouldn't be too early to ring Kevin so she needed to find a phone box. They crossed the Strand to Charing Cross Station where Pam said goodbye and went to catch a train home while Amy rang Kevin.

She was surprised when he answered the phone straight away. They arranged to meet at Victoria Station in an hour's time so that they could catch a train down to Brighton.

Amy waited impatiently at Victoria Station until Kevin finally arrived looking sheepish at being late.

They arrived at Brighton late morning and mingled with the crowds of Mods wandering along the promenade. Amy was beginning to feel really depressed. She realised it was only a reaction to the high she had been on all night. The energy was being leached from her legs and all she wanted to do was lie down and rest.

"Let's go down onto the beach and sit for a while," she urged and, tugging Kevin's arm, headed for the steps leading down from the promenade. On the beach they stumbled across the pebbles to get to a groyne where they could sit and relax on its sheltered side. Kevin was concerned at Amy's pallid complexion.

"I'll be fine," she reassured him, "stop fussing like an old mother hen - think I'll try to take a nap." She lay down and used Kevin's knee as a pillow. The warm sun beating down made her feel drowsy. She closed her eyes and dozed off into a fitful sleep. Kevin sat leaning against the groyne watching the groups of people - mostly Mods - wandering aimlessly down near the water's edge. Some, in a playful mood, tried to throw their friends into the sea accompanied by much shrieking and laughter. There didn't appear to be any friction with the few Rockers that lurked around, who were wisely keeping a low profile.

A particularly noisy group of Mods passed nearby crunching the pebbles underfoot. Amy sat up and yawned while Kevin massaged his numb legs. He hadn't dared move in case he disturbed her. "Feeling better?" he asked.

Amy smiled. "I'm OK - told you I would be. Have I missed anything?"

"Haven't seen a single punch up," Kevin informed her sounding a little disappointed.

Amy felt a bit more energetic so suggested they take a stroll along the promenade. The place was crowded with Mods but not like it had been at Easter. They walked round to the Zodiac coffee bar and sat sipping cappuccinos. Amy was still feeling depressed from her come down but tried to hide it from Kevin.

"I don't think we should stay down here all night," Kevin said. He could tell Amy was not her usual self and he didn't much fancy the prospect of sleeping rough. "If we catch the train back up to town you could stay at my place."

Amy didn't need much persuading in her present delicate state. She also didn't like the idea of roughing it especially after the dire night spent in the cliff gardens at Easter. She definitely didn't want a repeat of that experience.

"Yes, maybe we should go back to London," Amy agreed and grinned, "it would keep you in your parents' good books and we don't want your dad calling out the Brighton police force to hunt us down do we? Are you sure it'll be OK for me to stay at your house?"

"Mum and dad will be so relieved to see me come home that they'll welcome you with open arms and assume you're having a good influence on me - shows how wrong impressions can be!"

Amy gave him a playful kick under the table. "Come on then, let's go home and please your mum and dad."

Back at Kevin's maisonette his mum was only too happy to make up a bed for Amy on the divan in the lounge before shooing Kevin upstairs to his room, which he shared with his younger brother.

Amy slept intermittently and woke early so she got up, washed and tidied away the bedding before anyone else stirred. She went into the kitchen and made a pot of tea and was just pouring herself out a mug when Kevin peered round the door, his hair all tousled, wearing a dressing gown.

"Got one for me?" he asked coming over to give her a hug and a kiss as she reached to get another mug from the cupboard. "I think mum and dad definitely approve of you."

Amy smiled. "Let's hope I don't disillusion them." Just then Kevin's mum came bustling into the kitchen.

"Right, I'm going to cook egg and bacon for everyone, so Kevin, go and get dressed and kick your brothers out of their pits. Tell them they must be down here in twenty minutes if they want breakfast."

Amy made herself useful by laying the dining table in the lounge while Kevin's mum started the cooking. Kevin's dad came in carrying a newspaper and after a cheery greeting, he settled down in his armchair to read it. Amy thought he was quite good-looking, tall, well-built with very dark hair and a moustache. She could imagine him taking no stick from his sons.

Although she didn't have much of an appetite, especially for a fried breakfast, nevertheless Amy enjoyed sharing the meal with Kevin and his family. They made her feel at ease and afterwards Kevin took her up to his room to show her his electric guitar.

"I can only play a few chords and it really needs a new amplifier," he said putting the leather strap round his neck. "I'm not supposed to play it loud as it would upset the neighbours." He plugged the shiny red and chrome guitar into the amplifier and turned the volume down before giving it a few quiet strums.

"If you learnt to play it you could join a group," Amy suggested giving the strings a gentle pluck.

"Don't think I've got the patience or enough talent to do that." He stood up and put the Who's record of 'Can't Explain' on his record player, turned the volume up and then did a good impersonation of Pete Townshend doing his windmill swings with his arm.

Trevor came in, sat on the bed, and pretended to be Keith Moon madly smashing at his drums.

Amy sat on the other bed enjoying the performance until Stuart arrived and switched the record player off. "Dad says you're making too much noise."

Trevor and Kevin both groaned. Kevin took off the guitar. "What's the use? We can't do anything in this flippin' place."

"It was good while it lasted," Amy said, "but it's time I headed back home. I shall have to try and make my peace with my parents as they will be wondering where I have got to."

Kevin walked with her to the tube station and promised to meet her at the Scene the following evening.

At work Tuesday morning Amy discovered she had been transferred to F division on the opposite side of the large office. Four married men worked there with just one other woman. Amy felt nervous - she hadn't worked with men before and now she had Philip as her head of division and Paul as his deputy. They very soon put her at ease with their relaxed, friendly ways, which took Amy a while to adjust to, after the strict regime of Vera and her sidekick, Audrey. Amy felt sure that once she got to know her new work colleagues better, she would find the change a big improvement, especially as now she had a different workload doing policy transfers and changes of address which was a bit more interesting than entering receipts into dusty ledgers.

Philip sat nearest the wall on the long bench, with Paul in the middle and then Amy next to the gangway.

Paul leaned across to Amy and whispered, "I'm surprised you stuck it for so long over on A division with those two wretched old witches making everyone's life a misery."

"I had been thinking about handing in my notice," Amy admitted, "I think they knew I wasn't very happy there."

"Well you can forget about leaving now - we'll look after you - won't we Jeannie?"

Jeannie was just returning to her seat in the middle of the long bench in front of Amy. She was smartly dressed in a bright red suit, wore plenty of make-up and her platinum blonde hair was cut into a neat bob.

She flashed Amy a dazzling smile. "Don't take any nonsense from him - or any of this lot come to that, Amy. If they give you grief just tell me and I'll sort them out." Jeannie was a big sturdy girl in her mid-twenties and Amy didn't doubt she could sort out any man.

Amy met up with Kevin at the Scene that evening and he persuaded her to book a day off work on Friday so that she could go over to his maisonette in the afternoon, as they would have the place to themselves.

Trevor had asked Kevin to bleach his jeans jacket while he was at work on Friday so when Amy arrived in the afternoon they took it up to the bathroom and filled the bath with a bleach solution before dunking the jacket and leaving it to whiten. "Better not leave it soaking for too long - if I ruin it for him he'll kill me," Kevin said.

They returned to the lounge and Amy left Kevin sorting out what records to play while she popped into the kitchen to make some coffee.

"Do you realise it's one month we've been going out together now," Kevin said as Amy put the mugs down on the coffee table.

"Doesn't seem that long - I'm surprised you've been keeping count."

Kevin pulled her down onto the settee beside him and kissed her. "How about we go to the Goldhawk Club tonight to celebrate? I don't know who will be playing though." Amy liked the idea of seeing the much talked about club even though it would be quite a journey to get there.

Stuart arrived home from school, shortly followed by Trevor who had finished work early.

"Did you bleach my jacket?" he asked as he burst in the door.

"Oh, we left it soaking in the bath a while ago," Kevin said looking guilty, "and then forgot about it."

"What! You idiot!" Trevor shouted in dismay and dashed off upstairs to rescue it.

Kevin looked at Amy and shrugged. "He should have done it himself instead of palming it off onto me."

Trevor reappeared with the jacket dripping on the carpet. He held it up and grinned. "You're lucky - it's bleached just right." He took it into the kitchen to put in the spin dryer.

"I knew it'd be fine," Kevin called after him while pulling a face at Amy that said, "Phew – that was lucky."

After tea with the rest of the family, Kevin and Amy caught the tube to the club in north London. It was packed, hot and stuffy. Amy held onto Kevin's hand as he led her through the tightly packed gloom to some seats at the far side. They were in luck because the Small Faces were playing on stage and had a great repertoire. The atmosphere in the club was good and they managed to find enough space for a few dances. At the end of the evening, Kevin took Amy to Charing Cross station just in time to catch the last train home.

"Pat and Mary have invited me and Pam over to Pat's house tomorrow evening," Amy said as she boarded the train and leaned out of the window to say goodbye. "Mary said you and Trevor are also invited - she's not holding a grudge against Trevor any more."

"Is it a party?"

"No, just coffee and records. Do you think you'll be able to stay out all night tomorrow so that we can go down the Scene?"

"I'm sure I can work it somehow, but if dad puts his foot down then I'll just walk out."

"Let's hope it doesn't come to that," Amy said, adding, "I might get the blame!"

The whistle blew and the train moved off. They just had time for one quick kiss before Kevin was left behind on the platform.

Amy had arranged to meet Pam on the London-bound train Saturday evening, but as the train drew in to the station there was no sign of Pam. It wasn't like Pam to not turn up. Something must have happened. Amy wondered whether her friend was ill. Should she get off and walk round to her house to find out? She was meeting Kevin and Trevor at Finsbury Park tube station and would be very late if she had to catch a later train.

As she tried to decide what to do, the train made up her mind for her by pulling away. Amy leaned out of the window hoping to see Pam dashing onto the platform at the last moment but it didn't happen.

She arrived at Finsbury Park to find Kevin waiting for her along with Trevor and Ken.

Kevin greeted her with a hug and a kiss. "I've done it," he said smiling, "I told the olds I'm staying at Ken's tonight. He'll back me up if needs be so I brought him along." Amy didn't really see why Ken needed to come along but as he was doing Kevin a favour she didn't mind. They walked off down the back streets of Finsbury Park in search of Pat's house. The boys were in a boisterous mood with Trevor and Ken prancing about playing silly buggers. Mary had given Amy directions to Pat's house and they soon found her street - a wide road of large detached and semi-detached houses.

As they wandered down the middle of the road Trevor suddenly swooped on Amy. "What are you hiding in your handbag Amy?" he asked with a grin as he suddenly tugged the bag away from her and ran up the street with a furious Amy in hot pursuit. He thrust his hand inside and gave a triumphant yell as he pulled out her diary and waved it above his head.

Amy flushed with indignant rage at his audacity. "Give me that back," she shouted jumping up to try and grab it from Trevor's hand. Trevor tossed it to Ken who whooped with glee before throwing it to Kevin. Amy's angry threats fell on deaf ears. Even Kevin joined in the fun, tossing it back to Trevor.

By now Amy was furious. "That's it, Kevin," she stormed, "I don't expect any better from those two, but you're behaving just as badly, so we're through - I've finished with you." She stomped off to the side of the road and sat down on the kerb with her head on her knees. She could feel the hot tears threatening but fought to hold them back. Maybe she was overreacting, and the last thing she wanted was for them to see her defeated and crying. Kevin came over and sat down beside her.

"Here," he said and dropped her bag and diary into her lap, "I'm sorry but it was only a bit of fun - we didn't mean to upset you."

"Well you did!" Amy snapped. She stood up and thrust the diary back into her bag. "I'm going home!" She turned and walked back down the road. Kevin hurried to catch her up and tried to get her to change her mind.

"Let's go to Pat's now that we're here," he coaxed, "she's expecting us and will wonder where we've got to."

"Too bad. Send Trevor in to explain and apologise."

Kevin accompanied Amy on the train back to the West End. He looked contrite and kept apologising and begging Amy to forgive him.

"I promise I'll never do anything like that again. It was all my stupid brother's fault - he started it."

"Yes, but you didn't have to join in."

It took the whole of the journey to the West End before Amy grudgingly agreed to go to the Scene for a while with him. She didn't really want to carry out her threat of going home so she held out for several hours before capitulating and finally agreeing to stay all night with him. Eric was down there and sold Amy five doubles. Kevin tried to dissuade her from buying them so she deliberately ignored him and took them regardless.

Sunday morning they walked to the coffee bar in the Strand and sat at a table upstairs sipping coffee. Then an idea struck Amy. "Why don't you come home with me? Mum and dad are going to Suffolk to visit Granddad, so they'll be gone all day."

"That'd be great!" Kevin said with a grin, "but I'd better ring home and let them know I shan't be back for the rest of the day."

They huddled into a kiosk on Charing Cross station so that Kevin could make his phone call home. It went well with no awkward questions asked about his stay at Ken's house. They came out of the kiosk and dashed along platform two just in time to catch the train before it pulled out.

"There will only be my irritating younger brother, Ray, at home but we can ignore him," Amy said snuggling up to Kevin and resting her head on his shoulder.

Kevin smiled. "I'm used to having irritating brothers around so it won't bother me."

They walked up the hill to Amy's house from the station and, whether real or imagined, she could sense the neighbours net curtains twitching and curious eyes gazing out from behind them. She held Kevin's arm and proudly paraded him round the Crescent, but was nevertheless relieved to reach the privacy of her home. They went in the back door and Amy took Kevin through to the lounge.

He relaxed on the settee while Amy sorted through her records. "We can play these as loud as we like and no-one will complain," Amy said brightly. She was still feeling a bit high from the doubles she had taken whereas Kevin was looking a little jaded.

Just then the door opened and Ray poked his head in. "Oh, you're home at last. I'm making some coffee - do you two want a mug?"

"That's a rare treat from you," Amy said in surprise. She decided his thoughtfulness deserved an introduction to Kevin.

He reappeared five minute later with two mugs.

"Mum has left food ready prepared so I'll make the meal today if you like?" he offered setting down the mugs on the coffee table.

"Didn't know you could cook but that would be great," Amy said, amazed at her brother's good behaviour. "I'm suspicious - he must have some ulterior motive," Amy whispered to Kevin after Ray had gone, "he's never usually this helpful."

"It gives us more time to ourselves," Kevin said pulling Amy into his arms for a kiss and a cuddle.

Several hours later they were still snuggled up together listening to the Kingsmen's LP with a worrying aroma of burnt food coming from the kitchen, when they heard a tap on the door and Ray entered carrying a tray laid out with plates of food and more coffee.

"Er - the chops got a bit charred but they're still edible - I think," he said putting the tray down in front of them. He had managed to cook lamb chops, potatoes and peas.

"Wow - that looks almost good enough to eat!" Amy declared with a hint of sarcasm. "Pity about the lumpy gravy though."

"I thought it was a pretty good first attempt," Ray said defensively.

"It looks great to me," Kevin said lifting the tray onto his knees, "I'm starving so I'm not complaining." He grabbed a knife and fork and began tucking in and gave a relieved Ray the thumbs up verdict. Ray left with a satisfied smirk on his face. Amy wasn't feeling very hungry so she just picked at her food and let Kevin finish off hers after he had eaten his meal.

Afterwards Kevin leaned back and yawned. "That meal has made me feel really tired."

"Why don't we go upstairs and relax?" Amy suggested, standing up. "We can borrow Ray's double bed - I'm sure he won't mind." She took Kevin's hand and led him up to Ray's bedroom. A thin counterpane covered the bed so they took their shoes off and snuggled up underneath it.

"This is more comfortable," Kevin said appreciatively but no sooner had they resumed their snogging than there was a knock at the front door.

"Ray will get it," Amy mumbled. The next minute there were footsteps coming up the stairs and Ray's bedroom door was flung open. Amy turned to find Pam standing there looking as though steam was about to erupt from her ears. "What on earth's up?" she asked in consternation.

Pam came in, shut the door, flung off her coat and shoes and walked over to the bed. "Shove over," she said climbing in beside Amy.

Pam was so wound up that it hadn't occurred to her she might be an unwelcome intrusion. "I've had it with my parents," she ranted, "last night dad stopped me from going out. I'm sure my mother was behind it. We had a flaming row and I stormed off to bed."

"I wondered where you'd got to when you didn't show up at the station," Amy said.

"I've decided to leave home just as soon as I can find a flat," Pam continued, "I'm going to an agency tomorrow."

"Have you told your parents that you're leaving home?" Kevin asked.

"No way! Mum would have forty fits and try to stop me. I shan't tell them - I shall just pack my things and go."

"Well if you're going flat hunting then I'm coming with you," Amy declared resolutely.

Pam gave a sigh and visibly relaxed. "I was hoping you'd say that," she said with a smile, "I didn't really fancy doing it on my own."

"We'll have a great time, Tibs, in our own place with no more parents to answer to."

"Mm, yeah - I can't wait," Pam agreed. Then she glanced across at Amy and Kevin as though the situation was only now registering with her. "By the way, what are you two up to here in your brother's bed?" she asked suspiciously.

"Nothing!" Amy retorted, "we were feeling a bit tired after being up all night. Ray's been waiting on us hand and foot with food and drinks - goodness knows what's got into him!"

Amy was a little disappointed that Pam didn't seem to be in any hurry to leave, in fact she appeared unconcerned that three in a bed was one too many. The three of them lay in the bed discussing flats and the best areas in London to look for one. They eventually roused and trooped downstairs in the early evening to make some coffee and then it was time for Pam and Kevin to catch their trains home. Amy walked to the station to see them off and then returned home to find her parents were back and hopping mad because Ray had dutifully informed them that Amy and her boyfriend had been up in his bed all afternoon.

Amy glared at him. If looks could kill he would be stone dead. Her father ranted and raved at her, ignoring his daughter's vigorous protestations, he insisted she couldn't be trusted. She eventually managed to appease him by explaining that Pam had been there too so it had all been completely innocent.

'Thank goodness I'll be out of here before too long,' Amy thought as she stomped off to bed.

After work next day Amy and Pam visited an accommodation agency to see what flats were on offer that they could afford.

"I quite fancy living in West London," Pam said as they perused the flats advertised in the agency window.

"Yeah, that would be great," Amy agreed, "but most are way out of our price range."

A lady behind a large desk handed the girls particulars on a couple of flats situated in the Bayswater area and then the girls headed for the station.

"Let's book a day off work on Wednesday so we can do some flat hunting," Pam suggested as they relaxed on the homeward bound train. Then she suddenly leaned over and tugged at Amy's polo neck sweater. "Ha, I thought so," she shouted triumphantly, "Kevin must have been feeling hungry yesterday judging by all those love bites you're hiding."

Amy grinned and quickly readjusted her polo neck. "Can't keep anything from you can I? After all the ear bashing I got last night from my parents because my darling brother told on me, I'll be relieved when we find a place, and the sooner the better."

Tuesday evening the girls headed for the Scene as usual only to find a crowd loitering around in Ham Yard looking at a loose end because the Scene was closed for redecorating. A large notice was nailed to the door stating that the club would reopen on Saturday.

They found Kevin, Trevor and Len in the crowd and Len suggested they all go back to his house at Stockwell and listen to some music. They caught a bus to Len's house and were pleased to find they had the house to themselves as Len's parents were out. Pam and Amy went to make coffee in the kitchen while the boys sorted through Len's album collection.

"Me and Pam are taking the day off work tomorrow to go flat hunting around Bayswater," Amy announced as she came in with the tray of coffee mugs.

"Hope you're gonna have a house warming party," Trevor said eagerly.

"Mm, maybe," Pam said doubtfully, "only we don't want to go upsetting neighbours and get ourselves chucked out as soon as we're in."

"My cousin mentioned something about a flat near him that's being advertised," Len said, "I can find out about it for you if you like - I'll be seeing him tomorrow."

"Yeah, do that and I'll ring you tomorrow evening," Amy said.

Next morning the girls headed up to town after the rush hour and Amy stopped in Oxford Street to buy some material and a pattern for a dress before they caught the tube over to Bayswater to look at the two flats which the agent had given them details of. They were disappointed with both of them as one was too cramped and the other too grotty.

"Maybe Len will come up trumps with this flat he mentioned last night," Amy said as they made their way to another accommodation agency to see if they had anything suitable.

The agent rummaged through her filing cabinet and produced typed details of a flat which was also in Bayswater.

"I can arrange for you to view it on Friday," she said curtly.

"It'll have to be after work," Pam told her, "we can't take any more time off."

The agent made a brief phone call to arrange the appointment and then it was time for the girls to make for the station in order to miss the rush hour home.

Amy popped into a phone box on the platform to ring Kevin. He tried persuading her to catch a train over to his house but Amy insisted she must go home and wash her hair. She agreed to meet him and Trevor at the Scene on Saturday evening instead.

Then Amy rang Len and he gave her the address of the flat in Warrington Road. She just had time to jot it down on a scrap of paper dug out from the depths of her handbag before Pam was dragging her out of the box and yelling at her to hurry because their train was about to leave.

After work on Friday, Amy and Pam hurried across town by tube to Warrington Road to look at the flat Len had told them about.

"What a dump this area is," Pam said in disgust as they turned into Warrington Road with wrecks of cars littering the roadside. They searched for number 61 among the gloomy, tatty facades that had seen better days.

Pam gave a shudder. "It's no good, Bat, I couldn't live in a rundown area like this."

"No, neither could I," Amy agreed, "it'd be like living in a ghetto! Fancy Len's cousin living somewhere around here. Let's not waste any more time and head over to the other flat in Bayswater."

They arrived in a wide well-kept tree-lined avenue and found the first-floor flat bright, clean and quite spacious. The bathroom was shared with another flat on the same landing.

Amy thought the landlady who showed them around seemed rather snooty. She emphasised the list of rules to be adhered to, and mentioned that she had several more viewings booked over the weekend.

Amy glanced at Pam questioningly. She grinned and nodded, so Amy turned to the landlady. "We'd like to take the flat," she said on impulse, "when could we move in?"

"First there are forms to sign," the landlady said coldly, "you must both come back on Monday when I shall have them ready for you."

The girls bubbled with excitement as they headed home on the train.

"It's six pounds ten shillings a week though, Tibs. Do you think we'll be able to afford it?" Amy asked.

"We'll just have to be very careful and keep the rent money to one side," Pam said. "I'm not going to say anything to my parents," she added, "I know they'll kick up a stink - especially my mother."

The following evening Pam called for Amy and as they walked around the Crescent on their way to the station, they met Ray cycling home.

Amy flagged him down. "Tell mum and dad I won't be home tonight - me and Pam are going up West."

"Coward! You should have told them yourself," he retorted.

"I didn't fancy getting into another row. Tell them I'm staying over at Pam's if you like."

"You know they don't believe that one any more."

"Well I don't really care since we won't be around here much longer."

"You've found a flat then?"

"We're signing the forms on Monday, but you must promise not to say a word to mum or dad."

"My parents think I'm staying at yours tonight," Pam said as they continued on their way, "but I'm not sure they really believe what I tell them."

"I wouldn't be surprised if my dad is still meeting up with your dad to check up on our stories," Amy said, "but it won't matter any more once we leave home. I'm *so* looking forward to it, Tibs."

"Yeah, me too," Pam agreed, "It'll be great not having to make up stories and tell lies."

They arrived at the Scene early and saw Eric and a couple of his mates sitting in his old convertible in Ham Yard. Eric leaned out of the window and beckoned them over.

"I've got some gear here if you two want to score," he whispered as Amy bent down next to the window.

"I think we need something to get us through the night," Amy said, ignoring Pam tugging at her arm. The back door swung open and Amy climbed in. She squeezed next to a boy whose name she didn't know and Pam reluctantly got in beside her.

"I'm not sure I want to take anything," she whispered in Amy's ear.

"I've got doubles and blues," Eric said, producing some small brown packets.

"I'll have some of each." Amy fished in her handbag for her purse.

Pam sighed. "Oh well, if you're going to be dancing all night then I'd better have some too."

Their purchases made, the girls went down the Scene and found it looking fresh and a bit lighter in its newly redecorated state. They went to the ladies and took some of the pills. After half an hour they began to kick in and the girls had to dance, as they couldn't keep still.

Nearly an hour later Kevin arrived with Trevor and Ken. Kevin put his arms around Amy and kissed her.

"Guess what!" he whispered excitedly, "I can stay down here all night. My parents think I'm staying at Ken's. Trevor's going home later, so he's going to cover for me too."

"Do you trust him?" Amy asked suspiciously. She wouldn't put it past Trevor to drop Kevin in it.

"'Course I do - I'd do the same for him," Kevin said defensively.

"Well if you want to keep going all night, I've got some blues you can have," Amy offered, "but don't let on to Trevor or Ken."

Kevin looked doubtful. "I've never taken any pills before, but if you've taken some then maybe it would be OK for me to take some too."

Amy led him to the snack bar in the far corner and bought a coke. They sat on a bench in the darkest alcove and Amy rummaged in her bag until she produced a small packet. "There are five doubles here - they should be plenty for you," she said, discreetly emptying the packet into his hand. Kevin glanced down at them and hesitated, but only for a moment. With one swift movement he tossed the pills into his mouth and took a long swig from the coke bottle.

"What are you two doing lurking in here?" Amy looked up to find Pam standing in the entrance looking quizzical.

"Oh, er - nothing," Amy said hastily, "Kevin was thirsty."

They got up and went onto the dance floor to join Ken and Trevor who were bopping with several girls. After half an hour the pills started to take effect and Kevin began dancing wildly. His feet moved twice as fast and he flung his arms around above his head. Amy tried persuading him to modify his dancing so that he didn't attract so much attention, but to no avail. He was enjoying himself far too much to curtail it.

Pam tugged Amy's arm and frowned at her. "Have you been giving that boy pills?" she demanded.

"Kevin's old enough to decide for himself whether or not he wants to take pills," Amy said defensively. "Still, I think I'll give him a wide berth for a while until he quietens down," she added after watching his antics.

As she walked away Ken tapped her on the shoulder. "How about a dance - promise I won't show you up like Kevin," he said with a grin. He took her down near the stage out of sight from Kevin where they danced together for several numbers until Trevor came over.

"I think it would be best if you stopped dancing with Amy," he said to Ken, "Kevin has seen you and it has put him in a bad mood."

"Too bad," Ken said casually, "he shouldn't have shown Amy up." Amy looked around the dance floor until she spotted Kevin still dancing frantically with arms and legs flaying in all directions.

"Perhaps we shouldn't dance together any more," she said, "and besides I need some fresh air - let's go up to the yard." She headed for the exit followed by Ken.

Outside they perched on the top fence rail of the car park and puffed on cigarettes watching the comings and goings of various groups of Mods. Then Trevor appeared through the doors from the club followed by Pam.

He walked over and leaned on the fence. "I'm going to head off home now as the last bus leaves in a few minutes. Mind you ones keep an eye on Kevin."

"We're not his keeper," Ken retorted, "it's not up to us to look after him."

"You're his cousin so I'm holding you responsible," Trevor snapped glaring into his face. Ken shrank back surprised at Trevor's ferocity.

"OK, OK, keep your hair on. He'll be fine; I promise to bring him home safe and sound."

Trevor left to catch his bus and the others returned down the Scene to find Kevin. A slow number came on so Amy walked over to him and put her arms around his neck. He seemed relieved to see her and held her close as they smooched around the floor. He gave Ken, who was dancing with Pam, a dirty look each time they made eye contact. Amy was glad to see that he had calmed down a little but it was short lived because as soon as a loud lively record was played he began leaping around again. Amy danced with Ken and Pam, pretending to disown Kevin who was oblivious to Amy's discomfiture.

It wasn't until closing time Sunday morning that Kevin finally collapsed on a bench exhausted. Amy found it hard to believe that five pills could produce so much energy in him.

The four of them walked down to the Strand for a coffee and then strolled round to St James Park as the sunshine promised a warm day ahead. They found a quiet spot beneath a tree and lay on the grass to rest and try to get some sleep, but after an hour of chatting and giggling they gave up and decided to wend their various ways home.

Pam and Amy met up after work on Monday and dashed down the tube to catch the train to Bayswater. The landlady met them at the door and took them up to the first floor flat so they could sign the necessary forms.

"You can move in next weekend," she informed them coldly, "I'll give you the keys then and the rent will be due each Saturday."

With the forms signed the girls duly agreed to meet her there on Saturday morning before hurrying back to the station in order to catch the train to their typing lesson. As it was their last lesson, they needed to be there because from then on the typing course became a postal course.

Tuesday lunchtime Pam found Amy and Jeanette in the canteen minus Mary as she was on holiday in Italy. She sat down at their table looking excited.

"Guess what, Bat," she said and then continued without waiting for Amy to hazard a guess, "an agent rang me this morning about a great flat in Finsbury Park and it sounds really nice. I think we ought to go and take a look at it."

"But we've already signed the forms for the flat at Bayswater," Amy reminded her friend.

"I know, but this flat has its own bathroom making it self-contained *and* it's a lot less rent. I really think we should go and see it after work today. It's only just become available and will probably get snapped up quickly."

"OK, Tibs, ring the agents and tell them we'll go and view it after work today. If it's cheaper to rent and has its own bathroom then it sounds too good to miss."

The girls found the address in Finsbury Park. It was a semi-detached house on a corner hidden behind a high neatly clipped privet hedge. Pam rang the doorbell and a smartly dressed middle-aged lady answered it with dark hair piled up on top of her head. She introduced herself as Mrs Hodges and ushered them into the hall, which housed a large aquarium occupied by brightly coloured tiny tropical fish. They followed her upstairs to the first floor flat, which consisted of a good-sized lounge with a bed settee and a small kitchen with a bathroom leading off from it. The girls thought it was ideal and booked it without further ado. Mrs Hodges took them downstairs to her lounge to sign the necessary forms and the girls arranged to move in on Saturday.

"I'm afraid your bath is currently out of commission - I'm waiting for a plumber to come and clear a blockage," Mrs Hodges explained apologetically, "but you are welcome to make use of our bathroom down here until yours is fixed - I'm sure it won't be for too long." She led them back to the front door and shook hands. "There's only myself and my husband living here," she informed them as they walked out into the porch, "he's out at work all day and I run the corner shop opposite." She pointed over the hedge to the other side of the road.

"That'll be handy for our bread and milk and other essentials," Amy remarked and then they thanked Mrs Hodges and left for the station.

"I think we're really lucky to get that flat," Pam said excitedly, "it's much better than the one at Bayswater."

"Pity about the bath though," Amy said.

"Oh that'll soon be fixed," Pam said dismissively adding, "I must ring up and cancel the other flat."

The girls caught the tube to the West End and headed for the Scene. Inside they found Kevin and Ken. They told the boys all about the flat they had been to see.

"It can't be far from Pat's house as she lives in Finsbury Park," Ken pointed out.

"She lives in the posher part on the other side of the station," Amy said, "we had to walk past some pretty grotty houses to get to this flat."

"At least the house looks very respectable and is on the corner of a more upmarket road," Pam commented.

Amy noticed Kevin glaring at Ken from time to time so she took him away for a dance.

"What's the problem you've got with Ken?" she asked as they smooched together.

"Oh, you noticed. If he's not careful I'll land him one before the evening's over."

"Why? You know I hate violence," Amy said crossly.

"I'm sure he wants to try and get you away from me. He keeps winding me up."

"You must be imagining it," Amy said, "besides, I don't fancy Ken so you've got nothing to worry about."

Kevin smiled and gave her a kiss. "Still it doesn't stop him trying and if I catch him chatting you up - he'll cop it."

Amy made a point of keeping her distance from Ken for the rest of the evening, not wanting to be the cause of a fight. By the time Kevin walked Amy to the station and saw her onto her train, he had calmed down and apologised for his jealous behaviour earlier.

"It's only because I think so much of you and don't want to lose you," he said earnestly.

"Well I hope that's true since you'll be off at the weekend on holiday for two whole weeks. I shall miss you, so you had better behave yourself and not go having a holiday fling with any girls you meet."

"I don't even want to go - Butlins Holiday Camp isn't exactly my idea of a great holiday," Kevin said glumly, "and I'll have mum, dad and my brothers to irritate me all day and every day."

Amy kissed him goodbye and joined Pam in the carriage. She wasn't looking forward to being without Kevin for a whole fortnight but felt reasonably sure that he wouldn't be chatting up any girls at the campsite.

After tea Wednesday evening, there came a loud knocking at the front door. Mr Brown went to answer it and found a near hysterical Mrs Tibton standing on the doorstep. He brought her into the lounge and sat her down.

She immediately pointed an accusing finger at Amy and started ranting. "I've found out Pam is planning to leave home on Saturday and I'm sure it's something you have talked her into. No good will come of it, mark my words. There's only one thing girls want flats up in London for - and that's men!"

"It's not true," Amy protested, "we just want some independence."

"Yes, independence to entertain men in your flat!" Mrs Tibton yelled and pulled out a hanky to dab at her eyes. "You're all men mad at that age."

Amy realised Pam's mum was in no mood to be reasonable or listen to anything she had to say so she discreetly edged out of the room and left her parents trying to calm her down. Amy had mentioned to her parents that she intended moving out on Saturday and had been surprised how well they had accepted her news. 'Maybe they'll be glad to see the back of me,' she thought somewhat ruefully, 'after all the staying out all night.'

After half an hour Amy heard the front door open and close. She peeped out of her bedroom window and saw her dad accompanying Mrs Tibton across the green to his car. He was taking her home. Amy decided to lay low in her bedroom in case her mother took a leaf out of Mrs Tibton's book and started having a go at her.

She didn't get a chance to speak to Pam until after work on Thursday when they met up to go to the Scene. Pam was full of apologies for her mother's behaviour.

"Why did you tell her you were leaving home on Saturday? You must have known how she would react," Amy said as they walked along arm in arm.

"I didn't tell her," Pam said, "but I made the mistake of telling Ronnie and he grassed on me, dropping me right in it!"

"I think dad managed to calm her down after I left the room. My presence seemed to make her worse. I'm obviously no longer flavour of the month with your mum then," Amy added with a wry smile.

"She's convinced you've persuaded me to leave home and get a flat with you."

"It was actually the other way round if you recall the other Sunday when you came round in such a bad mood with your parents."

"Anyway, I'm going to keep out of her way as much as possible until I leave. Dad has been pretty reasonable about it and hasn't said much."

"I can't believe how calmly my parents have taken the news. They have even offered to bring the bulk of my things up in the car on Sunday."

"Probably want to check out what sort of place we're living in," Pam said. "Make sure it's a respectable establishment."

"I'm certain Mr and Mrs Hodges' clean and neat house with its clipped hedges will give the right impression," Amy declared.

They met Kevin and Trevor down the Scene. Trevor was in a particularly irritating mood and kept teasing Amy about all the girls they would meet at the holiday camp. Kevin took Amy onto the dance floor to get away from his brother.

"Take no notice of him," Kevin whispered, "he's only winding you up."

"Well, he's succeeding," Amy said crossly, "he's really getting on my nerves - he should grow up."

Kevin changed the subject. "Tell you what, I'll see if I can get you and Pam my cleaning job while I'm away on holiday."

Amy brightened up. "That would be great if you could."

They spent the rest of the evening making the most of their last few hours together by smooching on the dance floor or cuddling up together on a bench at the side. Pam danced with Trevor but found his company tedious in his present mood.

The next day was Friday and it was also payday, which arrived opportunely for the big move on Saturday. Kevin rang Amy at work to say his final goodbye for two weeks and told her the disappointing news that he was unable to get the cleaning job for her and Pam.

Saturday was a bright sunny day and Amy felt excited at the prospect of finally gaining her independence. She spent the day sorting out her things and packing them into suitcases and boxes. All she needed overnight was her weekend case; everything else could be brought up on Sunday.

When she was finally ready to leave she found the house strangely empty. She hunted for her mother to say goodbye but there was no sign of her. Amy was late and she had arranged to meet Pam at the flat at four thirty. She eventually reached the flat just after five o'clock and found Pam busy unpacking her clothes.

"I had a terrific row with my mother so I walked out leaving a lot of my stuff behind," she informed Amy.

"But we've done it, Tibs, we're free at last," Amy said dropping her weekend case and doing a twirl. "No more parents to answer to."

"Yes, it hasn't really sunk in yet," Pam said with a sigh, "we'd better pop down the road to the local parade of shops before they close and stock up on some essentials."

The girls enjoyed the novelty of doing their first shop for the flat: Food and cleaning materials to get them over the weekend. Back at the flat they made themselves some beans on toast for tea and then opened up the divan and made up the bed.

"How about we pop up West to the Macabre?" Pam suggested, "the bed is all ready for us to fall into when we get back." They quickly got ready and headed for the tube. At the Macabre they enjoyed a cup of cappuccino and bought a pair of skeleton hand ashtrays.

"Let's wander round to the Pic to see if there's anyone there we know," Pam said.

"OK, but I don't fancy going down the Scene tonight since Kevin's not there," Amy said.

At the cafe they peered through the window but couldn't see anyone they recognised. As they turned to go they found themselves confronted by Ken.

"What are you two doing lurking around here?" he asked with a smile.

"We're just about to head home to our new flat," Amy informed him.

"What a waste of your new freedom," he protested, "come down the Scene and enjoy yourselves."

"He's right Bat," Pam said, "let's go and have some fun."

Amy reluctantly agreed and they walked through the subway of the multi-storey garage and emerged in Ham Yard.

As soon as they entered the Scene Ken asked Pam for a dance and they vanished onto the dance floor. Amy gazed around. How she missed Kevin already. She spotted Dick standing nearby with a mate so she went over to chat to them. Dick introduced her to Bill - she had seen him before but didn't know his name.

Pam spent the rest of the night wrapped up with Ken, which annoyed Amy somewhat. She hadn't shown much interest in Ken before tonight and now, suddenly, they were inseparable. Amy danced with Dick and Bill and was surprised at how well she kept going without the help of any pills.

Sunday morning, after a coffee in the Strand, Pam kissed Ken goodbye and he arranged to come round in the afternoon.

The girls crept up the stairs to their flat. They didn't want to get off on the wrong foot by waking the Hodges early on a Sunday. They collapsed into bed and slept until after midday when a ring on the doorbell woke them up. Amy scrambled out of bed and peered out of the window. Down below she saw her dad's car parked up with all her things piled up on the back seat next to Ray.

"Quick, get up Tibs. We must dress and look as though we've been up for hours. My parents mustn't guess we've been out all night."

The girls flew into frantic activity throwing on clothes, ripping bedding off the bed and pushing it back into a divan. A knock came at their door and Mrs Hodges' voice called out: "Your parents are here with your things, Amy."

"Oh, right, just coming," Amy called back raking a comb through her hair while Pam drew back the curtains.

Amy opened the door trying to look bright eyed and bushy tailed to find her mum and dad standing on the landing with Ray hovering behind them.

"Thought we might find you still asleep in bed," her mother said walking in and gazing around the room.

"Oh, we've been up for some time," Amy lied, "er - did you find the address all right?" she asked, changing the subject.

"I drove straight here - no problem," her father said setting down a suitcase by the divan.

"It looks like a nice little flat you've got for yourselves," mum observed peering through the doorway into the kitchen.

"It's got a bathroom too," Amy informed her, "would you like a cup of tea or coffee?" she offered and felt relieved when they refused.

"We can't stop, dear," her mother said, "it will be quite a long journey home again. If you can help unload the car then we'll be on our way."

Pam and Amy went down to the car and everyone helped carrying boxes, the record player, it's stand and the records.

Amy heaved a sigh of relief as she waved goodbye to her family. "At last we've got some music," she said to Pam as they hurried back upstairs.

They had barely got everything straight and put away when another ring on the doorbell announced that Ken had arrived.

Amy put some records on while Pam gave Ken a brief conducted tour of the flat. Then Pam and Ken cuddled up together on the divan so Amy tactfully went into the kitchen and made some coffee. Feeling 'de trop', she decided to spend the afternoon in the kitchen cleaning the cooker inside and out. Every time she popped into the lounge to change the records, she found Pam and Ken snogging. It made her miss Kevin even more.

Ken went home early in the evening - to Amy's relief, and the girls spent the rest of the evening finding homes for all their things and then fried some eggs and bacon for supper.

Mary was back from her holiday in Italy and arrived at work Monday morning looking really sunburnt, making her naturally olive skin darker than ever. She wanted to hear about everything that had happened while she had been away so Pam and Amy spent the lunch hour with her in the canteen catching up on the news and Mary told them all about her holiday in the toe of Italy staying at her grandmother's remote rustic house.

After work the girls caught the train back down to Kent to collect the remainder of Pam's things. She had arranged for her brother to bring them along to her friend, Christine's, house, as she didn't want a confrontation with her mother. They stayed for a while chatting to Christine and Ron before leaving to catch the train back up to London. They found a shop open in the local parade and bought some chops for their tea.

"You know, Tibs, now that we can go out every night all night if we want to, I actually quite enjoy having a night in listening to music and just relaxing," Amy said stretching out her legs on the divan after they had finished the washing up.

"That's because we appreciate being in our own place now," Pam said bringing in mugs of coffee and handing one to Amy.

As Pam was meeting Ken down the Scene Tuesday evening and Amy didn't fancy playing gooseberry again after Sunday, she decided to stay home and wash her hair.

"It's been four days since Kevin went on holiday and I've not heard so much as a peep from him," Amy complained as Pam gathered up her handbag and headed for the door.

"That's not long at all, Bat, I expect you'll get a card in the post any day now," Pam said trying to console her.

Amy gave a deprecatory snort. "No chance of that because I'm sure I forgot to give him this address."

"Well maybe he'll ring you at work. Anyway I won't see Ken tomorrow night - I'll stay in and we can practise our typing 'cause we've been neglecting it lately."

The prospect of another evening spent indoors was far from the lively London life Amy had envisaged prior to leaving home.

Chapter Twelve

July - The Bedsit

Amy stood at the kitchen sink up to her elbows in soapsuds lethargically washing dishes. This was definitely not how she expected to spend a Friday evening in London. She was thinking of Pam enjoying herself now at the Goldhawk Club with Ken. Flat sharing was fast becoming mundane with all the washing and cleaning it involved. True she had been to the Scene with Pam the previous evening but once Ken arrived Amy found herself having to dance with Jim, a friend of Eric's, who danced with jerky movements as if someone was pulling his strings. She gave a sigh. She desperately missed Kevin but felt annoyed because he hadn't been in touch.

Saturday morning the girls vacuumed and dusted the flat and then caught the bus to Holloway Road to do some shopping. On returning home they found Ron, Pam's brother, on the doorstep. He had just arrived from the opposite direction.

"I found a few more of your things that I thought you would need," he said handing his sister a carrier bag. They all went upstairs to the flat and Pam showed him round while Amy made the coffee. Pam quizzed her brother on the state of things back home.

"Mum and dad are gradually coming round to accepting that you have really left home for good. Dad thinks it'll make you more responsible, but mum still doesn't trust your motives."

"Time will prove to her that I can be trusted," Pam declared defiantly.

Ron stayed to tea and then left when the girls needed to get ready to go to the Scene.

"I really don't fancy playing gooseberry all night to you and Ken," Amy said as she sat by the window applying her make-up.

"Tell you what I'll do then," Pam said, "I'll pretend to Ken that we're coming home at the end of the evening but once he's caught his bus home we can sneak back down the Scene and enjoy ourselves."

Amy brightened up at this. "We'll have a great time, Tibs. It seems ages since we last went clubbing on our own."

Pam's plan worked well and midnight found the girls back down the Scene preparing to dance the night away.

"It's a good job Ken's not devious like us else we might have bumped into him sneaking back down here too," Amy said with a giggle, "he thinks we're home by now snug in our bed."

Eric and Jim were there so the girls spent some time with them and they all went round to the Piccadilly for a coffee. Eric apologised for not having any spare pills for the girls.

"Oh we're managing fine," Pam quickly assured him, "I think our bodies have got accustomed to no sleep on a Saturday night."

Amy unwrapped two sugar lumps and dropped them into her coffee and then scooped a handful of sugar lumps out of the dish and discrectly stashed them in her handbag.

"Now we've got the expense of a flat to run, we have to economise wherever we can," she said by way of explanation as Jim gave her a quizzical look, "by the way, Eric, where have Mick and Dick got to these days? Mick hasn't been down the Scene for ages."

"I haven't seen so much of them lately myself," Eric said, "Mick was courting a girl who lives on the coast so he spends a lot of time travelling down there. Not missing him are you?" he asked with a wry smile.

"You must be joking," Amy said scornfully, "but I am missing Kevin - it's another whole week before he gets back from holiday."

They returned to the Scene and danced until it closed when Eric suggested they drive to a cafe for an early breakfast. Jim had his car parked in Ham Yard too so Amy climbed in next to him while Pam got in Eric's car. The boys decided on a race to the cafe with the last to arrive paying for the food.

They zoomed off down Shaftesbury Avenue two abreast on the wrong side of the road. Fortunately there was no other traffic around at that hour on a Sunday. Jim's car just made it to the cafe first as it was a lot newer than Eric's and had more horsepower.

After some toast and coffee the girls said goodbye and headed home to their flat to get washed and changed as Ken was due to call round in the afternoon and they needed to give the impression of having had a good night's sleep.

Ken didn't suspect a thing as they sat in the lounge playing records and drinking coffee. Amy felt she just wanted to curl up and go to sleep but there was no separate bedroom to escape into.

Ken left at teatime and after Pam had closed the front door behind him, Mrs Hodges poked her head out of her lounge and told Pam she wanted a word with her and Amy. Pam dashed back upstairs to get Amy.

"I expect we're going to get a lecture because we were out all night," Pam whispered as she and Amy arrived down in the hallway and tapped on the lounge door.

The girls entered to find Mr Hodges sitting in a chair hidden behind his Sunday paper and his wife standing primly in front of the fireplace.

"I've asked to speak to you both because Mr Hodges and I have some concerns," Mrs Hodges began and gave the newspaper a meaningful glare. "Firstly you are coming and going at all hours of the day and night. We don't want to be killjoys - I know you girls are enjoying your freedom but I'm sure your parents would not approve of the hours you keep."

"But.....," Amy began to protest.

"And secondly," Mrs Hodges continued cutting Amy short, "we don't mind you entertaining in your flat but must insist you keep the volume of your music at a reasonable level as we often struggle to hear our television down here."

"Sorry Mrs Hodges, we didn't realise the sound carried down here," Pam said quickly, "we'll try not to disturb you." She turned to leave giving Amy a discreet tug on the arm.

Back in their flat Amy exploded. "What a miserable old bag! We left home to get away from being nagged. She can't stop us from staying out all night if we want to."

"Maybe we should stay in for a while to keep the peace and get back in their good books," Pam suggested.

"Why should we?" Amy demanded, "we pay good money for this flat. They're happy to take our money but don't want any inconvenience attached to it. Why should we make concessions for her or her hen-pecked husband?"

After tea they listened to their music though Pam did turn the volume down a little when Amy was out in the kitchen. The lecture from Mrs Hodges had put

Amy in a bad mood for the rest of the evening. She felt restless until finally at eleven thirty she stood up. "It's no good Tibs, I'm in need of some chocolate to cheer me up. Let's go and hunt for a vending machine."

Pam sighed. "Are you sure you're not just doing this to annoy the Hodges?"

"'Course I'm not," Amy said scornfully, "I need a pick-me-up and chocolate is the only answer. Once I get a craving for chocolate nothing else will do."

The girls crept out trying not to disturb their landlady and headed for the shops and station in search of chocolate. They discovered a vending machine at the rear entrance to the station and made their way back home with several bars of chocolate each.

After work on Monday the girls hurried home and got ready for an evening at the Marquee. They were bubbling with excitement because the Animals were topping the bill. When they arrived in Wardour Street they were dismayed to find an enormous queue snaking back towards Leicester Square. "I doubt we'll be able to get in," Pam said as they joined the end of the queue. The Marquee was a fair sized club but Amy was inclined to agree with her.

Just then two youths arrived next to them. "Want to buy a couple of tickets and beat the queue?" one of them asked with a grin.

"Let's see them," Amy said suspiciously. He fished in his inside pocket and produced two tickets with a flourish. The girls studied the tickets and decided they certainly looked bona fide.

"How come you don't want them?" Pam asked.

The youth shrugged. "Changed our minds. 'Course if you don't want them there are plenty here who do."

"We'll take them," Amy said quickly getting out her purse.

"Now you can go straight in with no queuing," the youth said handing over the tickets and eagerly pocketing the money.

The girls wasted no time; they hurried to the entrance and waved the tickets at the bouncers on the door and then they were inside checking their coats into the cloakroom.

"That was a stroke of good luck," Pam said as they headed for the bar to get a drink.

"And now we can get a good position near the front before it gets too tightly packed in here," Amy added.

They thoroughly enjoyed watching the Animals perform. There was no room to dance but that didn't matter. During the mid-evening break they walked down to the Macabre for a coffee and then returned to find Paul Jones of Manfred Man had joined the Animals on stage for a few numbers.

At the end of a great evening the girls walked round to the Piccadilly for a coffee so that they could stock up on sugar cubes before catching the tube home.

The next evening, being Tuesday, they went to the Scene as usual. Pam had arranged to meet Ken but Amy noticed, as the evening wore on, that Pam was getting more and more irritated with him until at times she seemed downright nasty towards him.

"What's the matter with you two?" she asked Pam as they stood in front of the mirror in the ladies brushing their hair.

"Oh I don't know, Bat. He's just annoying me tonight. I'm not sure I really want to go out with him any more."

"But Ken is pretty keen on you - I can tell," Amy said.

"Yes I know; perhaps that's why I keep being nasty to him in the hope that he'll get fed up and pack me up."

"That's just being cowardly," Amy said with a hint of disapproval, "just tell him if you don't want to see him any more."

Pam sighed. "Maybe it's not Ken. Maybe it's just me being tired and crotchety. I'll make an effort to be nicer to him for the rest of the evening," she promised.

The girls had heard that the Who were appearing at the Manor House on the far side of Finsbury Park the following evening and were determined to go. They trudged across the park sheltering under a brolly against the persistent rain.

"We're not doing much to appease the Hodges," Pam said side-stepping a puddle.

"Cobblers to them," Amy retorted, "maybe we'll stay in tomorrow night. I need to wash my hair and we haven't done any typing practise lately."

They arrived at the Manor House only to find an even longer queue than the one at the Marquee on Monday. It went down the road round a corner and stretched along the next road. The girls thought they would never reach the end of it. After waiting in the rain for twenty minutes the queue had barely moved. Then an official came along to tell those at the rear that they wouldn't be able to get in, as the club was already nearly full. Everyone groaned. There was nothing left to do but trudge back home in the rain.

"At least now we can have two nights practising our typing," Pam said gloomily.

"I'd much rather be watching the Who," commented a disgruntled Amy, "Kevin would be so jealous if I could tell him I'd been to see his favourite group perform while he was away on his hols."

"I noticed a poster outside the Manor House advertising Charlie and Enez Fox. They're appearing there on Friday evening," Pam said, "so why don't we go?"

"Could do I suppose," Amy said unenthusiastically, "seeing as it's only a walk across the park, but they aren't particular favourites of mine."

Saturday evening Amy was impatient to get to the Scene to see Kevin now that he had returned from his holiday. Pam on the other hand was dragging her heels and refused to be hurried.

"I've decided to pack Ken up," she announced as they walked to the station, "I'm fed up with him."

"That's a pity what with Kevin coming back - we could have gone out in a foursome."

"Sorry Bat but I can't live a lie."

"Oh well, never mind. That boy you were chatting to last night in the queue outside the Manor House - didn't he ask for your phone number?"

"Yeah, but I doubt whether I'll hear from him." They arrived at the Scene and discovered Trevor and Ken there but no Kevin. When Amy asked where he was Trevor just shrugged and seemed keen to change the subject. Amy dragged Pam into the ladies.

"That's it!" she stormed, "I've finished with Kevin. I've heard nothing from him and now he doesn't even bother to come here to see me."

"Perhaps there's a good reason why he couldn't get here tonight," Pam suggested trying to calm her friend down.

"Huh, he could have given Trevor a message but clearly he didn't and Trevor was obviously embarrassed when I asked him about Kevin's whereabouts."

"I shall tell Ken we're through and then me and you can enjoy ourselves for the rest of the night," Pam said, opening the door.

"I'm going to see if Eric has got some spare pills - I need something to get me through tonight," Amy said, following Pam back into the club.

"Get me some too would you, Bat? I think I'll need a boost after dropping Ken."

Amy spotted Eric with his mates near the record booth and made her way over there while Pam went to collar Ken. Amy was in luck because Eric had plenty of spare pills. She bought two packets each containing ten blues and then made her way to the snack bar in the corner and bought a coke.

As she went back into the ladies she felt a tug on her arm. It was Pam. "I've done it," she said, "he took it pretty well."

"That was fast. Do you realise we are both free agents again, Tibs?"

The girls had a packet of pills each and quickly swallowed them with the coke while the ladies was empty. After half an hour the pills began to kick in making Amy want to dance but Pam started to have a bad reaction.

"I feel really peculiar," she said, holding her head, "I think I need to lie down for a while." Amy could see how white she looked and took her up the stairs into Ham Yard to get some fresh air. She couldn't find Eric but his mate Dave was lounging against the railing so Amy went over to ask him if he knew where Eric was. She mentioned that Pam was feeling ill.

Dave shook his head. "He took off a little while ago. If Pam needs to lie down then my van is over there," he offered.

Pam gratefully accepted and they all climbed into the back of Dave's van. Dave spread some matting out to try and make it more comfortable but Pam's condition was steadily deteriorating. She was now sweating and moaning.

"Do you think she needs to go to hospital?" Amy asked anxiously.

"No, she'll be OK in a while once the effect of the pills wears off. I've seen people get the horrors before."

Amy was having difficulty keeping still. She desperately wanted to be back down the Scene dancing the night away instead of being cooped up in a van.

Dave gave Amy a cigarette and as he lit it with his lighter Pam suddenly opened her eyes and yelled: "Don't use the matches - we need them to light the gas."

"She's delirious," Amy said, trying not to giggle at her friend's outburst. "It's no good, I can't stay here - I've got to get out."

Amy clambered out of the van and went back down the Scene. She found Ken and told him what had happened. He was immediately concerned and demanded to see Pam. Amy led him outside to the van and he sat with her for the next couple of hours while Amy went back down the Scene to dance off the effects of the pills.

A boy called Roger came over to dance with her and he told her that he knew she had a boyfriend called Kevin. He insisted on referring to him as her husband. Amy quickly enlightened him that they were no longer together.

Roger just grinned. "I bet you anything you like, you'll be back with him before too long. I can tell when a couple are really suited to each other." Amy shook her head but secretly hoped that he was right.

At four in the morning Amy went to see how Pam was doing outside in the van. She was relieved to find her more lucid with a bit of colour back in her cheeks.

"Bat, those pills I took must have been bad," she said, "how come you're OK?"

"Don't know, Tibs, but they were in separate packets."

"I'm feeling thirsty - let's go round to the Pic for a drink."

"Are you feeling well enough to walk?" Amy asked, surprised at Pam's rapid recovery.

"I'm feeling a bit shaky but if I hang on to you I'll be OK."

They walked slowly through the garage to the coffee bar while Dave and Ken went back down the Scene.

As they sat sipping coffee, Blocker Tony came in with a friend and sat at the adjoining table. He introduced the girls to Ray who turned out to be a right charmer and a complete nutter to boot.

He launched into a confession of his immense and undying love for Amy, extolling her beauty and declaring adamantly that she ought to be a top model. Amy giggled helplessly at his tirade of tosh and Pam even managed a smile.

Back down the Scene Pam was feeling much better and wanted to dance. She now had far more energy than Amy, having spent most of the night lying down.

When the club closed Sunday morning they went down to the Strand and continued to dance at the Last Chance until nine o'clock when they left to get a coffee. The coffee bar was crowded as usual but the girls found a couple of seats at a table next to Graham and his mates. They had been down the Flamingo all night. Graham introduced his mates; some of them Amy and Pam had met before but hadn't known their names. One, a diminutive Jamaican, was a very likeable character who had the strange name of Rupert Bear.

"My mum and dad have an odd sense of humour," he explained with a wide grin, "and fortunately I've inherited it."

While they were all chatting and joking, a longhaired bloke came and sat on the spare seat next to Amy. He took a swig of coffee and then lit a cigarette. Amy glanced at him and then did a double take as she recognised him. He was one of the guitarists from the Birds though unfortunately not Ronnie Wood. She kicked Pam discreetly under the table and inclined her head in his direction.

Pam looked surprised then leaned across the table. "Er, excuse me, but don't I know you?" she asked, "aren't you Moggsy who plays with the Birds?"

"Yeah, that's me," he said and gave them a long hard stare. "Didn't you two come down the 100 Club? You look familiar."

Pam and Amy smiled, pleased that he actually remembered them. They chatted to him while he drank his coffee and then he said cheerio and disappeared down the stairs. "Pity it wasn't Ronnie Wood," Amy said wistfully.

Rupert leaned across towards the girls. "We're going to the afternoon session at the Flamingo," he said, "why don't you two come too? Should be good as John Mayall will be on stage."

"Yeah, we might do that," Amy said.

"We've just got to kill some time until it opens," Graham added.

Amy glanced at Pam. "Why not come back to our flat?" she offered impulsively and Pam nodded in agreement.

"That would be great!" Graham exclaimed, "me, Rupert and John can come home with you now and the others can call round later as they've got to go and see someone first."

Amy jotted down their address on a napkin and handed it to one of the boys who would be coming round later. Outside the coffee bar they split into two groups. Amy, Pam and the others headed for the Piccadilly Line up to Finsbury Park.

At the flat they crept upstairs trying to be quiet but Mrs Hodges poked her head round the kitchen door and gave them a frosty look. They hurried into their flat and closed the door before she had a chance to say anything.

"Don't go much on your landlady," Graham said dropping onto the divan. Rupert went over to the records and sorted through until he found the Kingsmen's album and put it on.

Amy made the coffee and then they sat in the lounge chatting and listening to the music. After half an hour there came a loud knock on the door. Amy answered it and found Mrs Hodges standing there looking slightly agitated.

"Mr Hodges would like a word with you and Pam downstairs now please," she said, giving Amy a cold hard stare. Amy turned and called to Pam and then they followed their landlady down the stairs.

Mr Hodges was pacing in front of the fireplace with his head bowed. He stopped and cleared his throat as Pam and Amy came in accompanied by his wife. "Er, I understand you have taken some boys up to your flat," he began rather hesitantly. "Well I'm afraid you must ask them to leave."

"But you told us only a week ago that you didn't mind us having friends round," Amy protested.

"Yes, but this is different," Mr Hodges snapped glancing at his wife who backed him up with a nod.

"How is it different?" Pam asked.

"Well, because one of them is coloured. We do not permit these people in our house." Mr Hodges glared at the girls.

"They are our friends and guests. We invited them in and we are not going to ask them to leave!" Amy shouted

"Why do you live in an area that has such a high percentage of blacks if you don't like them?" Pam demanded, adding, "you obviously don't mind taking their money in your shop 'cause if you tried to ban them from there, you'd be out of business within a week."

"That is beside the point," Mrs Hodges cut in curtly, "we want that boy out of our house - the others are welcome to stay but he must go."

"I said there is no way we will ask him to go," Amy reiterated, her face flushed with anger.

Mr Hodges studied the girls for a moment and then puffed out his chest. "You leave us no alternative," he said flatly, "either he goes or you go."

"If that's how you want it then we will leave," Pam replied defiantly. "Come on Amy, let's go 'cause there's a bad smell in here." Pam turned on her heel and stomped out of the room with Amy close behind.

Back upstairs they received curious looks from the boys.

"Everything all right?" Graham asked, "only we heard raised voices downstairs." Reluctantly the girls related what had happened.

"I can't let you lose your flat because of me," Rupert said in alarm, "I'll just leave."

"You're not going anywhere," Pam said firmly.

"Anyway they can't just throw you out, they've got to give you at least a week's notice," John piped up.

"I wouldn't want to spend another night under the same roof as those prejudiced bigots," Pam snarled, her eyes flashing, "I'd rather sleep on a park bench."

"It might well come to that," Amy said with a sigh.

Just then the doorbell rang. It was the rest of the boys arriving. They were let in and came galloping up the stairs. When they heard what had happened they were up in arms, full of indignation at the way Rupert had been victimised and applauded the girls' defiant stand. A loud pounding on the door interrupted them.

"I want you all out of my house now," yelled a furious Mrs Hodges through the door and then they heard her stomping back downstairs.

"John's right," Graham said, "they've got to give you time to find another flat. I'm going to go down and try to talk some sense into them."

"We'll come too," chorused the rest without hesitation.

"OK, but it's probably best if Rupert stays up here out of the way," Graham stipulated.

"I think you'll be banging your head against a brick wall with that evil pair," Amy said, "but we appreciate the gesture."

"I really don't want to stay here a moment longer than I have to," Pam said. The boys trooped off downstairs and it wasn't long before raised voices could be heard coming up into the flat.

"Doesn't sound like they are having much luck," Pam said. The shouting got louder as tempers frayed and the argument raged until footsteps on the stairs heralded the boys' return. They came in looking as if they had just gone ten rounds with Cassius Clay.

"They are the most narrow-minded bigoted bastards I have ever had the misfortune to meet," Graham snarled as he flopped down in a chair.

"I did warn you that you'd be wasting your time," Amy said.

Suddenly they heard loud thumping on the door followed by an irate Mr Hodges yelling at them to pack up and get out.

"He's just doing what his wife has told him to do," Pam declared scathingly.

"Still, we had better do something positive instead of just moaning about those two buggers," Amy said, "I think we should phone Pat and Mary to ask for their help. They might even be able to put us up temporarily."

Pam agreed. "That's not a bad idea, and you boys had better get going if you want to get to the Flamingo on time."

"But we can't just leave you in this mess," John protested.

"Nonsense, we'll sort something out," Pam insisted, "and besides you've already done your best to help."

They all clumped down the stairs and as they reached the front door Mrs Hodges appeared down the hallway at the kitchen door.

"I've called the police," she shouted, "they are coming round and bringing police dogs with them."

By way of response she received a chorus of jeers. Outside they went their separate ways and the girls headed for the local parade of shops where there was a phone box. They rang Mary and explained what had happened. Mary said she'd go and collect Pat and they would come over in Pat's car.

"I got the impression Mary wasn't exactly champing at the bit to help us," Amy said as they emerged from the phone box.

"I'm sure they wouldn't see us left homeless on the street," Pam declared trying to sound optimistic about the predicament they were in, "meanwhile let's go along to the newsagents and see if there's any flats advertised on the notice board."

The girls stood peering at the jumble of adverts when they were suddenly startled by a muffled voice close behind them mumbling: "Are you two lovely ladies looking for somewhere to stay?" They jumped and turned round to find a tall, bearded, bespectacled man hovering near them holding a handkerchief over the lower half of his face as though he was trying to conceal his identity. He looked like an ageing beatnik wearing a scruffy duffel coat, brown-corded trousers and scuffed suede shoes. Amy thought his manner appeared to be somewhat shifty and a bit lecherous.

Then he removed the handkerchief and apologised. "I've been having a nose bleed," he explained. "I just happened to overhear you mention something about a flat as I was walking past and I may be able to help."

Amy glanced at Pam unsure whether they ought to speak to this dodgy-looking bloke let alone believe what he was telling them.

"Um, yes we are looking for a flat to rent actually," Pam said eyeing him warily.

"Well that's a coincidence because I've got a bedsit that's available," he drawled. "If you want to take a look at it, I'll drive you round there. You can find me next door in the launderette." He turned and walked away.

Pam nudged Amy and whispered excitedly, "this is too good an opportunity to miss."

"But I don't think we should drive off with a total stranger," Amy said, still suspicious about this bearded man's motives.

"There's two of us - he wouldn't stand a chance," Pam declared, "come on Bat, let's take him up on his offer - we've got nothing to lose." She hurried along the pavement to the launderette and tapped on the window, beckoning to the man inside. He came out and smiled broadly.

"How much is this bedsit of yours?" Pam asked him.

"It's three pounds a week and has a kitchenette and a telly," he said, adding, "by the way my name is Don." The girls exchanged excited smiles on hearing how little the rent was and then introduced themselves.

"My Minivan is just here at the kerb," Don said ushering them across the pavement to a shabby grey little van, "If you can both squeeze into the passenger seat, I'll run you round to take a look at it." He climbed into the driver's seat and leaned across to open the passenger door.

"He doesn't seem too bad after all," Amy whispered as they walked round the bonnet. They managed to squash inside, but it was far from comfortable. As Don pulled away from the kerb he gave a wave to a young woman with long blonde hair standing at the launderette window with a puzzled frown on her face.

"Who's that?" Pam asked.

"Oh that's my wife, Joan," he said casually, "I forgot to tell her where I was going."

"Won't she think it very odd for you to be driving away with two girls?" Amy asked in surprise.

"Not really," Don said with a smile as he indicated and attempted to change down a gear, fumbling for the gear stick under Amy's legs, "she's accustomed to me doing the unexpected. I'll explain when I go back to collect her and our laundry."

Pam and Amy recognised the road he drove down because it went past the Hodges' house and shop. They pointed the house out to Don and told him all about their argument with the Hodges which had necessitated their urgent search to find another flat.

"They sound like pretty horrendous people," Don surmised, "you're better off out of there."

At the end of the road he turned right into a wide tree-lined avenue where expensive-looking large detached Victorian houses stood back from the road. Most had been converted into flats. Before Don reached the far end of the road, which looked like a dead-end, he pulled up outside the only property that stood out from all the others - for all the wrong reasons.

Pam and Amy clambered out onto the pavement and gazed at the colourful, ornate house before them.

"That is genuine Italian mosaic decorating the front of the house," Don informed them, "the previous owner was a bit of a crook and stole it. He thought it improved the look of his house, and I quite like it now that I've had time to get used to it. 'Course when he was arrested he didn't have a leg to stand on - there was the loot plastered all over his house for all and sundry to see. He couldn't have had much between his ears. He got sent to prison for seven years and I got the house at a bargain price."

"Obviously the rightful owners didn't want their mosaic tiles back," Amy said as they walked up the untidy concrete driveway to the steps that led up to the stained glass double front door.

The door opened into a wide hallway with the original black and red tiles on the floor. It was empty except for a hall table and a large grandfather clock. Don opened the first door on the right.

"This is the room," he said and ushered them inside. Amy gazed around, pleased with its spaciousness. It contained a double and a single bed, a large wardrobe with drawers and a telly. An enormous bay window overlooked the neglected front garden and filled the room with plenty of light. Brightly coloured curtains hung from wooden rings and a rush mat hid most of the worn and faded carpet. In the corner opposite the door was the kitchenette. It was very compact and housed the cooker, a sink with drainer, and a worktop plus a few cupboards on the wall. Outside the kitchen door stood a small table and three chairs.

"This will suit us just fine," Pam pronounced, "and I bag the double bed," she added sitting on it and testing its springiness.

"Er, there is one small snag," Don said shuffling his feet, "this room actually belongs to three girl students. They have gone off to work in Italy for the summer holidays but I promised they could have the room again when they return in September."

Amy gave a groan. "I knew it was all too good to last."

"Well you can have the room for six weeks and I'm sure something else will turn up by then," Don said encouragingly.

"Yeah, it's not that bad, Bat," Pam said standing up, "at least we've got somewhere to stay for now and that's the main thing."

"You're right," Amy agreed, "six weeks is long enough for us to look around. Who else lives here?"

"It's mostly students - some go to Hornsey College of Art. There are nine rooms that we let out while me and Joan have got our flat in the basement. There's only one bathroom though - it's on the second floor with a separate toilet and then there is a third floor above that."

"Isn't there a queue for the loo in the morning?" Amy asked feeling a little disappointed at the lack of bathroom and toilet facilities.

"It's not that bad," Don said with a chuckle, "there is an outside toilet which we use along with the two tenants who occupy the basement bedsits. There's also a pay phone and vacuum cleaner down there outside our door."

"We'll manage just fine," Pam declared, "but we'd better get back to the Hodges house and start packing. I expect Mary and Pat will be arriving at any moment."

"Oh, I forgot to mention our house rules," Don said as he handed over a front door key and room key to each of them, "no boys are allowed in your room." The girls groaned in unison but then they noticed Don's eyes twinkling. "Except me of course," he added. "Actually there are no rules here - everyone does pretty much whatever they like."

"Well that's a relief," Amy gasped, "we've had our fill of rules and bigots lately."

"Joan will sort out the rent and a rent book with you later," Don said as they walked outside to the Minivan. He drove them back to the Hodges house and dropped them off. As he drove away with a toot on the horn, so Pat's Mini Countryman came into view from the opposite direction.

"That was good timing," Amy said as Mary and Pat got out, "we've just found ourselves a bedsit and now we need a hand getting our stuff moved round there."

They took the girls up to their flat and made some coffee. Amy played records and deliberately turned the volume up.

They enjoyed banging and crashing around as they packed up and stamped up and down the stairs shouting and yelling as they took boxes and suitcases down to the car. Mary and Pat joined in, loving every minute of it. Mrs Hodges came out of her kitchen and shouted at them to be quiet but the girls just laughed and made even more noise.

"I wonder where the police and their dogs have got to?" Pam yelled as she stamped back up the stairs.

"Must have got lost," Mary yelled back from the front porch. Mrs Hodges retreated to her kitchen and slammed the door.

Finally everything was crammed into the car. Amy flung the keys into the tropical fish tank as a parting gesture and yelled: "Good riddance to bad rubbish," as she slammed the front door for the last time.

"I could do without having to change flats on a come down after a night of clubbing," she complained as she squeezed into the rear seat beside Pam, "I feel terrible!"

"Mm, me too," Pam agreed, "and we've still got to get unpacked as yet round the corner."

"At least you're only moving a very short distance," Pat said after Amy had given her the directions. She drove down the road and turned into the wide avenue.

"This is nice," Mary said appreciatively.

"You might not think so when you see the front of the house we're moving to," Amy warned her.

Pat drew up and gazed in disbelief at the gaudy frontage and burst out laughing. "I see what you mean."

"Well I think it's bloody great!" Mary declared approvingly, "now show us your bedsit."

It didn't take long for the girls to unload the Mini and carry everything inside.

"I like this room," Pat said putting a box of records down on the table, "not quite as large as the last place but it's got a lovely big bay window."

Pam put the kettle on for coffee while the others unpacked and found homes for everything.

Mary spotted two old biddies tottering along the pavement with arms linked. She gave a mischievous chuckle and opened the lower sash. Hidden behind the net curtain she yelled through the window: "You brazen hussies!"

The old ladies stopped in their tracks and looked around trying to discover who had yelled at them.

Mary closed the window and collapsed on the bed in paroxysms of laughter.

"You'll get us thrown out before we've had a chance to move in," Pam said reprovingly.

With the room straight and the girls settled in, it was time for Mary and Pat to head home for their tea. Pam and Amy thanked them for their help and invited them round the following evening.

"We'll get some wine and celebrate our good fortune at finding this place," Pam promised.

On their own at last, exhaustion finally overcame them, as they lay flopped out on their beds.

"I think we deserve a holiday, Bat," Pam announced drowsily, "everyone else has had one except us. How about we get some brochures tomorrow at the travel agents? With all the rent we are saving, I'm sure we can afford it."

But Amy wasn't listening - she was sound asleep.

Printed in the United States
By Bookmasters